SECOND LIVES

SECOND LIVES

A Journey Through Virtual Worlds

TIM GUEST

 RANDOM HOUSE | NEW YORK

Published in the United States by Random House, an imprint of
The Random House Publishing Group, a division of
Random House, Inc., New York.

RANDOM HOUSE and colophon are registered
trademarks of Random House, Inc.

This work was originally published in Great Britain by
Hutchinson, a division of Random House UK, London, in 2007.

LIBRARY OF CONGRESS CATALOGING-IN-PUBLICATION DATA

Guest, Tim.
Second lives: a journey through virtual worlds / Tim Guest.
p.   cm.
ISBN 978-1-4000-6535-6
1. Virtual reality. 2. Shared virtual environments. I. Title.
BD331.G77 2008
006.801'9—dc22   2007032065

Printed in the United States of America on acid-free paper

www.atrandom.com

2 4 6 8 9 7 5 3 1

First U.S. Edition

Book design by Katie Shaw

CONTENTS

1
Exodus: *Leaving the real world behind* 3

2
Virtual Worlds, Real Selves: *Life on both sides of the screen* 26

3
Linden Lab: *Dreamers of the dream* .50

4
Hacking Matter: *Changing the world for fun and profit* 62

5
Virtual Mafia: *My life as a foot soldier* 79

6
Cyber-Terrorists: *Attacking thought* 97

7
Virtual Riches: *Where there's money, there's an addiction* 121

8
Virtual War: *Join up and see the imaginary world* 147

9

Us: *Together in electric dreams* 163

10

Virtual Sex: *Boys who are girls who like boys who are girls* 171

11

My Virtual Sister: *Beyond the nuclear family* 189

12

Corporations: *Branding virtual dreams* 199

13

Virtual Art: *Creating ourselves anew* 217

14

Korea: *King of the world* 231

15

Conclusion: *Back to life* 255

SECOND LIVES

1

EXODUS

Leaving the real world behind

In August 2004, Derek LeTellier, then a nineteen-year-old student teacher from Chicago, entered a competition on some land near his home, to see who could stack objects the highest. Derek's entry was a skyscraper, forty stories tall, built entirely out of wooden blocks — a triumph of effort and will over gravity and friction. He didn't win the competition, but the land was empty and so LeTellier began to come back every few days to see what else he could stack. At the end of each day, he knocked the towers down. His experiments became a kind of regular neighborhood sideshow: Each week, a handful of locals would gather to watch his towers fall. Derek worked out how to stand on the towers as they came crashing down, and surf the tumbling blocks to the ground. Then a friend, James Miller, mentioned that the tower reminded him of the World Trade Center. Another friend who came along that same week had lost a relative in the real 9/11 attacks. He mentioned he would like to see what it was like to be inside the towers as they collapsed. So, at his friend's request, Derek built a second tower, next to the first. The two men, along with a handful of others, climbed inside.

Derek's intention hadn't originally been to re-create the World Trade towers. "A lot of what looked like symbols for 9/11 mostly were due to practical reasons," LeTellier told me. "The shape of the buildings, the size, and the placement of people inside them." I asked Derek if he had been wary of any controversy the collapse might cause. "A little bit, especially when we put that second tower up," he said. "At that point I got a little disturbed about what we were doing. How eerie it looked. Before that, it's only an experiment. At that point, it became something more."

Derek had also developed a tradition: As he knocked over his towers, he shouted a single word. The day he and his friend sat next to each other inside the tower, he shouted it aloud—"Die!"—and the two towers fell again.

And, as a result, the world ended—or at least part of it. The two buildings, which had taken Derek just five minutes to build, were among the largest constructions that area of the world had ever seen, and when they fell, as if in a rising pall of smoke, the world went black.

Literally. Because all of this was nearly, but not quite, happening. Derek was in his apartment in Chicago. Others were in their offices in San Francisco, and all across the United States. Derek's re-creation of the World Trade Center attacks took place in the Olive district of a virtual world called Second Life. The towers, which had taken just a day to build, were the largest constructions Second Life had ever seen. When they fell, the world crashed. Every player was ejected.

Second Life is a virtual world: a computer-generated place, created by real people from all across the world who log on to live other lives online. The players—known in Second Life as "residents"—see these worlds as 3-D computer-generated images on their screens. They can watch their virtual selves on their monitor as if through the eyes of their online self, or, more often, from behind their head, a perspective called the "third-eye view." Using their keyboard and mouse, they can watch their virtual selves wander over digital terrain. In the real world, of course, Second Life exists only as ones and zeros on the hard drives of seven hundred Debian Linux servers in a San Francisco data warehouse. The Second Life computers function like Web servers, only, instead of serving up Web pages, they serve up a whole 3-D world. All the buildings, objects, and terrain Derek and his friends could see on their computer screens were digital; the other people, who also paid to inhabit this virtual world, also looked computer-generated, but at the helm of each was a real person, somewhere on the real globe.

In virtual worlds, you are born fully grown: Each new character is an adult, albeit one who doesn't yet know how to "be." In every virtual world, you can walk, talk, and move things around using your keyboard and mouse—but in each world these controls are different, and have to be learned anew. Second Life's solution to this problem is for each character to appear first in Orientation Island, a jumble of tropical hills and beaches where, like rehabilitation in fast-forward, you learn how to operate your self and inhabit the world. When I first logged on, under the virtual sky—perfect shades from blue to white, like the sky seen from a 747—I wandered the island. Here and there, placards—which I clicked on to read, and which appeared as text on my screen—taught me how to walk, how to talk, how to move objects at a distance, how to fly. (If the first part felt like rehabilitation, the second part felt like superhero school.) At the end of the final lesson, a teleport button transmitted my virtual self into the wider virtual world, where all the other people were.

In Second Life, you can move around, talk with others using the keyboard or a microphone, interact physically with others' second selves–hug, wave—and, although I didn't know this when I began my journey into virtual worlds, you can get married, make money, commit crime, and almost forget the real world even exists. And although only a handful watched Derek LeTellier's towers fall, the dream they shared, of entering a new place and leaving the real world behind, had already begun to colonize the imagination of millions.

Derek's experiments were a local affair, but virtual worlds were already on the scale of entire nations. By 2004, around twenty million people were regularly logging on to virtual worlds like Second Life; at the time of this writing, that figure has more than doubled. Between fifty and seventy million people worldwide—far more than passed through U.S. immigration at Ellis Island in the whole twentieth century—now regularly log on to these new online spaces to abandon reality in search of a better place. This time, though, our new lands have no indigenous inhabitants to dispute our claim to the territory. Virtual worlds are empty except for us, and are shaped entirely to our desires.

In the past, mankind could only dream of such utopias. Heaven, Eden, Oz . . . lands somewhere over the rainbow. But now, through computer technology, we have built ourselves a new kind of heaven: perfected virtual worlds, where we can finally move in and take up residence. Through computer screens in homes, offices, libraries, cyber-cafés, military bases, colleges, and schools, more people than inhabit Australia have stepped through the electronic looking glass to create second lives. In virtual worlds, it seems, we can finally break free of the forces of nature: We can shed gravity (in most games, you can fly) and we can rid our lives of friction (in online worlds, nothing takes any physical effort at all).

For the most part, these millions play what are known as massive multiplayer games: playful but constrained virtual spaces like Sony Online Entertainment's Dungeons & Dragons–style world, Ever-Quest—the planet's fifth-largest virtual world, with half a million players—or Blizzard Entertainment's World of Warcraft, the most popular game in the United States, with 8.5 million players worldwide. In Southeast Asia, I discovered, the numbers are huge. In 2005, one South Korean game series, Lineage and Lineage II, boasted four million active accounts, and the numbers are rising exponentially. More people reside in Lineage and Lineage II than reside in Ireland. The population of virtual worlds seems to almost double every year. "I expect there will be two to three million more people in the U.S. that come on board in the next two years," David Cole, president of the multimedia research firm DFC Intelligence, told *Salon* magazine in July 2002. The actual figures were in the top range of his guess—and eight million more residents have joined since then, attracted by a freedom of movement and expression that is harder to find in the real world. (And that's not even counting the millions in Southeast Asia.) In 2002, game designer Brad McQuaid, one of the creative forces behind EverQuest, predicted virtual worlds "will rival the movie industry in the next five to ten years." We're well on the way. In 2005, Hollywood took in $9.2 billion in U.S. box-office receipts (worldwide, that figure rose to $23 billion). In the same period, the combined annual revenues from these new virtual worlds were estimated at $3.7 billion, a figure predicted to rise to $19.3 billion by 2009. By then, if current trends continue, virtual worlds will make more money than American football, baseball, and basketball combined, and, each year, more people worldwide will visit a virtual world than will visit a McDonald's restaurant.

The economies of virtual worlds, I discovered, ran far beyond the income of the people who created them. In each world, there were virtual currencies, and the mass exodus from the real world had brought with it such a mania for virtual items that people were now willing to pay real money to acquire them. People who want, say, a more powerful sword, or their own virtual Frank Lloyd Wright–style cantilevered home by the virtual seaside, but don't have time to construct it themselves, will pay substantial sums of real-world money instead. The money is paid via credit card, on websites in the real world, and the goods are delivered inside the game. I knew virtual worlds had their own currencies (in EverQuest, I had killed rats for a week to scrape together a single gold piece), but I had had no idea how these initially fictional currencies had begun to affect our own real-world ones. The largest virtual items broker, Internet Gaming Entertainment—a bit like a hedge fund, with a collateral of virtual swords and property instead of stocks and bonds—will sell you virtual currency from one of fourteen nonexistent places, for real-world cash.

The income had become so reliable, I discovered, and the exchange rates between virtual currencies so stable, that enterprising businessmen in poorer areas of the world—Mexico or China, for example—had set up "virtual sweatshops": offices where employees worked (and sometimes slept) at their PCs, working in virtual worlds to make gold and other items for their bosses, in exchange for a real-world salary.

In 2001, economist Edward Castronova, then a professor at California State University, studying welfare, spent many evenings online, inside the virtual world of EverQuest. He noticed that players were selling virtual items and virtual currency for real money on eBay—the game had an economy, which intersected with the real one. In his 2002 study *On Virtual Economies*, he examined this economy of EverQuest, then the planet's second-largest virtual world, with just under half a million residents. He found that EverQuest had a real, consistent U.S. dollar exchange rate, which put the average wage of each player—the virtual money he or she earned while playing the game, hunting for virtual booty and creating new virtual items—at the equivalent of $3.42 per hour. One EverQuest platinum piece, he found, was worth about one cent: more than one yen or one lira. From that, Castronova calculated the virtual world's gross national product (GNP): $135 million. EverQuest, he concluded, had a per capita GNP of $2,266—richer than India, Bulgaria, or China, and almost on a par with Russia. By these measures, the world's seventy-seventh-largest economy was a subcontinent that only *nearly* existed. Since Castronova's study, virtual business has boomed. In 2002, virtual game items—nonexistent things—were sold for more than $15 million on eBay alone (despite a ban, instituted by eBay in April 2000, at Sony's request, on sales of EverQuest items). In October 2004, Castronova, by then an economist at Indiana University, estimated the global market in virtual goods at around $90 million. By 2005, a company that specialized in trading virtual goods put the market at over $700 million. (By then, Castronova was hedging his bets; he placed the market at between $200 million and $1 billion.)

These online worlds offer a powerful enchantment: an entire alternative life. To some, the liberation afforded by these second lives is seductive to the point of obsession. When I began my journey, one in ten Second Life players spent eighty hours or more per week logged into their online alter egos. When I spoke with the EverQuest design team in 2002, they told me EverQuest residents inhabited their virtual selves for an average of twenty hours per week. In another Castronova study, from 2001, a third of EverQuest residents claimed to spend more time in their virtual world than at their real jobs, a figure supported by studies of other virtual worlds. In interviews with Castronova, one in five players claimed they thought of EverQuest—not their house or apartment—as their actual home. For these people, the real world was where they worked in order to buy time to really live online.

The word *virtual* has roots in the power of certain qualities—virtues—and has come to mean possessing essence and effect without possessing form; something not quite physical, but with a measurable impact on the real. True to their name, virtual worlds had begun to have an effect on the real. Virtual residents hold online weddings, where they swear devotion to partners other than their offline spouses. In the summer of 2005, Sony, as makers of the sequel EverQuest II, launched a competition to find a real-world look-alike for the queen of that virtual world, Firiona Vie. But they were too late; Firiona already had a real-world incarnation. In January 2005, Tabitha Ayers, an American virtual world resident and committed EverQuest player, named her real-world daughter after the virtual elf queen. The devotion to virtual selves isn't always so harmless. In June that same year, two twenty-nine-year-old South Korean parents were so enchanted by their favorite virtual world, World of Warcraft, that they left their four-month-old baby alone so they could sneak off to the local Internet café. When they returned five hours later, their baby had suffocated. In China, a runaway boy had supported himself by stealing entirely virtual objects and selling them for real money. In the United States, a husband hacked into his wife's game account and staged her virtual suicide, in order to make her seem unbalanced and influence a real-world custody case in his favor. In Korea, where game scores are read out on television news, there is an entire police division dedicated to cyber-crimes, almost all related to a single virtual world—Lineage: The Blood Pledge—that has four million Korean residents. Elsewhere, others have used virtual worlds to plan their dominance over the real world. The U.S. Army, I read, had commissioned one virtual world company to build a model of the entire real world (built to half scale in relation to the virtual size of each soldier) where thousands of virtual soldiers could rehearse conflict anywhere on the globe at a moment's notice.

It was the scale of the movement that seemed most revealing. One morning, I visited my local Blockbuster video store and took a walk along the shelves. There, among the DVDs, were rows of these interactive shared fantasies: boxes of software for your PC that allow you to log in to virtual worlds and abandon your self for any different kind of new self you could wish for. There were dozens of worlds, each ripe with a different possibility of reinvention. The advertising slogans all encouraged me to move to a better place. In City of Heroes ("There is a place we can all be heroes!"), you could shed your own clothes for the cape of an aspiring superhero, free yourself from gravity, and leap across the tall buildings of a Metropolis-like city to save old ladies and fight crime. "You're in our world now," the EverQuest box's sales pitch declared. There was an online version of the Sims (previous versions of which, offline, had become the bestselling computer game ever), where you could join thousands of others to buy furniture, go on a date, or even, by mistake, set your virtual house on fire. If you wanted to fight, you could log on to worlds with names like Battlefield, Counterstrike, and Planetside, where pitched battles of various sizes were played out over and over, forever, all at no real cost—except the pocket change you paid to play.

If you were disappointed with NASA's fading space program, you might choose to journey not to Mars, but to a more interesting place entirely: another universe, like Star Wars Galaxies ("Visit a Galaxy far away—right now!"), modeled meticulously on the films of George Lucas. In this patented galaxy resembling a colossal residential theme park, you could become an alien, fly between the stars, meet Darth Vader or Jabba the Hut, and—after years of practice—become a Jedi knight.

In many virtual worlds, the world's makers decree the purpose of your new virtual self. These worlds offer a specific, restricted path: You fight monsters, make deals, and practice your skills in order to become a more powerful wizard, warrior, or Jedi master. In these worlds, the purpose is to advance up a series of levels, to become a more powerful character by hunting animals and other computer-generated characters—bandits, evil wizards—controlled by the game. Essentially you track down, attack, and kill stronger foes, a repetitive and lengthy process players have christened "grinding" because of the time and effort involved. (One resident of another fantasy virtual world, World of Warcraft, set his sights on a single suit of rare "Enchanted Thorium" virtual armor. He timed the quest: It took ninety-five hours.) The developers fine-tune the games into a kind of virtual Skinner box: They deliver just enough reward to keep you playing. My own time in EverQuest had mostly consisted of working in this way, as a computer-generated Orkin operative, hunting virtual rats until my wrist was sore.

I was particularly interested in other, newer worlds, including Second Life, where the purpose was less defined. There were no foes to defeat, no levels to progress through. In these brave new online worlds, the players themselves make the universe and dwell within it. There is often no goal except simply to live a virtual life. You build an "avatar"—a virtual you—that you can dress like a doll and inhabit as your second body. You can act out your original self, or build a whole new one, online. In real life you might be a taxi driver, but in your second life you can be an architect, fashion designer, superhero, wizard, or king. Through these worlds, almost anything is possible. You can set up a spaceport, be crucified, become Conan the Barbarian.

Through your second self, in accelerated time and with accelerated ease, you can build houses, make and sell things, work, get married, divorce, and die. People wear virtual clothes, drive virtual cars, and construct virtual flat-pack furniture. There are virtual garages, virtual tax collectors, virtual art shows, virtual war memorials, virtual courthouses, and virtual strip clubs (because *virtual* doesn't necessarily mean "virtuous"). If you haven't got the money or contacts to buy virtual land, you can rent rooms in virtual apartment complexes, to shelter your virtual self from the virtual rain. The writer J. G. Ballard, the notorious doomsayer of the dark side of urban sprawl, has envisioned a future where people "abandon reality for virtual worlds, like they once abandoned old Europe." That morning, I discovered they had already done that—and even for some of the same reasons: to rediscover a freedom of movement and expression that in their native lands had become a struggle.

There is room for everybody. The only limit to the geographical size of virtual worlds is the number of Internet servers used to store them. By 2000, the landmass of EverQuest, to scale with the size of each player's online self, was roughly three times the size of Manhattan. In the multiplayer world of Star Wars Galaxies, there were nine planets, each with more surface area than all the land in EverQuest. To walk the equator of each Star Wars planet, one after the other, would take a week.

Just like the cinema screen, virtual worlds such as Second Life have the capacity to entrance us, to make us forget ourselves. Unlike with film, though, the new digital pilgrims journey further: through their computer screen, and into the ideal world on the other side. These people don't just watch their virtual selves, they *become* them.

Of course, whenever we try to create heaven, we also can't help but create a kind of hell. Despite their efforts to abandon the real world, players often find that they have in fact brought their troubles along for the ride.

—

Like most people who remember the occasion, Derek LeTellier saw 9/11 on-screen. He had been in the middle of first period, in history class, when his school made an announcement for all teachers to turn on the news. His history teacher turned on the TV, "and we just sat there the whole period watching and listening."

Derek decided to pay tribute to this witnessing, too. After the virtual World Trade Center collapse, the servers were restarted, and LeTellier and his friends logged back in to Second Life. As the crowd gathered again, Derek built a virtual screen, on which he displayed images of his own towers falling. More people gathered to watch. Then the crowd began to argue. Was knocking down the virtual Twin Towers in poor taste? Should people be allowed to bring such traumatic events into Second Life?

In June 2003, when Second Life was launched, there were just five hundred residents, who spent an average of twenty hours a week in their virtual selves. By the end of my journey into virtual worlds, in May 2007, Second Life would be virtual home to 5.6 million. Other worlds would have millions more—for an estimated total of around 70 million people worldwide. Back in August 2004, when there were ten thousand residents, Derek LeTellier had been a Second Life member for a year. (He'd seen an interview on G4, a niche gaming channel on television, with Philip Rosedale, the CEO of Linden Lab, the company that made Second Life, and he thought he'd give the budding virtual world a try.) "Second Life was smaller then—twenty 'sims,' as opposed to over three hundred two years later," Derek told me. "For a while there were only about one hundred people who were online at a time, and it wasn't hard to know everyone who was online." Back then, when a controversy erupted, everyone heard about it. "Mostly just people who felt that it was offensive to collapse the towers because they had loved ones who had died in the towers and they felt it was disrespectful."

In his real life, Derek LeTellier was working toward a degree to teach high school history. In his virtual life, Derek was making history. "I haven't noticed it as much in the much larger Second Life," he told me, "but when it's difficult to be in Second Life without seeing things like the towers collapsing, then there's always bound to be people who are offended. It's that type of event in history where a lot of people remember exactly where they were when the towers fell. And watching what we did brought back those memories for people. People had interpreted it as kind of a re-creation."

Later, on the Second Life bulletin boards, the argument raged on. "Damiana Domino" called the project "really tasteless." She argued that painful memories should be left out of Second Life. "It's unfortunate that in a place where no physical harm can come to us, we still find ways to hurt each other," wrote Ananda Sandgrain, a Manhattan resident in her first life.

Others disagreed. "It was closure for me," Derek's friend, who had lost a relative in the real-world collapse, told Linden Lab's in-house reporter, James Au. "I wanted to know just what he went through. How it would have felt for him. Second Life allows me to do that and live to tell the tale."

"If you didn't like what was going on then you could just go elsewhere," "RisingShadow" wrote.

We share a multicultural world of diverse ideas, added "kohne Kato." "For our own sanity, we must be tolerant."

This is just a game, said "Brad Lupis."

"Yet another one who just doesn't get it," "Grim Lupis" (no relation) replied. "This is just a game to you. To others, it's something completely different."

By October 2006, when I met Derek in virtual person, I had been living part of my life in Second Life for nearly three years. I had set up a virtual office, and I invited Derek to come talk about the fall of his towers and the subsequent controversy. In Second Life, LeTellier was known as Derek Jones. Dressed as his usual virtual self—a short, cartoon-monkey-headed man, in an Imperial Stormtrooper uniform, with a single pearl earring—he told me how it felt to be inside a collapsing building.

"When the building begins to fall underneath you, the floor starts going down, columns collapse all around you," Jones told me. "It was quite a sensation even though it obviously wasn't real. All that could be heard was the constant clanking of the blocks hitting each other. For me at least, it just made me wonder how terrifying it would be if this was actually happening, with the floors falling from underneath, watching pieces of the building scatter away."

As we spoke, the sun set. It was a foggy night, and outside my office, snow was still falling. I asked if he wanted to re-create the second falling of the twin towers. He said yes. Derek Jones winked out of existence, and I accepted his offer of a teleport. In the sandbox, an area of Second Life kept aside for virtual building practice, I watched as he pulled a skyscraper, floor by floor, from his pocket. And there it was. A tower of wooden blocks, like the one he'd built two years before.

When the tower was built, we stood inside, near the top floor. The walls were open to the virtual elements; the noise of the wind was louder up here. We stood, up in the clouds, lit from the side by the last rays of the virtual sun. I looked down to the ground, far below, and for a moment felt dizzy. "Die!" Derek said, and the towers fell for a third time.

As we fell, the air filled with the sound of building blocks collapsing around us. In the two years since he'd first knocked the tower down, Second Life technology had improved; this time, the server managed to stay online.

In Second Life you could build what you liked, be what you liked, say what you liked, as long as you didn't offend others. And that's where the problems really started. "In football, everything is complicated by the presence of the other team," Sartre wrote. We had developed our perfect worlds, and what attracted us was that other people lived there, too. But the problem was, other people lived there, too.

One by one, Derek Jones picked up the blocks, which now covered the plain, and I flew off. I looked down, and an earringed monkey wearing a storm trooper uniform waved at me from among the rubble.

After September 11, EverQuest II players held an in-world candlelit vigil, but in the years following Derek Jones's reenactment, Second Life responses to the attacks were varied—and still controversial.

In 2005, Second Life residents constructed hundreds of 9/11 memorials. Most avoided controversy: They built virtual memorial gardens, or virtual memorial plaques, or virtual memorial statues of New York firefighters raising the American flag. One man, "Rusty Vindaloo," listed the names of all who had died that day. But another resident, "Sexy Casanova," bit the bullet, and constructed a much more detailed replica of the World Trade Center. Perhaps crucially for his popularity ratings, he didn't knock them down. Even so, many residents took a while to accept it. "At first I thought it was morbid," "Olympia Reebus" said about the towers' third incarnation. "But now I realize it's a way to 'never forget.' "

Through the millennia, mankind had dreamed alone. Now, suddenly, in our virtual worlds, we are able to share and inhabit one another's dreams. But wherever human beings share things, fights break out, and our virtual worlds are no exception. In moments like the second World Trade Center crash, what should have been a virtual utopia descended into yet another struggle over right and wrong.

"I have a question," "Emericus Phaeton" wrote, in the final comment on a Second Life website's coverage of the event. "When does Third Life come out so we can escape our second one?"

My own journey to feeling alive in a virtual world took years. When I was nine years old, my favorite thing in the world was to go with my father to the video arcades. We traveled through air-conditioned malls to rooms full of blinking game cabinets, where we entered simple, line-drawn science fiction and fantasy worlds—Gauntlet, Indiana Jones and the Temple of Doom, Marble Madness—paying our way a quarter at a time. We yanked on the joysticks and bashed the plastic buttons as fast as we could, and we became other people, and other things: a wizard battling ghosts and thieves; Indiana Jones garroting thuggee guards; a marble, lost in a crazy checkerboard maze. For me these games were ecstasy, our time in those air-conditioned arcades a kind of rapture. I was transported. I could become someone else, but remain myself. I could kill, but go unpunished. I could die, but live.

In later years, I persuaded my father to buy a home games console. After my real-world martial arts class, I plugged in our Atari console to practice kung fu on the living room television. I preferred the ease of my virtual kicks to the hard work of stretches and push-ups in the real-world community hall. (I wasn't alone—our type of console, the Atari 2600, eventually sold forty million units.) I wouldn't have been able to articulate it then, but the thrill I felt was from my first shaky steps into virtual reality. I had dipped my toe into that perfect world. There I was—look, that was me—*inside the TV*.

In later years, my father and I lived mostly apart, but when we were together, we played computer games again. By then they were more complex: 3-D worlds instead of 2-D side-on views. We explored dungeons; I took control of our computer-generated self while he traced our steps on graph paper. To find our way together, we drew careful maps of nonexistent places. During adolescence, though, the real world became more complex and demanding, and for years, I left computer games alone.

Then, in the mid-nineties—in my mid-twenties—I began to play games again. I had a boring job, I was broke, and my relationship was a struggle, so, as an experiment and a distraction, I bought a PlayStation console. Most games, though, seemed to transport me into a world as dull as my own. But I gave them a chance: I mowed down demons with machine guns, though I turned down the death-metal soundtrack. Most of the games felt like spending time in the company of an angst-ridden teenage boy. But here and there, within these budding virtual spaces, I caught glimpses of something more perceptive and revealing. Games offered us the experience we desired—adventure, importance, ease of motion—without any physical challenge or change. It seemed a world both full and hollow. "Nought's had, all's spent / Where our desire is got without content," wrote Shakespeare in *Macbeth*—a quote repeated by the agent handler Colonel Campbell as he guided the bandanna-wearing black-ops mercenary Solid Snake to destroy a top-secret undersea robot, in Metal Gear Solid 2, a PlayStation 2 game released in 2001. When, after destroying a power plant that had been commandeered by operatives from the renegade terrorist group Dead Cell, I read this quote—delivered to my in-game character through an in-ear microphone—I was intrigued. It seemed to show a new kind of self-consciousness about video games: their gift (experience without risk) and their curse (experience without risk).

Soon, though, I gave up on the PlayStation. Games left my life again, replaced by friends and work and other more social urban addictions. Then, as I approached thirty, pressures seemed to exponentially increase. I looked for distraction again inside another game: EverQuest, an online fantasy in which you sit in front of your PC (logged on as a gnome, dwarf, or human) and hunt animals and the undead. I of course knew what EverQuest was, and that up to half a million players paid fifteen dollars a month to share the game world, logging in for an average of twenty hours a week. I knew, too, that many players had found their online lives so compelling the game had soon been dubbed "EverCrack"—but I assumed EverQuest would be much the same as the games I already knew. Instead, I entered what seemed like an entirely new world. I discovered that players gathered in tunnels to create their own bazaars in which they traded gold and armor for magical items and pieces of information. I discovered that some players identified so much with their EverQuest characters that they held marriage ceremonies, traded virtual rings, and shared virtual bank accounts—with people they'd never met in real life. (This last part worried my then-girlfriend, who insisted I play as an ugly gnome; to make the point clear, she christened my new, squat self Funnyface.) Without thinking, I assumed most of these players were the kind of people who pitched tents to see science fiction film premieres, and who spoke invented languages. Then again, I was there, too.

I played Funnyface for months, hunting rats, then lions, then bears, until I trekked across the world—it took hours—to the desert, where I hunted crocodiles. The world was repetitive—more repetitive, in fact, than the world I was trying to leave behind—but compulsive, too. Somehow, being liberated from my particular anxieties made the smaller, safer anxieties of the online world infinitely more appealing. I began to play other online games, too. For a few months I logged on to Star Wars Galaxies, another multiplayer world, billed as a chance to live inside the Star Wars universe. I rode land-speeders across deserts and seas, met Jedi knights, and bought my own droid, which beeped and followed me around.

I had no idea of the scale of these worlds, or the number of people who inhabited them. In 1962, Canadian critic Marshall McLuhan predicted that with the rise in communications technology, a "global village" would emerge. By the end of the twentieth century, with the arrival of virtual worlds, this global village was a real place, although it was more of a global nation, populated by millions. In these new virtual spaces, free from many of the pressures of the modern world, I could see something was being born, something that would reveal, and perhaps help reshape, our sense of who we are.

In the affluent West, we sometimes forget how much of our experience is already virtual. The radio we listen to in the car, the music on our headphones, the TV we turn on when we get home—even the print we read in books and newspapers—are all means to simulate human company. We can buy and download movies, music, books; we can watch TV online; we can listen to radio on our cellphones. Through technology, we have placed ourselves at the center of a kingdom of choice and self. We choose our company from remarkable people spread across the world, instead of suffering the company of the normal people nearby. In our "reality" TV shows, audiences involve themselves in the creative process—or at least, they buy the illusion of involvement for the price of a telephone call. Through marketing, we inflame our desires, but we can't contain them; we project our desires out into the world, and call them market forces. Advertising enrages our senses by convincing us to buy things that promise what we desire, but that in fact also undermine our needs. Cars promise ease, freedom, and access to nature, but also deliver traffic, fines, and asthma. The Internet promised us connection and self-expression, but it also separated us: A 2006 survey showed that, over the period since the Internet entered our lives, the average number of close real-world friends has fallen from 2 to 1. With our new global digital consciousness we have made a kind of Faustian bargain, buying freedom partially at the price of our loneliness. At the same time, we are snared in a barely visible web of concepts, brands, advertising, and persuasion, all carefully crafted to enchant us into material acquisition. We've seen too much, but not done enough. We are prisoners of our expectations, caught in the lethal trap of experience without risk.

As I began to enter into virtual worlds, I could see they offered the same kind of addictive enchantment. Somewhere, it seemed, I would find people so entranced by the possibilities of the world within the screen that they would become reluctant to spend much time at all in the real world.

There was also a personal motivation to my curiosity. It was a time in my life when the daily tasks of the Western world threatened to drag me under. Taxes, car insurance, parking fines, finances, deadlines: No amount of personal organizers (I went through five) and no time management plans seemed to stem the tide of paper and fines. E-mails went unanswered, parking tickets went missing, bills went unpaid. I couldn't remember the last time I'd seen the end of my to-do list. At any given time of day, it seemed, the odds were even that I would be on hold to a utility company. Even without a mortgage, I was seriously in debt. For at least two weeks, my main source of nutrition seemed to be leftover olive oil. The modern world was overwhelming me.

Underneath the endless tasks of real life, I felt something else, too: a kind of sorrow, never far away. For years I had struggled with my own difficult history, with the sorrow my past had planted in my chest, like an old bruise. It arose almost every day, lodged in me, and it refused to be disgorged. I could distract myself for a moment from this sorrow: by smoking, or listening to music, or watching films. All these activities surrounded me with ghosts, gave me the impression I was warm and belonged, instead of out here alone. But always, when the cigarette was out, the song over, or the movie finished, the sorrow returned. It felt like a flaw that couldn't be removed, a grain of sand that no amount of advertising or distracting entertainment or imagined perfection could rinse from my self.

I couldn't figure out where the sorrow came from. Did I somehow have implanted in me, because of my idealistic childhood, the idea that life could be easy? Or did we all, somehow, feel this way? Did we all want, as these virtual worlds seemed to offer, to reach up, to let go of our skins and find a new place—a heaven—without sorrow and loss?

I knew I had had an isolated childhood. I knew I had inherited various breeds of sorrow and struggle from the tangled roots of my family. I knew I had chosen a solitary career. A writer's life is perhaps more virtual than most; my contacts with agents, editors, often even friends, took place mostly via e-mail. Most days I sat at my desk and hoped that if I pressed computer keys in the right order checks might arrive in the mailbox. It was hard to discern how much of this struggle was a reflection of me—my personal history, my own particular losses—and how much was a reflection of our society: isolated, set apart, in doubt about our feelings. It seemed to me that the sorrow wasn't just inside. It also surrounded me. I waded through it, and other people around me seemed to wade through it, too. People in the streets, on buses, and on subways seemed hedged against some loss: hunched into newspapers and books, but now also blocking out the world with iPods and cellphones (as well as even more direct medication: between the late eighties and late nineties, prescriptions for antidepressants in the United States tripled). We were unhappy, but we weren't supposed to be. Immersed in a constructed world, we sought comfort in record stores, in the mall, in the movies. Technology meant we were always in touch, but, I read, since the seventies the number of Europeans living alone had doubled. We were all more connected, and all more separate, than ever.

Virtual worlds weren't the only way people were connecting online. As I began to journey into virtual worlds, a new kind of Internet community rose to prominence. On websites such as MySpace, launched in late 2003, users could write notes, describe their lives—their interests, favorite songs and films; style their 2-D Web page to reflect their personality, and make connections with Web links to people with similar interests. Today, social networking sites such as MySpace and its imitators have hundreds of millions of users. MySpace is currently the sixth most popular website in the world (third in the United States). After the success of MySpace, a whole raft of imitators arose, including the most popular MySpace rival, Facebook. Launched in February 2004, by February 2007 Facebook had twenty-five million accounts, and an estimated revenue of $1.5 millon a week.

In 2006, to acknowledge the way these communications technologies were reshaping society, *Time* magazine nominated an unusual Person of the Year: "You" (the magazine's cover was mirrored). Much of the edition reflected on the ways the new, interactive websites—christened "Web 2.0" because of the way they involved the user, instead of just giving out information—were empowering people to take part in new, online communities.

The thing about the Internet, I noticed—even the new social networking sites—is that no one else is actually there. We can read the traces people leave behind—the book reviews, the diary entries, the photos on a MySpace page—but at no time do we encounter the people themselves. Virtual worlds, though, were different. In Second Life, you didn't just rifle through people's notes; you bumped into people. That was why, for me, virtual worlds were far more compulsive, even though they were far more opaque—harder to sign up for, more error-prone, harder to navigate—and therefore growing more slowly. In just under three years, MySpace grew to one hundred million accounts. In roughly the same period, Second Life grew to around six million. The slow growth didn't mean, though, that virtual worlds would always be eclipsed by these more basic, easier-to-use social network sites. In April 2007, Stanford-based Gartner, Inc. technology analysts predicted that, by the end of 2011, 80 percent of Internet users, and the same percentage of Fortune 500 companies, would have a "second life," although not necessarily in Second Life. They would have an avatar of some sort, in a shared virtual world.

Although I was on the early end of this exponential virtual growth curve, I knew I wasn't alone as I spent late nights on the Internet finding a way to transcend my solitude through an electronic connection. At night, when the calls stopped and the offices of the people I was supposed to call back closed, I could relax, log on to virtual worlds, and spend some time elsewhere, away from my struggles, in a safer world where death, and therefore anxiety, was gone. In Second Life, there were no taxes, and so no tax returns to be late with. In World of Warcraft, you didn't even have a home to care for, much less a landlord who held your belongings hostage against four months' missed rent.

Millions of others were joining me. (In late 2006, a survey showed U.S. residents spent fourteen hours a week online—the same amount of time as they spent watching TV.) Isolated at home, these people came together online. Were these new virtual émigrés, like me, escaping the suffering of the world? Or were they forging new worlds, building a new perspective on our plight?

There was something else, too. The first time I had heard about Second Life, I had created an account—named Errol O'Flynn—but I had never actually logged on. Then, some months later when I decided to actually log on, my previous virtual self seemed to have expired. I couldn't log on. I e-mailed Linden Lab to see if I could reactivate the account; they mailed back, explaining that my virtual surname—O'Flynn—had expired. They had given me a new name: I was now Errol Mysterio.

It wasn't the first time I had been given a new name. The dream of a perfect world was a dream that I knew intimately, from a childhood spent living in communes in India and Oregon, with my mother, her guru, and her friends, as they dyed their clothes orange and hunted heaven. They, too, left the world behind to find something better; what they found was a kind of heaven, and also a kind of hell. When my mother was twenty-nine, she decided to leave our family home and enter into a commune headed by the Indian guru Bhagwan Shree Rajneesh. I was now also twenty-nine and escaping pressures similar to those that had plagued my mother so many years before. Only now, perhaps, they were worse. Twice as many people lived alone, bankruptcy filings had doubled. People were folding under the pressure. The system to which my mother had tried to create an alternative—the system of global free market capitalism—was now the dominant global dream.

Something else about the spirit of virtual worlds reminded me of the idealized and troubled communes. My first few excursions into them had uncovered a new kind of experimental attitude, which reminded me of the freedom sought by my mother: freedom of space, creativity, motion, and sexuality. Back in the seventies, they called their communes places "beyond the frontiers of the mind." The virtual world émigrés were traveling beyond a new kind of frontier, and virtual worlds seemed to attract the same kind of pioneer spirit.

And so I decided to finish what I couldn't complete when I was nine: to journey into these perfect worlds and see what consolation and trouble I could find there. My journey would take me to Naboo, to fight Jedi; it would take me to ancient Rome, to speak with the first barbarian to be crucified on the virtual cross. A short conversation about virtual cheating would later lead me into an entire virtual underworld, where hackers and even virtual mafia hitmen used computer skills and intimidation to make small fortunes. I would work as a mafia foot soldier, and nearly get banned from virtual worlds for my crimes. In the real world, I would travel as far as Korea, to meet the king of the largest virtual universe, who in real life looked over his shoulder each morning, in fear of his online foes.

The word *utopia* contains within itself its own impossibility. Coined by the fifteenth-century writer Thomas More, it means both "perfect place" and "no place." And when we try to override that impossibility, when we try to create heaven, we can't help but also create hell. Oz had its wicked witch; Eden had the snake. My mother's guru ended up in jail for immigration issues, and a group of his disciples poisoned eight hundred people and plotted to murder an Oregon district attorney. I knew that the journey into virtual worlds, too, would take me to both the dark and light sides of the story. (I knew, from my childhood, that wherever people traveled to extremes of experience, others would be quick to judge.)

I wanted to venture further into these worlds, to see what I could discover. I wanted to meet the real people behind the screen, and discover the ways their virtual lives both extended and complicated their actual ones. Our new virtual worlds seem at first to be a perfectly imagined heaven: full of abundance; the best of all possible worlds, outside of gravity and beyond scarcity and loss. In virtual worlds, even death was conquered: You could simply click the mouse to be reborn. I wanted to explore how we had begun to inhabit virtual worlds, to examine why so many people yearned to be elsewhere, and to discover what that said about the actual world in which we live.

2

VIRTUAL WORLDS, REAL SELVES

Life on both sides of the screen

When I began my journey into virtual worlds, I expected that their residents would fit the stereotype of video gamers: lonely, lazy, depressed, addicted, using shared fantasies to kill one another and to kill time. But, as I already suspected, the loneliest world was the real one, and while these "loners" may have been isolated at their computers, virtual worlds were crowded. The people I met seemed sensitive, thoughtful, and fascinated by the possibilities of the new spaces they had discovered.

Many virtual world companies, cautious about endangering their profits, are careful about revealing customer information. Because Linden Lab's philosophy is more open, with some work it is possible to find out more precisely who is spending time inside Second Life. The real-world gender split is close to even: in fact, men make up 59 percent of Second Life players, but women tend to play for longer, so any particular person you meet in Second Life is just as likely to be male as female. That is in the real world, of course: Linden Lab keeps no records of how many of those people decide to become different sexes in their virtual life. Linden Lab reports qualitatively that women tend to be "facilitators," encouraging others to gather together. In early 2007, the most common age group was 25–34 (39 percent), followed by 18–24 (27 percent), 35–44 (21 percent) then 45 and over (12 percent). (The remaining 1 percent was 13–17, restricted to a private, under-18 version of Second Life called the Teen Grid.) By 2007, Second Life growth across the world had made U.S. players a minority: 31 percent, about 2.4 million, were American, and just over half (51 percent) were European (of these, France had the highest European Second Life population, followed by Germany, then the United Kingdom). Other research from outside Linden Lab revealed more: a survey by EPN, a Dutch technology think tank, showed Second Lifers tended toward an above-average income, with the median of U.S. players earning $43,000 a year. They also tended toward technical vocations: the most common area of real-life work was information technology (20 percent), followed by the service industry (16 percent), either studying or working at universities (15 percent), and fields of creative and communication (14 percent). Interestingly, in the same survey, slightly fewer Second Life residents reported they were "very happy" than a control group of U.S. and European Union residents (58 percent to the control's 60 percent), but more reported they were "neutral" (35 percent to the control's 25 percent), and almost half the percentage of Second Life residents reported they were "very unhappy" (8 percent to the control's 15 percent). The EPN survey also delved into why people spent time in virtual worlds. "Doing things I can't do in real life" ranked first, followed closely by "making friends," "learning," "killing time," and, strangely, "sex." (I wouldn't understand this last reason until later in my journey.)

So, Second Lifers tended to earn a little more, to want to do things they couldn't do in real life, and to rate themselves as more neutrally happy—but less unhappy—than the rest of us. Later, I would meet some of these people: In my hometown of London I met Todd Robertson, a seventeen-year-old who made his own virtual world, and ran it like a god. I would meet Noah Burn, the twenty-four-year-old South Carolinian forger-gnome, who made a killing running a virtual forgery press, copying virtual objects and selling them for a real profit. But the real lesson I learned is that there is no one typical player. I would have to build my own, impressionistic picture of virtual world residents, by meeting the people themselves.

I decided to begin with a trip to meet the real people behind two very different virtual residents, who were driven to explore virtual worlds for very different reasons. I would begin with John Lester, a religious studies graduate and ex-hacker who found in virtual worlds the perfect place to test his ideas about community and about "soothing harm." Then I would meet Wilde Cunningham, a group of severely disabled men and women for whom virtual worlds were a long-yearned-for release.

John Lester was a hacker kid, who had grown into a thirty-five-year-old hacker man. In May 2005, I met with him at his hacker den in Cambridge, Massachusetts, near Harvard Square. The room was like a stage set from *The Matrix*: a jumble of wires, hacked computers, black-light rave props. We climbed through a trapdoor and he showed me his basement server room, a spiderweb of cables and makeshift racks packed with gray boxes and blinking lights, sprinkled with fans to keep the servers cool. We sat upstairs and sipped coffee as he explained how his interest in virtual communities, which began as a child, led him to buy a whole virtual island.

In 1979, at the age of twelve, John bought his first computer, an Atari 800. In 1981, he discovered his first online communities—bulletin boards, or BBSs. BBSs were modems people could dial up and connect with in order to exchange software and messages with other members of the community. They were like virtual youth clubs or hangouts, early, localized versions of the Internet, except that often only one person at a time could be connected. (Recently, some of these original servers were discovered: text-world ghost towns, uninhabited for twenty years.) Back in '81, Lester hung his home phone on the cradle of his three-hundred-baud modem (six thousand times slower than his current Internet connection), and dialed the numbers of local bulletin boards. "I realized, wow! On these bulletin boards you would talk to people, you could communicate with people all around the world," he told me, "and it was like you were in the same room." One bulletin board led him to another, and another. Soon he began to log on to these early virtual communities all around the world. But even back then, our virtual liberation had a real-world cost. "Once you start getting into this virtual, cyberspace environment, it's very postgeographic," Lester told me. "You get into a sense of, 'Oh, I'll just call this number.' And you don't think where it is. You just want to get there. So the first month I had discovered all these bulletin boards, we got a phone bill. I remember my father saying, 'We have to talk, John. You're on the computer all the time; I guess you've been using your modem.' " The bill was four hundred dollars.

Lester begged his father not to take away his computer. Rather than stop using the modem—it wasn't an option—he worked out how to dial up local computers to reroute his international calls for free. "And that's when I discovered the whole sort of shadow world of people online. I discovered this whole underground who had exactly the same problem as I did. People who wanted to connect with other people on all these long-distance bulletin boards, but didn't want to pay. Not criminals, but people who were interested in trying to communicate more with people."

Through the BBS underground, Lester learned ways to make long-distance calls for free. "The simplest ways were special codes that would allow you to bypass the local telephone company's billing, and actually have it billed to some other company. There were other tricks: You could call the local computer at a university, because their security was always really crappy. That computer would have a modem connected to it, and you would use that modem to then call long-distance. So next time the phone bill came there were like no long-distance calls on the bill." Lester persuaded his father he was making only local calls, and his time in these early virtual communities continued. "We had one phone line, and I was busy on it every night."

He played some bulletin board games, including Trade Wars, but these were turn-based; you had to log off before someone else could log on and play their turn. They were competitive, too, which didn't fit with Lester's excitement about the cooperative possibilities of these early virtual worlds. "I was never into fighting," Lester told me. "I was always very much interested in people working together toward a common goal." Then, in 1983, a friend who was a freshman at the University of Massachusetts in Dartmouth, where Lester grew up, showed him a "dumb terminal"—a basic computer hooked up to the college mainframe computer—and he had his first experience of a truly interactive, live, populated virtual world.

Virtual worlds, in the sense of computer-generated places we can inhabit, have been with us for nearly a third of a century. In the spring of 1979, on Essex University's DEC 10 mainframe—an early computer with 128 kilobytes of storage space, and which came in four refrigerator-size boxes—a young student named Roy Trubshaw constructed a text-based world that people could share: the first Multi-User Dungeon, or MUD. Back then, there was an experimental packet-switching system linking Essex University to ARPANET, the U.S. Department of Defense network that later became the model for the Internet. People who logged on were given a description of their starting place, our first view into virtual worlds: "You are stood on a narrow road between The Land and whence you came. To the north and south are the small foothills of a pair of majestic mountains, with a large wall running around. To the west the road continues, where in the distance you can see a thatched cottage opposite an ancient cemetery. The way out is to the east, where a shroud of mist covers the secret pass by which you entered The Land. It is raining."

Despite the world's limitations, MUD was compulsive. Within a year, people were logging on from halfway around the world. Even if they had never met in the flesh, in this new text-only space, up to thirty-six players at once could meet, talk, and fight. They could even alter the structure of the world by changing room descriptions and adding objects, described in text, that other people could use and in turn alter. (Their modifications soon filled up the DEC 10's fifty kilobytes of usable memory; the assembly code had to be completely rewritten.)

Over the next several years, a few people made some profit. For example, developer Alan Klietz wrote a game, Milieu, using the computer language Multi-Pascal on a CDC Cyber mainframe, an early supercomputer. Klietz sold Milieu as franchises for a few hundred dollars, an amount that now seems extremely modest.

Richard Bartle, who took over MUD development from Roy Trubshaw in 1980, has fond memories of those early, text-only virtual worlds. Decades later, in an industry dominated by graphics, Bartle argues that the text-only form could handle concepts such as multiple perspectives, or more abstract narrative experiences, that graphical games struggle with. "In a textual world, I can stand in my own mouth, seeing my surroundings get light and dark as I open and close it," Bartle wrote. "I can be part of a painting I am carrying under my arm. I can have internal organs. I can photograph an opinion. I can un-erupt a volcano, store the world in a box, hold a soul in the palm of·my hand, dance with the color cyan. Do that in your 3D world.

"I prefer text: the pictures are better," he wrote.

My own introduction to technological worlds was through singleplayer versions of these MUDs. In 1980, when my father worked at a technology mall in San José, California, I would visit him on weekends, spin on a swivel chair, and type, in the game's code, "Go East." "Hit Dwarf," I'd type, and laugh as I read about the dwarf knocking me dead in turn. I learned to type that way: rattling out basic instructions to my new virtual self. Lester, too, was captivated by these textonly virtual worlds.

"That totally blew me away, because you were communicating with people, but then you were also part of a game," Lester says.

Around 1987, however, Lester took a break from computers. At the University of Fribourg, Switzerland, he studied religion, then evolutionary biology. It wasn't until 1991, when he found himself working at Massachusetts General Hospital in Boston, that he bought himself a computer and "started calling bulletin boards again. I re-plugged into the computer underground scene. 'People said, Count Zero! Where have you been!' " (Many of Lester's real-world friends still call him Zero, after Count Zero, his bulletin board "handle.") It was as if he had never left. For a while, he and a friend ran their own virtual community bulletin board. They set up the Boston branch of *2600* magazine, a hacker monthly. Lester still remembers their first meeting—the first time he encountered his virtual friends in the flesh. They spread the word about a meeting in Harvard Square: "I re-member I wrote '2600' on a piece of paper, and I folded it and put it on the table." And people arrived. "It was really intense for me. I mean I remember thinking, Wow, this is the person behind the text on the screen."

Throughout all this, Lester was working as a technician in the neurological department of Massachusetts General Hospital. In 1991, his chief of department, Anne Young, asked him to find cre-ative uses of computer technology to support medical practice. He looked online to see what seemed to be needed. "What I found, pri-marily, were patients and caregivers trying to find each other." He then decided to found an online community to support people with neurological conditions and their carers. He named it BrainTalk, after the cult NPR radio show *Car Talk*. In 2004, Lester, by then a re-search assistant at Harvard Medical School, moved BrainTalk, now one of the largest neurological websites, with two hundred thousand members, away from Mass. General. It is now a nonprofit organiza-tion funded entirely by donations and Google ads.

Back in his cluttered den, John Lester stood and pulled down a wall-size projector screen to show me the BrainTalk website, a message board crowded with discussions on conditions ranging from ADHD to vascular malformations. "What excited me about BrainTalk was the intense sense of community. Every group is differ-ent. Some are about handling disabilities in real life. Some are about starting the staircase of getting back to where you were. We're trying to empower people, raise awareness, and let them know they're not alone. I'm not an encyclopedia. I'm a hotel manager," Lester told me.

In 1999, while Lester was still working on BrainTalk at Mass. General, EverQuest launched. EverQuest was one of the first virtual worlds to offer a first-person perspective, and at the time it was by far the largest. Norrath, as Steve Clover, co-creator and lead programmer, christened the EverQuest continent, now stood at millions of square feet of virtual real estate; at one point, EverQuest would have a per capita GNP greater than that of China. At the start of development, though, the project team had no idea that their creation was to become such a phenomenon.

Clover and his co-designer, Brad McQuaid, had been working as database programmers, developing a single-player role-playing game together in their spare time. The few offers they had for the game fell through, so they posted the demo on the Internet. John Smedley, who co-founded Verant, the company that first developed EverQuest, saw the demo and offered them a job. "As much as we loved database programming," Clover told me in 2004, "we jumped at the chance."

As Bill Trost, senior game designer, remembered, the team's saving grace was that they had no idea what they were getting themselves into. "When I joined the project, EQ [EverQuest] was just an idea," he told me. "They wanted to create a graphical MUD, and had some idea about how it would look, but not many specifics. We had lofty goals but we were lucky: We were too young and too new to realize how difficult it would be."

Clover created the original map of Norrath, inventing the city names—including the branded capital, Qeynos (*SonyEQ* spelled backward)—and, with McQuaid, wrote the main design document. They sketched three continents, accessible by boat, where players could fight, loot, barter, and even learn a trade. "No one had ever made zones of that scale in a 3-D game before," Scott McDaniel, EverQuest's art director, said. "We didn't know what the impact of open geometry or ten thousand polygons would be. The programming and art teams got together, and through sheer trial and error we banged out a system that was robust enough to take dozens of players in a zone, but still allowed the freedom to create very different landscapes."

The geography near the team's offices in San Diego (Clover told me he could "go surfing and skiing in the same day without driving too far") offered inspiration for Norrath's varied terrain. And the eventual population explosion that made the EverQuest phenomenon unique was mirrored in the way the staff ballooned within their small office. "Early on," McDaniel remembered, "there were maybe fourteen people attached to the project. All seven of the artists shared one cube. . . . It was a bonding experience."

McDaniel told me that Norrath, EverQuest's landmass, was Leviathan. "We shipped with seventy-eight zones. Half of those were outdoors and averaged three thousand by three thousand feet across. After that came the Kunark expansion, which had zones that averaged eight thousand by eight thousand feet." When we spoke, five years and hundreds of millions of dollars' worth of revenue later, a team of forty-three developers, supported by over one hundred customer service staff, continued to expand this virtual world—which had more than doubled in size. At peak times, the EverQuest servers exceeded one gigabyte per second of bandwidth—a DVD's worth of data every five seconds. "You're in our world now" was the game's tagline, and they meant it. "Our games aren't about playing for an hour and being done," McDaniel said. When I spoke with the EverQuest team, there were over 430,000 residents, who averaged twenty hours per week as their EverQuest selves.

Soon after EverQuest launched, John Lester began to explore the possibility of more visual communities for BrainTalk. He spent some time in EverQuest, but he felt the world was limited: more like a 3-D story than an entire world. Then, in a meeting on virtual worlds at MIT, he met Mitch Kapor, who had founded the software giant Lotus. Mitch told him about a new project he had invested in: Second Life. "It's the beginning of the metaverse," Mitch told Lester.

Lester—whose Second Life persona, John Prototype, I later discovered, was as lively and as bald as his real-world self—was irrepressibly excited by the possibilities of this uniquely flexible virtual world. It was important to Lester that his communities have the possibility to remain private, but as soon as that facility was added to Second Life—through the ability to buy a private virtual island, in which you could choose whom you allowed to visit—he picked up the phone. "As soon as the private islands were set up, I called Linden Lab, and I said, this is great. I want to get a virtual island. They asked, 'What do you want to do with it?' And I said, 'Hmmm, I'll get back to you.' " Lester began to explore ways to build communities inside Second Life to help people from BrainTalk connect with one another. He created a community for one group, people with Asperger's syndrome. Then John came across a virtual kiosk, inside Second Life, with some writing by a Second Life resident, Wilde Cunningham, played by a group of nine men and women with cerebral palsy. Lester decided to buy Wilde an island.

I first read about Wilde online, in a journal written by Wagner James Au, then employed by Linden Lab, the producers of Second Life. In his blog, Au interviewed Wilde and June-Marie Mahay, the woman who cared for the group in the real world. I e-mailed June-Marie. For days we missed each other's calls, until finally she suggested we meet online, "at her place": her own plot of land inside Second Life.

To prepare for my meeting with June-Marie, I logged in to Second Life, and I built myself anew.

When you first log in to a virtual world, you sculpt your own virtual self to define how others will see you. In some worlds the process is basic: You choose from a set of premade characters, then you choose from a range of preselected paunches, chins, and haircuts. It's a kind of virtual Mr. Potato Head, which can lead to a world full of oddly similar people. In some worlds like Second Life, the process is more complex. In these places, you can customize hundreds of details—eye color, face shape, height, even pot-belly width—to suit your ideal self-image. When I joined Second Life, I hadn't spent much time on my virtual appearance. To prepare for my meeting with June-Marie, I decided to spruce up my Second Life self and re-create my actual appearance as accurately as possible. I stretched my character up to be tall and skinny, and pulled the virtual muscles of my new face until they resembled my real self. Then I added muscle tone (perhaps just a little more than my actual body).

Before I met June-Marie I had a few hours to kill, so I spent some time inhabiting my new virtual shoes. First, though, I had to choose them. In most virtual worlds, including Second Life, you can choose your clothes as well as your self. Each new Second Life character comes equipped with a range of basic clothes, free. I donned a gray T-shirt and blue tennis shoes, and placed a virtual flatcap on my virtual head. After a few adjustments to the T-shirt size, I moved my virtual viewpoint back to check out my new self, then I quickly clicked back to change the size of my love handles.

I had an hour or so to kill, so I took a wander. When I made my second self, I had tried to re-create my real body, but I quickly saw, from the virtual residents I passed, that most virtual residents were eager to liberate themselves from their real-world limitations. There were robot-headed monsters, cartoon-faced clowns, spiky-haired punks, leather-clad dominatrices. There were flying figures, with fairy wings instead of arms.

The landscape, too, was as varied as a dream. I flew over cartoon-ish architecture—fairy-tale castles, blocks of primary colors, upside-down houses in the air—interspersed with some pieces of meticulous realism: office blocks, malls, more than one seaside home of can-tilevered steel and glass. I flew over what looked to be a flying Scrab-ble board, each square as large as the virtual me. I landed near a sign that said "Skydiving." I sat in a seat and traveled up until the sky grew dark and the virtual earth below turned blue. I jumped and fell for long seconds, until I realized I didn't have a parachute. Still, this was the virtual world, and my worries were unfounded. I hit the ground flat, stood up, and brushed myself off.

I could see that, in virtual worlds, people felt freer to experiment in all areas of experience. Near the pool, what looked like a French chateau offered "sub/slave collars." Opposite, a floating golden cube advertised "Ayesha's Antiques Heaven Yard Sale." Under the sign was a virtual furniture store, where, among antique-style Louis XV chairs and vintage crossbows to mount on your virtual wall, you could buy a series of sex positions (including "BJ Push-up") for your virtual self.

Near Antiques Heaven was a fairy-tale castle. The portcullis was down, so I strolled in. Inside was "Mistress Tala Fate," decked out in full virtual dominatrix gear. Tala graciously showed me around her new mansion—it took her three "pets" (subservient players) two days to make it, she said—including a medieval banqueting hall, a waterfall, and a fully equipped torture dungeon. ("I don't know how much you know about 'the lifestyle,'" she said. "Not a whole lot," I replied.) She insisted I stick around for the longer tour. Unwilling to appear rude—and I had the sense someone named Mistress Tala would know how to be persistent—I logged off, waited five minutes, then logged on again somewhere else.

Like most virtual worlds, in Second Life you interact with all the objects around you using a mouse and keyboard. Your pockets, often infinite in depth, are opened in a window that contains everything you can own; in many worlds there's no limit to the size of objects you can carry around, and in Second Life it's a cinch to pull a castle out of your pocket, drop it on the floor, and walk inside. As I watched, a man called Hank Ramos pulled a hot-air balloon out of his pocket and offered me a ride.

Hank showed me the Globe theater, a full-scale re-creation of Shakespeare's original. Next to the Globe, a chessboard loomed out of the mist. "Someone's working on a Scrabble board," Hank told us. We drifted over a volcano, a tree house, a boatyard, and a towering billboard of a woman I didn't recognize. For a while, it looked like we were coming in to land over a virtual Los Angeles: suburban homes in rows, each with their own glittering backyard pool. I asked Hank how to buy some land. He explained virtual property was sold off in parcels by auction or lottery. I wondered aloud about how to get my own virtual seafront home. "Seaside property is much in demand, here as in First Life," Hank said.

The terrain became even more dreamlike. We drifted over platonic solids: a lone torus, a flock of dodecahedrons.

"Look, there's John Linden," Hank said. Every member of the Second Life production team has the surname "Linden"; John's surname—which, like that of every Second Life character, was displayed in floating text above his head for all to see—meant he worked for the people who made this world. I told Hank I would catch up with the balloon, and then I flung my virtual self from the side. I fell, my virtual arms flailing, into the virtual sea.

That day, John Linden had spiky red hair and deep black skin. He looked like the Silver Surfer after too long on a tanning bed. I asked John about his job. He helped shape the worlds, he told me. He asked me to follow, and he led me over the terrain, deep into the ocean—in Second Life you can breathe underwater—then high over a range of newly sculpted hills. As he showed me around, John Linden exhibited the same careful courtesy as had Hank Ramos; in virtual worlds, with many fewer physical cues, it is easy to be misunderstood, and most people seem to bend over backward to be civil.

I asked John Linden about the virtual money. Could people cheat in Second Life? In earlier versions of Second Life, he explained, during a limited test before it was released, people did find ways to create money. But Linden Lab could tell immediately; they monitored the economy closely, he said, and they could spot the appearance of large amounts of money. "That sounds like total surveillance," I remarked. John insisted they didn't monitor everything. "Only in cases of dispute, where it's absolutely necessary."

"That makes me laugh," I said. "That's exactly how everyone everywhere who uses surveillance feels."

In most virtual worlds, the residents communicate with more than just words. Each virtual self has a range of animations for everything he or she does. In Second Life, you can dance, wave, gesticulate, do a backflip. The animation for flying is Superman-style, fists in the air. As I spoke with John Linden, I noticed that certain phrases triggered animations in my virtual self, so that when I typed "That makes me laugh," Errol Mysterio bent forward double and clutched his belly with laughter. John Linden wrote "lol"—short for "laughing out loud." He, too, clutched his belly and dipped low. For a moment our laughter was identical, our two virtual bodies perfectly synchronized.

Then, high up on the hills, talking with the man who made them, I received a message from June-Marie. Her virtual self, Lilone Sand-grain, was online. She offered to teleport me to her location. I clicked "Accept" and seconds later I was by her side.

Lilone Sandgrain, it turned out, was a voluptuous virtual redhead, wearing a skimpy dress made from what looked like virtual crêpe paper. "Have a seat!" she said, smiling. She patted the sofa next to her. I chose a more cautious spot, on a nearby rainforest-print virtual arm-chair. Lilone smiled. "Welcome to my place!"

Around us fluttered a cloud of virtual butterflies, in every color of the rainbow. There were rainbows, too—three of them—as well as a multicolored fire, a waterfall, and a row of glittering fir trees. The air was thick with virtual dandelion seeds. "Peace to your soul," Lilone's scarlet and indigo "elven fire" told us automatically. "You are more than you think you are." In virtual worlds such as Second Life, it's not just your virtual body but also your sculpted virtual landscape that broadcasts your intended self. Here, in Lilone's hand-sculpted garden of New Age delights, I got the impression she liked to look on the bright, multicolored, fairy-lit side of life.

Among the butterflies, we began to talk about Lilone's work. In her real life, she explained, as June-Marie Mahay, she helped out in a Boston, Massachusetts, day-care center for the physically disabled, called Evergreen. Much of her time was spent handling and dis-cussing the challenges of disabled life. (On one occasion, she told me, it took an hour and a half to determine that John, a man in her

care with spina bifida—who could only nod to her questions—
needed a drink of water.) One afternoon, chatting with her group, she
mentioned her online hobby, playing Second Life. They all clam-
ored for a try. The group created a character by consensus, voting on
each element of appearance: spiky red hair, because they had always
wanted to show off, and orange skin as a form of racial compromise.
They called the character Wilde, after the rambunctious group's
nickname. Wilde loved their new online life. They met people, made
friends, and built an online gift shop, which brought them real-world
income. With Lilone's help, they began to spend as much time in
Second Life as the day-care center bureaucracy and their ailing computer network would allow. They were nine real souls inhabiting one
virtual body: multiple personality disorder in reverse.

Lilone told me she was amazed, even after only six months of Second Life, how much the group had changed. "They're so much more
confident now, even in the real world," she said. In the three years she
had worked with the Wilde group, Lilone told me, she had never
seen anything enrich their lives as much as the virtual world.

Then, as Lilone and I talked about Wilde, I realized that something had happened. I had forgotten my First Life self. Like a movie-
goer entranced by the screen, I had become what I saw. I was no
longer sitting at my desk, tapping on my laptop. I was sitting on an
armchair, surrounded by rainbows, talking to Lilone Sandgrain. I was
Errol Mysterio. I had entered the virtual world.

Over the next few weeks, I spent more time online with June-
Marie—more accurately, I spent time with Lilone Sandgrain. Lilone
showed me around Second Life, and told me more about her work
with Wilde. She showed me the virtual sixteen-acre tropical island,
owned and maintained by Wilde, a gift from John Lester, which they
had christened Live2Give. Another time, we met at a pair of virtual
swings hung over a tropical creek. In the background, as we talked, a
group gathered to practice their virtual construction skills on some
abstract shapes. Huge flashing cubes, filled with bright blue spirals,
billowed up behind us, as she explained how hard it was to give Wilde

as much time online as they would like. Hanging out on the swings with Lilone—a curvy redhead, her legs crossed—felt weirdly like a date.

On our final meeting before my real-world trip to Evergreen, Lilone and I met at the top of a tall white tower on Wilde's island. (Wilde liked to teleport to the top of the tower and then jump off, she explained.) We sat and sipped virtual Turkish coffee. Or at least, I tried to. In virtual worlds, it takes time to learn how to control your virtual self. In Second Life, for example, your virtual head turns to gaze wherever your mouse is pointing. If you do nothing for long enough, your virtual self's head slumps forward to let other people know you're not paying attention. I spent much of this particular meeting apologizing to Lilone for staring at her feet, or gazing off to the horizon with my head at ninety degrees, pouring virtual coffee down the side of my neck.

But Lilone had a surprise for me. "Hold on," she said. There was a pop, and, on the stool next to her, someone appeared. It was Wilde's avatar, or virtual self. The word *avatar* comes from the Sanskrit *Avatara*, meaning an incarnation, usually of a god in our mortal world.

"Wilde! Great to finally meet you," I said. I half-expected a chorus, but of course the reply came back as a single line of text.

"The room has filled with smiles," June-Marie typed back at Evergreen, for Wilde. "They are glad to see you too."

"You look a bit different from what I expected," I told Wilde. "You're a woman today."

Wilde laughed. "It's a bit tough for the men, but we alternate playing two months male and two months female. February is our last month as a woman." ("The guys feel funny dressing in dresses," June-Marie later told me. "Perhaps because we girls tease them; the girls don't have any problem being a man.")

Wilde was full of questions for me, about the life of a writer. When I had answered as many as I could, I asked them about Second Life. June-Marie reported on their behalf. "Scott says it's like opening a whole new world. He says it allows him to have a voice and to say things important to him—things he's always wanted to say." (In the real world, the group's lack of language can cripple their interactions; online, with June-Marie as typist and interpreter, they can hold real-time conversations, without all the confusion and anxiety of being misunderstood, or dismissed because of their appearance.)

Since my last online meeting with Lilone, I had shopped for virtual outfits. That evening, on Wilde's rooftop hideaway, I wore my first attempt at a virtual suit—a white tux and bow tie. I joked that I thought I should be serving the Turkish coffee, not drinking it.

In virtual worlds, where landscape is an extension of self, every man can choose to be an island; I asked Wilde how they felt about owning their own. "The room all agrees they love having the island. They love to have a single place to reach out from. The island becomes in a way like a voice for us. We hope in the future to have other people come and also build here." A new member had asked to join their island, Wilde told me. Their new virtual neighbor was a U.K. resident, who wanted to remain anonymous; he had cerebral palsy but could operate Second Life with his toes.

I asked the eight who were present that day if they enjoyed sharing the same virtual self. "Everyone enjoys playing together." There was a long pause. "We feel the most like the rest of the world that we've ever felt," Wilde said.

As Wilde, they were liberated from their daily plight. As Wilde, they could walk. As Wilde, they could dress themselves. As Wilde, they were eloquent, funny, and mobile. As Wilde, they could pilot an airplane, walk the seafloor, live on a tropical island, or hang out with friends.

I asked what the group had been up to in Second Life. "We went to hell yesterday." Wilde bent forward in laughter. "We looked everywhere for it. It's much harder to get into hell than people lead you to believe!"

I asked if they had tried virtual sinning. Wilde laughed again. "No, we didn't think of that! It was a hoot. By the time we found it and had a chance to be stabbed and have blood gush from everywhere it was time to leave."

After spending time with Wilde online, I decided to travel to visit them in person. Meeting online had taken two seconds: I leaned forward at my desk, and clicked my mouse button. Meeting in the real world took two days.

When I pulled up at the Evergreen Center—a single-floor, low-eaved building in Mattapan, on the outskirts of Boston, and daytime home for thirty-seven men and women, all severely mentally or physically disabled—the last thing I expected was mischief.

I was already stunned from the journey. Not long before, my London home had been burgled, and my laptop stolen. I had a last-minute work-visa problem, which led to a careful and selective explanation at U.S. immigration. At JFK Airport in New York, I had rented a cellphone; in the cab from JFK Airport, I had lost the cellphone. I spent a sleepless night slumped at a coffee shop in New York's Penn Station. Above me, a wall-mounted TV played *Fear Factor*: a gaggle of models and actresses who hoped to boil away their sorrows in the bright light of celebrity shut their eyes, dreamed of a better life, and ate cockroaches by the bucket. My train left at 4 A.M. After an hour's nap, we arrived in Boston and I followed my directions all the way to the wrong end of the Red Line subway. I called to report the loss of my cellphone, and headed back to the other end of the city.

So when I slid down a bank of gray snow and into the passenger seat of June-Marie Mahay's dented silver Mercury Lynx, with all my bags in tow (there had been no time to check into a hotel), I was exhausted.

June-Marie, a freckly, frizzy-haired redhead of about forty, hunched forward over the steering wheel and cackled. "You think you've had it bad!" she said. She told me about the last trip she had made with Wilde. At the Logan Airport security checkpoint, all members of the group were lifted from their wheelchairs and thoroughly searched because, she told me, "there are so many places they could hide something." The searches, in full public view, took the better part of an hour. Then, on the return journey, the nine were searched again. Their humiliation was such that June-Marie swore it was the last time. "I'm never taking them on a plane again," she said. But Wilde had found other ways to conquer distance.

At the Evergreen Center, June-Marie led me along a series of blue-walled hallways to the main playroom. There, among the Evergreen residents busy with magazines, jigsaws, or portable radios, she introduced me to the group. Almost immediately, the mischief began. June-Marie led me first to a woman in a wheelchair, in a shiny red down jacket, her black Smurf hat pulled low. "This is Johanna Goode. Johanna has severe cerebral palsy," June-Marie said. "She's in her sixties. Would you believe it?" I shook my head. Johanna's arms twisted, and her jaw writhed in pleasure. "Watch out for her," June-Marie said loudly. "I call her Johanna Bad." Johanna giggled. "She does bad things. Right, Johanna? Don't go near any open closets while Johanna's near. She's liable to lock you in." Johanna reached out to grab at my arm. June-Marie playfully batted her hand away.

A big, round black man strolled up. He wore large, thick-rimmed glasses, an oversized Super Bowl T-shirt, and a bushel of gold-plated necklaces. "I'm Micah. PlayStation, computers, and fuzzy posters," he said, by way of introduction. Micah looked puffed up: His chin rolled and his ankles were wide. His words were muffled, delivered half through his nose, but Micah could walk and speak. (Micah had "mild mental retardation," June-Marie later explained, "although he prefers the term *special needs*.")

After introducing me to the rest of the group, June-Marie straightened up and clapped. "OK guys! It's time to go through to the computer room." This room, twelve feet by ten, was just big enough for us all. Everybody jostled into place, until a jumble of wheelchairs faced the blank far wall. June-Marie squeezed around behind the door to boot up the computer. After a moment a projector, balanced on the edge of the one rickety table, flickered on. A scene appeared, stretched five feet square across the wall. It was a pastoral view: green grass, trees, a gray-brick church spire, all drawn in the clear, perfect lines and shades of computer graphics. Next to the church, piece by piece, a man appeared. First came his broad torso, then thick, spiky hair and long pointy ears. His skin, oddly gray, suddenly turned orange. His spiky hair bled with color, from gray into bright red. The group cheered. Like some virtual worlds, Second Life stores all its virtual objects and people as data on the servers—in this case those of Linden Lab, the world's San Francisco–based developers. Since every object, including every player's virtual self, is custom made, it can take a little while after you connect to Second Life for your character and your surroundings to download. After a few seconds, the man's clothes—baggy blue pants and a Boston Red Sox T-shirt emblazoned with "Who's Your Papi?"—materialized. The group cheered again.

"Look at me!" Mary Boucher, a member of Wilde with severe cerebral palsy, squealed. She pointed a crooked arm at her shared alternate self on the wall. "I'm so beautiful!"

While they were waiting for the background to load, I asked Wilde about their favorite memories from Second Life. June-Marie translated. The last time they had visited Second Life, they had danced with a friend, named Baccara Rhodes. They had come to the virtual church we could see appearing on the screen, to meet the bride of a virtual wedding. Baccara—a well-known Second Life resident who worked full-time as a virtual event manager, arranging celebrations inside Second Life—had wedded another resident, Mash Mandala. (The virtual bride and groom had never met outside Second Life.) Wilde had been invited, but the group couldn't make the date. So, the night before, Baccara dressed up in her wedding gown, which no one else had yet seen, and she danced with Wilde up the aisle.

Over lunch at McDonald's, June-Marie told me how Second Life had become part of the Evergreen routine. She had been working at the center for three and a half years, she told me. Before that, she had worked in a high-pressure managerial position until, hassled by her boss about a cigarette break, she finally quit to do something she felt proud of. She has never looked back. "No regrets, even when the rent's due," she told me. Back then, in her spare time, June-Marie played The Sims Online. But in March 2004, she left this community to become a resident of Second Life, and the following January—four months before my visit—her hobby came up, and the residents all begged to try. The management was reluctant, but after months of "pulling and tugging, lots of red tape and circles," June-Marie said, the center agreed to allow access to Second Life, for four hours each week.

Kathleen Flaherty, the Evergreen Center director, had not been enthusiastic initially about the group spending time on the computer. She told me she had been worried they would be disappointed. By the time of my visit, though, her opinion had changed. "I thought it was a little ambitious. I actually really underestimated the individuals. They've solved more problems than I ever thought they would.

"You and me, when we go to a party, we shake hands, and one of the first things we talk about is what we do for work. Danny will meet you and the first thing he'll say is, 'My name is Danny, I've got cerebral palsy.' And for Danny, it defines him. Now, when I come in the morning, I see Scott and I see Danny and I see Mary—and they're just more alive. Second Life defines them."

Over the next few days I got to know June-Marie, and I witnessed firsthand her constant and fierce support of Wilde. I watched her touch, encourage, and cajole each member of the group toward a feeling of self-esteem. In the hour or so each day they were allowed to inhabit

Second Life, June-Marie's relentless enthusiasm swept Wilde along through the daily chores of maintaining and updating a virtual island. At home each evening, June-Marie spent hours making tweaks or larger changes to the island, on Wilde's daytime instructions. (One member's pride and joy, which she kept upstairs in her pink and purple house on the north side of their island, next to a cabinet and a canopy bed, was her twenty-strong virtual doll collection. The day I arrived, June-Marie had been up at 4 A.M., working on a new doll.) June-Marie's job title at Evergreen was Senior Case Manager and Human Rights Officer, but she called herself their mascot. It was a self-deprecation that both belied and drew attention to her own importance. Without her, their virtual life would be impossible.

And, through June-Marie, I began to get to know Wilde. I saw their innocence, when June-Marie asked me to cover my notebook—a *New Yorker* cartoon depicting a partially nude mosaic. I saw their joy, when June-Marie's real-world boyfriend, who logged in to Second Life under the name of Ace Cassidy, suggested they hold a virtual wheelchair demolition derby, and they all roared with laughter. Also, I saw their burning drive to be understood. Wilde seemed to me guileless, forceful, and direct. Their inner life had been held in so long, it seemed, they had no time to play games or withhold. Their every effort was focused on expressing as fully as they could.

On my final day at Evergreen, when we arrived back in the playroom after their Second Life session, I asked if any in the group wanted to speak with me privately.

One member, Mary, nodded to June-Marie. Until now, Mary had been reluctant to speak. She tended to put the others first. (The previous April Fool's Day, June-Marie told me, a friend at Evergreen tricked Mary into believing she had won the lottery. She tried to run the same trick on Danny, but she had barely finished before she blurted out: "No sir! I can't lie to you!") In my group discussions with Wilde, Mary had always waited till last. Only when Scott raised his

hand, and asked Mary to talk for him—"Scott is Mary's most favorite," June-Marie whispered to me under her breath—had Mary
spoken up.

Mary had waited her turn, and now she wanted to have her say.
The group filed out. For the first ten minutes, Mary stuck to a famil-
iar line of conversation, and June-Marie had no trouble interpreting.
Mary began by describing her life. She owned her own apartment,
June-Marie explained. She liked computers—on a scale of one to
ten, computers were a ten. She didn't have one at home, but she
would like to if she could: She would spend three hours a day online.
She moaned, a long sound of distress. "I wish I could stand up," June-
Marie interpreted.

Mary talked on. She had been married and divorced. She had personal care assistants (Cynthia was her favorite) who came to care for
her basic needs a few times a day. She had had no contact with her
family for decades. "Not all family relationships are helpful," Mary
said.

Then Mary indicated she had something else to say. This wasn't
part of her usual conversation. June-Marie leaned in close to listen.

"You . . . Would . . . Like . . . To. Say. If everybody. Listens. To the
disabled. It could change the world. Is that right?" Mary nodded.
"You," said June-Marie. "Think. Your. What?"

"Feelings," June-Marie said. Mary nodded. "Are. Real."

Mary choked, coughed, and nodded.

"You," translated June-Marie. "Feel. People. Don't take you . . . seriously. You. Don't know. What. To do. To change things."

"Do you think Second Life will help in that way?" I asked.

Mary writhed her legs and arms, nodded, and groaned. "Yes,"
June-Marie said. "You. Love to play. Second Life. You. Feel. You.
Have. The right. To be who you are."

Mary coughed again.

"That's all," June-Marie said. Mary started to cry. "It's OK," June-
Marie said. "You can cry."

Mary cried herself out, and we sat in silence. Then Kathleen, the center coordinator, stuck her head in the doorway: It was two-thirty, and the van had arrived to take Mary home. As I followed Mary out of the room, she groaned something to me over her shoulder. Without thinking, I replied, "It was good to meet you, too."

"Did you hear that?" June-Marie said. "He understood you."

Mary nodded. She reached up and she pushed her fingers into mine.

LINDEN LAB

Dreamers of the dream

In July 2007, there were 7.7 million registered Second Life accounts. Back in May 2005, when I first visited Linden Lab, Second Life was home to just twenty-five thousand people.

Linden Lab was a small start-up company, named after the address of its first San Francisco offices, 333 Linden Street. Philip Rosedale, the CEO, had begun the business with his own capital, along with investors and entrepreneurs who had made fortunes from such tech companies as Lotus, Xerox, eBay, and Yahoo. When I visited, there were thirty or so employees. Most people in the real world had never heard of Second Life, but to Linden Lab employees, it was everything.

What made Second Life different from most virtual worlds was that Linden Lab sculpted only the landscape. Apart from some core elements (such as Orientation Island), everything was made by the residents. For Linden Lab, this was a coup. It avoided the immense effort and huge start-up cost required to build the contents of the world; they just laid out the territory, and let the inhabitants fill it.

This ability to create and to shape objects at will was the notion that first captivated Rosedale. He had always loved to build things, but, even as a child, he had been frustrated by the limitations of the real world. In fourth grade, Philip built his first computer from a kit. In eighth grade, he bought a retractable garage door motor, climbed into his attic, and sawed a hole in the ceiling so that when he pushed a button his bedroom door would slide up, *Star Trek* style, into the attic. It wasn't easy, though, to shape an entire universe according to his dreams. "I would imagine some neat thing and then try to build it in the real world, and it was rather difficult," he told me. "You run into problems like abrasion and friction and the fact that you can't just cut things." That year, frustrated by his growing ambitions, Rosedale began to yearn for a "magical machine," a super-technical tool belt that would let him build whatever he wanted, without worrying about all the real-world practical limitations that stood between him and his imagination.

By June 1999—after putting himself through college with the profits from his own software company—Philip decided that what he wanted wasn't the ability to change the real world, but to conquer it and replace it with something better: a virtual world with no barrier between thought and action. He left his position as chief technology officer of RealNetworks, which had bought out his video streaming software, and joined forces with an old colleague to form Linden Lab. Their vision was a renovation of Philip's childhood dream: a world where people could build whatever they liked, and become whoever they wanted.

Right from the beginning of online worlds, the players were quicker than the developers to recognize the possibilities in their new virtual lives. The designers of EverQuest were stunned when they discovered players were getting married online. In The Sims Online, you can combine objects, but not create new ones, and the residents worked hard to overcome this limitation. In one case, a group of Sims residents decided they wanted a piano, so they built one out of a desk and chairs, with cigars for piano keys. Linden Lab decided to harness that creative force and allow its users to build literally anything they liked. Compared to the amusement-park atmosphere of other games, where missions and goals are laid out like set rides—the same experience for everyone—this world would be more like a public park, with a minimum of rules. Linden Lab would create the physics, design the interface, and invent the basic ownership guidelines, and with luck, a whole virtual society would emerge. Linden Lab christened its world "Second Life," for what they saw as its unique benefit. "We agonized over the name," Philip told me. "We got into this classic marketing thing, where you talk about features and benefits. So the feature is a distributed computing environment in which you can build anything, but the benefit is a Second Life."

I met Philip at Linden Lab's latest real-world office, near the North Beach area of San Francisco: a gray stone-walled, high-ceilinged, loft-style building, with thirty or so desks grouped together in clover-like fours, with huge, high-spec PCs on each. On the wall were pinups that looked like holiday destinations—a Japanese temple, a tropical island—but were, of course, pictures of places in Second Life. The atmosphere was part cutting-edge start-up tech company, and part hardcore gaming café. (To our right, one employee was busy blow-drying his painted fantasy figurines.)

When Linden Lab employees first joined the company, they were given new virtual names. Many were already Second Life residents, and they kept their original selves, but for all official work, they used their "Linden" avatar. So, for example, Philip Rosedale's virtual self was called Philip Linden. In Second Life, as in most virtual worlds, each character's name is displayed above his or her virtual head, so that in Second Life, when you meet one of the world's creators, you know right away who it is.

I had met John Linden, another Linden Lab employee, inside Second Life, but not Philip. Philip Rosedale's Second Life self looked much like his real-world body—cropped blond hair, wide blue eyes. The real Philip had a wide mouth, and blond hair, and when he grew excited, his eyes widened. When he talked about Second Life, he grew excited a lot.

We sat at his desk, and Philip logged in. His other persona, Philip Linden, appeared on-screen. He hadn't been online for a few days, he explained. His last visit to Second Life had been for the wedding of two longtime Second Life residents, Mash Mandala and Baccara Rhodes. (The wedding was so well attended, Philip explained, that the server nearly crashed; to reduce the number of objects the server had to handle, the bride asked everyone to remove their hair.) Philip's avatar was still hovering beside the virtual chapel, dressed to the virtual nines: a tux and white bow tie, red virtual rose pinned to his virtual breast.

We talked about his clothes. He had bought them himself, from a virtual mall. Fashion, he said, was a great example of how Second Lifers created their world. In the two years since Second Life appeared online, the available outfits had developed from very basic to extremely sophisticated, some the work of successful real-world designers. Much of the in-world Second Life content that is for sale is also advertised outside the world, on websites such as http://shop.onrez.com, where you can use your real-world credit card, or in some cases even your cellphone, to buy virtual haute couture that is delivered directly to you online (with, of course, no shipping charges). Philip showed me a few garments—skirts, garters, gowns—and pointed out the complex visual tricks: realistic-looking effects that had surprised even Linden Lab employees. Residents can also shop inside Second Life itself; they can take a virtual stroll through one of the many virtual malls, hand over their virtual cash, and receive outfits from automated machines that let them try before they buy. It's not just clothes; you can buy vehicles—a virtual Ferrari will set you back 800 Linden Dollars, or about $2.40 in real money. You can buy accessories (a virtual Apple Blueberry iBook goes for 200 Linden Dollars), and, of course, there's the largest market: property. (A prefabricated virtual beach house goes for 1,800 Linden Dollars, about 6 real dollars, but that's before you've bought the land to put it on.)

Philip showed me maps of the Second Life landmass as it grew: from the virtual equivalent of around 140 acres, in March 2002, to around 11,200 acres when I visited the world in early 2004. Demand for virtual land was so high, Philip said, they were adding 160 acres a week.

And all this was exactly what they had hoped for. They would never have had the resources to create such a complex world themselves, but because of the free-form nature of Second Life, they didn't have to. Buildings, vehicles, clothing, even custom-made gestures—a dance, a wave, a different kind of laugh—all designed by residents, are at the center of most Second Life activity and trade.

As an example, Philip gave me a tour of third-party websites, run by Second Life residents, which sold virtual clothes. At these sites, with names like 2ndlook, you could input your credit card details and purchase a pair of socks (twenty cents), a ball gown (forty cents), or a furry bear suit (two dollars). (I asked if Second Life experienced fashion trends. Philip didn't have the figures, but from what I had already seen in virtual worlds, hemlines went up, and they stayed up. In Second Life, where perfect body shapes were the norm, people had it, and they flaunted it.) He took me through a gallery of images of community-made dresses; they looked as varied and as fashionable as those from the pages of *Vogue*. Philip explained how fast they had seen fashions evolve in Second Life, in a kind of arms race between designers for innovations that would attract virtual business. Early clothes were just 3-D shapes, but soon designers learned to make their dresses look like real cloth. At the time of my visit, the latest fashion was for hand-sculpted dresses, with carefully modeled creases and folds. The open attitude to currency exchange had created a whole virtual economy. Residents worked—as designers, event managers, pet manufacturers, hug makers, even virtual strippers—to earn Linden Dollars. "The market is getting very competitive," Philip told me. "There's money to be made." At the time of my visit, twenty or so Second Life residents sold enough virtual clothes, property, and animations to exchange their virtual profit for U.S. dollars and live off the result.

"All this really incredible stuff is coming from the community," Philip said. "I think that one of the surprises with Second Life is the degree to which people do tend to want to rebuild the world that they know. So people's first purpose is to make an avatar that looks like them, and their second one is to have a luxury car, or a house on a cliff, overlooking the ocean, built with wood, and with high ceilings. People first rebuild the world that they know, and only then do they defy it or experiment with it." Philip took travel as an example. In Second Life, you can walk, or fly, but you can also buy vehicles to travel faster and in higher style. "So people start with the Ferrari, and then after that they think, Well, where could I go from this? How about a floating car?" Only later do they realize they can grow wings. (Philip told me how, when they first opened their world to residents, they began with twenty people in 140 virtual acres; each one immediately built a virtual house, even though there was not yet any virtual rain.)

"We're trying to create an environment where any kind of stuff can happen. It's their world," Philip told me. He turned to his screen and showed me a Web page: Online photo albums captured Second Life residents' favorite virtual moments. Someone called Kit Calliope rode a giant green dragon; there was an arty shot of a flock of flying metal bubbles; someone else was dressed up as a cartoon squirrel. (The poster of the picture asked, "Is this the cutest squirrel in the world?") Philip likened Second Life to Burning Man, the festival in Black Rock, Nevada. Once a year, for eight days, around forty thousand visitors build a fantasy town on the dry plain of an ancient lakebed to create a place where almost anything goes. Inside his virtual world, Philip Rosedale hoped for the same freedom of expression, the same abandon of day-to-day concerns.

Above Philip, a beautiful woman with fairy wings looked down and waved. Philip grew animated. In the new digital frontier, he told me, people were *nice*. "I'm actually pretty introverted. I was a really nerdy kid and definitely not gregarious," he told me. To illustrate the friendliness inside virtual worlds, Philip imagined a situation where, in a strange place, he saw a beautiful woman. "In real life if I came out of the subway in Paris or New York or London, and I saw some beautiful woman, I wouldn't just go walk over to her. Yet in Second Life, you do that almost instantly."

"I don't know if the general public understands the fundamental love Linden Lab has for the community," Philip said. "When residents see a Linden, they think, They have god powers. They could delete me. But it's not like that." He laughed. "Well, we *can* delete them—but we don't. We are more like custodians. We make sure the trees grow, the land remains, the ocean flows. We're not so much gods—we're groundskeepers."

To Philip, the world of Second Life was a triumph of self over other, an opportunity to improve on the real. "Second Life is a world which is perhaps in many ways identical to the world we live in, but, in a number of significant ways, better."

Philip had a world to run, so he passed me on to Linden Lab's chief technology officer, Cory Ondrejka. In order to make Second Life run more smoothly, and reduce the number of objects each computer has to display, in Second Life there is a "mist" that fades in to cover distant terrain—you can only see people and objects nearby. Cory showed me a picture of the virtual world were this mist to disappear, and you could see forever: a seemingly limitless jumble of construction that looked as messy and as captivating as any real-world city. (Philip told me the ratio of residents to virtual land meant their world was "already as dense as Tokyo.") Cory in turn passed me on to Catherine Smith, the Linden Lab community manager.

As it happened, the day before I arrived, Catherine had called me. She was upset at my use of a quote in a U.K. magazine article about one of Second Life's best-known residents. (She'd called him a nut. "We love him, but he's a nut.") Another Linden Lab employee, Wagner James Au, was upset that some quotes of his I had used had been misattributed because of an editing error. The resident Catherine had called "a nut" was upset, and Au was annoyed, and some other Linden Lab employees—Catherine included—seemed far more offended than the situation warranted. Perhaps they felt their world was vulnerable: Second Life was a small world, with just twenty-five thousand residents (although two thousand new residents joined each week, and they added ten new servers each week to cope with the load). A bigger company wouldn't have cared—press coverage is press coverage—but Linden Lab seemed more idealistic and more protective over their world than most game companies. I faced a kind of immune-system response: Was I friend? Or foe? As the day went on, the immune-system response to my arrival softened into a kind of wary half trust, but I still sensed some resentment. Robin Harper, Linden Lab's vice president of community development and support, discussed how her work encouraged Second Life communities. She told a story of a group of students, studying a class inside Second Life, who posted conversations, including names, alongside some derogatory comments about Second Life residents, on a public Web page. The residents were hurt and angry, and the students were asked to come into Second Life and apologize in (virtual) person. "It was a very uncomfortable situation for a lot of people. They learned the hard way," she said, with a pointed look at me.

After I left Linden Lab offices, I slunk around the corner and nursed a coffee. I felt uncomfortable. I had made a mistake by not checking the magazine article edits, and although their response had been extreme, I felt culpable. I knew my journey into virtual worlds would become a journey into our own world. I knew, like any medium, they would change how we saw ourselves. What hadn't yet sunk in was how the world might change me.

On my way back from Linden Lab, I passed back through Boston to see Wilde again. After getting into Logan Airport at 6 A.M., I flagged a taxi and slung my bag into the trunk. Slumped in the backseat, I gave the address of the Evergreen Center. The driver told me it was a long way; it would cost over a hundred bucks, but I knew it couldn't be that far. Bleary-eyed from lack of sleep, I told him something was wrong, and asked him to stop. I leaped out, grabbed my cellphone to call Evergreen, and watched the cab drive away. Only after a few seconds did I realize I had forgotten my bag.

There was no sign of the taxi. I ran back to taxi controller, who told me there was no way to track down a cab without the license plate. He asked what it looked like. "Yellow," I said. He brayed with laughter. He gave me a list of the five main taxi firms, and told me to call each in turn. I walked back to the terminal door and dialed the first number. My phone beeped, then the battery went dead. I slid down the wall onto a pile of snow and held my head in my hands.

I bought a new telephone charger and called every taxi company in Boston. Although they all told me I would never see my bag again, I left my name and number with each.

To replace my belongings I needed a police report to give to my insurers, so I trekked through the slush past three terminals to the airport police. Then, bagless and cold, exhausted and feeling like a failure, I gave up. I walked a mile to the airport hotel and got a room. I stripped off my wet clothes, showered, and got into bed.

"You can hold yourself back from the sufferings of the world," Kafka wrote in his Blue Octavo Notebooks. "This is something you are free to do, and in accordance with your nature. But perhaps precisely this holding back is the only suffering you might be able to avoid."

I switched on the porn channel, bought some nonexistent company for the night, and held back my suffering for as long as I could.

On my final night in Boston, I took John Lester and June-Marie out to dinner. As we waited for our food, we talked about the decisions people make when they sculpt their virtual selves. John Lester, I knew, had modeled his virtual self exactly on his real body. I asked June-Marie why she hadn't made her avatar like herself. Too late, I realized my faux-pas. "You mean, why did I make myself hot?" There was an awkward pause. "Well, I meant, hotter . . ." I said. They laughed.

I mentioned the difficult time I had had with Linden Lab. John Lester insisted they meant well. "They'll come around. It'll blow over. I've told them: You're a friend." His language—us, them, friend, foe; the clear line between those who shared the dream and those who did not—reminded me of my childhood.

John announced he had some news. When we last met, Lester had told me he was in talks with Linden Lab to work with them in some capacity. Between my first and second visits, after an eight-hour interview in their San Francisco offices with eight of the top Linden Lab people—what Lester called "the gauntlet"—John had been hired by Linden Lab to help manage their community. "I am now Pathfinder Linden," he announced. He reached under his sweatshirt and pulled out a medallion: a pewter hand with a black leather strap. It was the Second Life logo: an eye inside a curlicued hand. Every new employee was given one, he said. "The eye observes the world, the hand shapes it," a card that accompanied the locket explained. "For this reason, many cultures embrace the eye-in-hand as a symbol of creation that springs from knowledge—as do we. Take it as your invitation to help create a Second Life that inspires ever more wonder, ever more imagination."

"The pendant flashes when I say something against the Linden Lab party line," John Lester joked.

We ate—when the bill came, John Lester joked about how virtual lobster was so much cheaper—and at Harvard Square station we waved goodbye. On the train, I couldn't help but still feel troubled about Linden Lab's overreaction to what they felt were misquotes. On my visit, Philip Rosedale's messianic zeal—which informed the whole Linden Lab endeavor—had become apparent. "We're not building a game, we're building a new world," Philip told me. "We can't understand why there aren't a million people in Second Life." In a way, he reminded me of my mother and her friends, who, in their mission to spread the word about the perfect new world they were building, sometimes ran roughshod over other people's feelings. Hidden behind Linden Lab's liberal attitude, it seemed, there was an unacknowledged moral superiority. They were, as Freud wrote about us all, "far more moral than they thought, and far more immoral than they could imagine."

Some residents resented the Lindens' power over the universe, and their tendency to make choices according to their own agenda about what was "fair." One resentful customer had already christened the company KremLinden Lab. And I wasn't the only one to receive Catherine Smith's wrath. In December 2005, CBC Radio reporter Lindsay Michael put out a request on a Second Life community website for Second Life residents in the Toronto area. One resident, known as Plastic Duck, wrote to Michael, announcing his intentions to "expose just how filthy [Second Life] is these days." Smith also wrote to Michael. "I noticed your call for interviews in the Second Life Herald and wanted to speak with you directly about Plastic Duck," she wrote. "You may or may not know that Plastic Duck has been banned from Second Life for griefing and generally anti-social behavior . . . you probably won't get a very balanced interview from him. And he is certainly not representative of our community." Linden Lab later amended their "Research Ethics in Second Life" policy to instruct any reporters who wanted to interview Second Life residents to contact the Linden Lab marketing department first.

Once more, their underground morality reminded me of the idealized communes of my childhood. I had felt the sharp end of Bhagwan's disciples' mania for positivity (at least before their foray into criminality): They labeled me "negative," the only sannyasin sin. Bhagwan's communes were intended as places of "Life, Love, and Laughter." Virtual worlds, too, inspired a similar, almost religious, devotion.

The parallels were uncanny. My mother and her friends, for the most part, declared their devotion to their guru, Bhagwan, in a letter. In return, Bhagwan wrote back: "Dear Beloved . . ." and, in his reply, gave them each a new name. And here, again, in this new, idealized corner of the universe, each Second Life employee received a new surname. My mother and her friends wore a locket with a picture of their guru. Linden employees, on becoming a Linden, were given a Second Life logo to wear around their necks.

I began my journey back to London with mixed feelings about my stay. At Boston's Government Center station, I changed to the Blue Line northbound. On the platform, a balding rocker in a green corduroy jacket set down a portable amp and plugged in an electric guitar. The empty station echoed to the mournful chords of Pink Floyd's "Wish You Were Here."

There was one more airport train, scheduled for 12:49 A.M. I saw the train's destination listed on the departure board and laughed. I closed my jacket against the cold and waited for the last train to Wonderland.

4

HACKING MATTER

Changing the world for fun and profit

After my visit to Wilde, I didn't return to Second Life for six months. I had begun my journey in a small virtual world and discovered a new mix of trouble and consolation. The trouble had become personal: I worried about Linden Lab's reaction, even though I didn't feel I had actually done anything wrong. I felt awkward about returning to their world when they weren't sure about my intentions. Also, the real world intervened with its own plans. On my return, all the loss and struggle of the journey—the plane flights, the insurance claims, the lost bags and cellphone, the 4 A.M. starts and the rainy waits for cabs—only added to my struggle with the daily tasks of real life. The world and its responsibilities reared up and threatened to swallow me again. In the burglary before I left, my laptop had been stolen. Disheartened, I began the slow process of reconstructing my notes from scratch. The relationship I had been in for five years broke up, and I began to search for a new home. The money I had spent on a PC, my gateway to virtual worlds, left a deeper hole in my pocket. I took up smoking and I was partying too much, on money I didn't have. Once more I was struggling to face up to the challenge of my mistakes and my history.

Virtual worlds had at first seemed attainable and inhabitable: a smaller, safer world where I might find some solution to the almost intolerable pressure of the real. But even there I had found strife. I was having trouble even spending enough time in the worlds themselves. Who had the time to lead two lives? I barely had time to live one.

To tell the truth, I was also ashamed. I had offended real people, and felt real wrath. I hid from Second Life in the same way I had always responded to this kind of thing. As a child, faced with the antagonism of a commune that didn't understand my resistance, I had armed myself with a science fiction novel and a Marmite sandwich, and taken refuge behind a commune sofa.

To add to my troubles, I discovered that the cellphone I had rented at JFK on my first visit to Massachusetts, and which I thought had been lost, had in fact been stolen. In the twelve hours before my call to report the loss, the thief had made more than two hundred calls to Africa. The cellphone company, Rentacell, billed my credit card thousands of dollars and my bank refused to reimburse me.

The theft made me think of the now-colossal economies of virtual worlds. Of the estimated yearly $400 million in virtual trade, I thought, there must be rich pickings for scammers and thieves. I logged on to EverQuest II—population three hundred thousand—and I took on the role of virtual gumshoe.

That was how I met Noah Burn.

Noah, a ponytailed twenty-four-year-old aspiring writer from Myrtle Beach, South Carolina, had discovered a way to alter the very fabric of the virtual universe itself. In his real life, Burn worked as a showroom salesman, selling what he called "upscale designer furniture." "It was well paying," he told me, "but not as well paying as EverQuest." For Noah, who journeyed to the murkier side of virtual trading, virtual furniture became more lucrative than real furniture could ever be. Noah, previously a resident of EverQuest, was new to EverQuest II, a revised and refurbished version: the same basic fantasy world, but with better graphics, new quests and areas, new foes, and new spells and weapons to discover. For many, the appeal of the more gamelike virtual worlds such as EverQuest and its sequels are the "trade skills"—ways to use your character to make and sell virtual things, for virtual money. In this way, characters can support each other by providing objects—weapons, armor—that they have made. I had always found this process tedious; I couldn't understand the appeal of spending hours fashioning virtual shoes, when I wouldn't for a moment consider spending my time that way in the real world. But others, including Noah, enjoyed the process. At least, Noah thought he would. Excited by the new ways of making virtual things in EverQuest II, Noah set up an account as soon as the game launched, in November 2004, but, like me, he quickly grew bored of making virtual things. ("I was promised that trade skills would be more fun in this game than the last," he said, referring to changes in the rules that supposedly made in-world construction more fun. "I tried them; they weren't. It was a no-talent, button-mashing marathon.") For a while, Noah set up a basic virtual gambling den, what he called "a ghetto casino," where people would pay him and, using a random number generator inside EverQuest II, double their money if they scored more than sixty–five. "The odds were horrible, but they kept coming," Noah told me. "It was like Vegas, really—except no free drinks, and the people weren't social." Bored of dealing with money-grubbing strangers, Noah decided to move into a variation of a business he already knew. He set up a virtual furniture store. Noah's character, a gnome called Methical, found places in little-known areas (what he called "the dark side of the game") to buy desirable virtual furnishings—an oil painting, an ornate chair, a wine rack—for fifty pieces of virtual silver. He turned his apartment into a virtual showroom, and sold his furniture to residents with less virtual nous, for twice the price.

One afternoon in early 2005, he bought a rare Gnomish Thinking Chair to sell at a slim profit. He opened his inventory—which appeared as a window on his screen—clicked "Sell" to put the item up

for sale, then closed the sale window to better see his virtual showroom. Normally, when Noah put an item up for sale, it disappeared
from his possession until it was sold, at which point the object reappeared in the possession of the buyer. Unusually, this time Noah
found he could return the chair to his showroom. He thought nothing of it, until later in the day when he got a message from another
EverQuest II resident, JimBob. "This chair isn't as cool as I thought it
was."

"What chair?" Noah—Methical—messaged back.

"The Gnomish Thinking Chair," JimBob replied. Methical looked
over: The same chair was still on his showroom floor. In his real-
world room, Noah started laughing. "It was the kind of laugh you
have when you're a kid and you just hit a house with an egg," he told
me. Noah contacted his "guild," a group of friendly players. "I think
I just duped something," he said. Noah had discovered a bug in the
game's code, which meant he could copy any virtual item whenever
he liked. He could buy one expensive item, copy it, and sell it to as
many buyers as he could find.

Uncovering a way to duplicate items was the equivalent of a virtual printing press for dollar bills, Noah realized. If he played his
cards right, he could find himself sitting on a very real gold mine. He
called on a friend from Oregon, Liz, also an EverQuest II resident,
and the pair set out to build a career as virtual forgers. They copied a
few items to confirm the Gnomish chair wasn't a fluke. Then they set
up a production line.

To maximize their profit, the pair focused on the most expensive
items, beginning with candelabras. (After all, Noah knew the virtual
furniture market inside out.) Noah offered ten candelabras for sale,
placed them in his showroom, and then Liz bought them; they had
twenty candelabras. Then they had forty candelabras. Finally, they
owned more candelabras than they could store in Noah's virtual
apartment. They sold them to other residents for two gold pieces
each. After a day of trading, they had sold a hundred candelabras,
which netted them two platinum pieces of virtual money. This was at

a time when virtual item trading sites sold platinum, one piece at a time, for three hundred dollars. The next night they copied furniture, Noah said, "until our eyes bled." Bored of candelabras, they switched to high-end paintings, which went for five gold pieces (about five dollars) each.

In virtual terms, the two were rich. The pair worried that the authorities—Sony Online Entertainment, which runs EverQuest II— might notice their forgery and confiscate the profits. To launder their virtual money, they bought virtual mansion houses, the best spells, the most expensive in-game horses they could find. "Hell, I even bought stuff and then just destroyed it. I had a crazy idea that the more I spread the money around, the less chance I would get banned. It started to feel like *Goodfellas*," Noah recalled. "You know, that scene where they rob the airport, then all the mafia members are told to lay low and not spend any money. Then one guy shows up with a fur coat and a Cadillac."

Each morning they prepared to discover they had been caught red-handed, and each morning they found they could continue their forgery. The excitement kept them in EverQuest II for up to twenty hours straight. "I can't even describe the almost magical feeling—of just being some mad scientist while everyone just walks past you on the server, not knowing what you're up to." Noah found the single most lucrative item: a rare virtual pet dog, called a Halasian Mauler, on which they focused their forgery. They bought more copies of EverQuest II, running multiple copies at the same time, all the better to forge their dogs. They were making two platinum pieces—worth six hundred dollars—every few hours. On six of EverQuest II's twenty-three servers, their level-5 characters (in the EverQuest II level hierarchy, which continues up to level 50, these were the virtual equivalent of preschoolers) were the richest in the game. They had so much money that they considered just copying items for fun: setting up a houseful of expensive baby dragons and simply giving them away. "We actually had about twenty or thirty baby dragons duped before we decided that this plan made no sense," Noah said. "And, well, money is cool. I like money."

The pair then took the step that would make them a real-world fortune. They began to sell the proceeds of their virtual counterfeiting
for real dollars. They hit the auction sites, selling at 50 percent of the
market rate just to shift more platinum. Noah knew he was doing
something questionable, and every day he expected Sony to fix the
bug that allowed them to copy items. But weeks later they were still
selling. They spoke on the phone to negotiate with virtual currency
brokers, sometimes ten calls an hour. Worried about real-world consequences, they confessed to many of the third-party virtual currency
brokers where they were getting their platinum; none cared. "They
said things like, 'We can't know that,'" Noah said. "And then they
would follow it up with, 'Keep cranking out the money.'" (No wonder. Judging by the buy and resell prices on some of the companies,
Noah probably made them close to $300,000.)

Noah and his co-conspirator sold so much virtual currency that
they flooded the market. Platinum prices dropped 60 percent. Of
course, they too were scammed: six times they sold virtual cash to
buyers who refused to pay, losing a total of around $5,000. But they
kept on selling. So much money began to accumulate in their real
bank accounts that Noah consulted a lawyer and an accountant to
make sure they weren't risking prosecution. Both professionals just
threw up their hands. "Needless to say, neither of them had any idea
what we were talking about," Noah told me.

Ultimately, the dogs were their undoing. Anyone who strolled into
Noah's virtual showroom—and there was no way to lock the door—
might see twenty-four of the most expensive dogs in the game lined
up ready to sell. When confronted by savvy buyers, Noah made ex-
cuses ("I'm quitting EQ2. I figured this would be a fun way to blow
my money"), but not everyone was convinced. On EverQuest II websites, players began to post complaints about the sudden deflation.
Then one morning, three weeks after Noah had copied his first
Gnomish chair, he logged on to find a message from Sony: "Mer-
chants will no longer have any interest in purchasing your pets."

It was a change aimed squarely at the pair's dog-forging operation. They knew the game was up. They decided to dump their virtual booty, and so sold their dogs, horses, and mansions at a quarter of the usual price. To cover their tracks, they destroyed whatever they couldn't sell. Nonetheless, the next day, some — but not all — of their accounts were banned. Sony e-mailed Noah. "Greetings. I regret to inform you that your account has been banned for duping items in order to generate large amounts of coin. Your account will be closed from this point forward."

Publicly, Sony announced they had tracked the duped money and made it disappear from the world, but they never contacted Noah or Liz again. Other residents who Sony believed had ties to the duplicated money — to determine who had received what, Sony sifted through their activity logs — also had their accounts banned. The company introduced a number of new economy reporting tools to avoid a repeat of the incident. But there was no way for Sony to recall the real-world money Noah and Liz had made. (When we spoke, Noah told me he still had nine virtual selves in EverQuest II — and some of them still possessed a share of their forged virtual booty.)

The problem of rectifying virtual deflation is not trivial. Sony decided to remove as much of the forged platinum as they could find; other virtual world makers have found different solutions. In 1997, a player in Ultima Online, a fantasy virtual world, discovered a gold-copying bug like Noah Burn's. The economy collapsed, and residents found their once-valuable virtual objects were worth almost nothing. After they fixed the bug, the Ultima Online team faced the challenge of how to remove the currency from the game. They decided to release a new item, a red hair dye, that altered the appearance of residents in a unique way. Because the dye was rare, everybody wanted it; prices rose. Slowly, the duplicated money leaked back out of the hands of residents and into the hands of automated shopkeepers. The economy stabilized.

—

I asked Noah how much money the pair had made. Initially he was reluctant to reveal the total. "It's allowed me to go to both Hawaii and Paris, as well as pay off student loans. Just know, it's more than some people make in a year. Hell, maybe three years." Later, he told me the pair made almost $100,000.

I asked Noah what he had learned from his days as a virtual forger. He compared it to a scene from *The Matrix*, in which a character inside a virtual world bends a virtual spoon with the power of his mind. "There is no fucking spoon," Noah said.

Similar loopholes have been found in other virtual worlds. One group of World of Warcraft residents discovered this method: They handed a friend a large amount of gold, but didn't click "Trade" to complete the transaction. They left that area of the virtual world, returned, and discovered that both residents retained the gold; they had doubled their money. The bug was fixed within days, but in the meantime they, too, made a profit. In another case, EverQuest II residents discovered another loophole and made so much virtual cash they caused a 20 percent deflation in the virtual economy; the amount of money inside the virtual world increased by a fifth in just twenty-four hours. To stop the virtual market crash, Sony temporarily closed the entire world.

With over a million residents now inside EverQuest II, tracking every potentially fraudulent transaction is unrealistic. In June 2005, Sony opened the Sony Station Exchange, where players could trade certain items without prejudice. In a statement explaining their decision, John Smedley, one of the original EverQuest designers, told his residents: "Dealing with fraudulent transactions of one type or another takes up roughly 40 percent of our customer service people's time." When word of his story got out, Noah told me, he received death threats from people whose virtual items lost real-world value in the massive deflation the pair had provoked. He accepted those as an inevitable consequence of his life outside the virtual law. "It is like the Wild West right now . . . and we're kind of like these outlaws," he told me. "I feel like Billy the Kid."

In Noah's case, it seemed as if he had made something from nothing. It wasn't immediately obvious that the real-world profit he made was at the expense of others who owned virtual items, which went down in value after he flooded the market. But in some cases of virtual profit, I discovered, the victims were clear.

Another twenty-four-year-old, Thomas Czerniawski, worked for his father's company, Exceltec Dental Laboratory, on the outskirts of Toronto, Canada, crafting crowns. In his other life, Tom's virtual alter ego, Istvaan Shogaatsu—who, along with one hundred thousand others, inhabited a space piracy universe called EVE Online—understood the technology of a different kind of pain. Shogaatsu, who described himself as "a cut-throat without morals or mercy," had long enjoyed causing havoc in virtual worlds. In his last virtual residence, a relatively small online space-combat universe called Darkspace, he claimed he had been single-handedly responsible for obliterating a quarter of the universe's players (he killed over four thousand). When we met, Thomas was Istvaan, the CEO of Guiding Hand, a mercenary corporation of ten EVE Online players that made their virtual living destroying other players' characters for profit.

In May 2005, Istvaan received an anonymous offer of one billion ISK, the EVE virtual currency (around $630 worth), for a "Pearl Harbor"–style attack—a massive, surprise assault causing irreparable damage—on another player's corporation, Ubiqua Seraph. The client had been scammed by Ubiqua Seraph and wanted virtual revenge. For the attack, Istvaan chose an accomplice, Arenis Xemdal, Guiding Hand's Valentine Operative—so named because of his charm, which enabled him to work his way into enemy corporations. Xemdal spent four months wooing the Ubiqua CEO, Mirial. They drew charts of Ubiqua Seraph's corporate structure, and found gaps where she was likely to be hiring. She hired Xemdal. To make him look good, Istvaan staged a number of artificially crippled raids, in which his Guiding Hand battleships underplayed their hand, and

Xemdal saved Mirial. Guiding Hand operatives fed their Valentine Operative secret information on competing corporations, which Xemdal fed to Mirial in turn; Mirial profited from the information, and her trust in Xemdal rose. Meanwhile, Guiding Hand plotted their attack. "We mapped the locations of their most bountifully stocked asset hangars," Istvaan told me. "We took down the locations of their privately owned stations . . . and we waited."

Four months later, Mirial appointed Arenis Xemdal as her lieutenant. She gave him access to the corporation's resources, and gave him the access codes to Ubiqua's warehouses: the key to her virtual safe.

When Guiding Hand received a message from Arenis with the attack signal, "Nicole," they made their move. A Guiding Hand battleship appeared near Mirial's position. Guiding Hand had a reputation for fierce piracy; the appearance of the battleship, far more powerful than her own ship, warned Mirial something was up. She fled for a nearby space station, but before she could reach safety, Arenis Xemdal turned his "Navy Apocalypse" battle cruiser's pulse lasers and combat drones on her. "She was killed by her lieutenant, who she trusted—dare say, even liked," Czerniawski told me. Across the galaxy, timed with the attack, Guiding Hand operatives looted six separate Ubiqua Seraph warehouses, stealing virtual minerals, cash, and all the Ubiqua Seraph corporation's valuable battleship blueprints. In a last-ditch attempt to save her virtual self, Mirial jettisoned an escape capsule, but she was quickly killed. Her frozen corpse was scooped on board by Istvaan himself. It was all over in fifteen minutes. Istvaan delivered Mirial's corpse to the client, but kept the stolen property as spoils of war. ("He still has it," Istvaan told me. "He treasures it.")

What made this different from just any space-fight inside a computer game? Now that virtual currencies had a real value, their haul was more than just pixels on a screen. The cash and merchandise stolen by Guiding Hand amounted to thirty billion ISK—about $18,000.

They decided not to sell, though; instead they invested the cash in rare EVE Online ships, which have since increased in value. "Overall, we've done very well with the money, multiplying it many times over," Istvaan said.

Thomas invited me on a tour of the crime scene. I logged in to EVE Online so he could show me where it all took place. I launched my new ship and Istvaan guided me to his own location in space—luckily a sparsely populated sector of the universe, where his virtual enemies were unlikely to pass by and attack while he was switching ships. He showed me the ships he had bought and stolen: a Raven class battleship, *Navy Issue*, with a regenerating shield and seven cruise missiles, each capable of taking out any enemy battleship. (The battleship was worth three billion ISK, Istvaan told me—about $1,800). He showed me another ship, which seemed ten times the size of the first. "This is an Apocalypse Imperial Issue. Only two exist in the entire game, and we [Guiding Hand] control both."

I flew my tiny trading ship in close to the war-scarred metal of Istvaan's prize ship, feeling like a fly on the hide of an elephant. "No more of these ships will ever be released, making them next to priceless," Istvaan said. Guiding Hand paid nine billion ISK (about $5,400) for each. "They've since appreciated in value to about twenty-five billion [ISK] apiece." That meant Guiding Hand could sell those two ships, together, for around $25,000.

The EVE developers, CCP Games, based in Reykjavik, Iceland, looked fondly on Istvaan's operation—not least because, as the story spread through the Internet, EVE Online gained thousands of new subscribers. But many players were outraged. After the heist, and back in the real world, Thomas Czerniawski received nine e-mail and telephone death threats. To Mirial and others connected with the Ubiqua Seraph corporation, the loss felt very real.

Istvaan's attack shone a bright light on the wild-frontier-style ethics of the virtual world. It had taken Mirial over a year to build up her virtual empire, but she had no recourse: The virtual items she lost had no legal value. And game developers need it to remain that way; otherwise every bug or server closure could be followed by a class-action suit by players for compensation. The games would become true economies; every player would have to fill in a tax return. CCP decided the scam was in the spirit of the game—after all, it was a space piracy universe. ("We would like to remind the players of EVE Online that game masters are unable to assist players who have been involved in any sort of scam," they announced. "We have taken measures to prevent scamming by making it easier for corporations to see exactly who has access to the shipyards and equipment pools, but it is up to the officers of the corporation themselves to ensure that they fully trust the individuals they recruit."

In spite of this, Czerniawski told me he and his Guiding Hand co-conspirators were concerned they might be accused of breaking a real-world law, such as wire fraud, so they were careful to keep all contact within the game. Others, though, haven't been so careful.

In October 2005, another player, a college student known as Nightfreeze, pulled off a more complicated confidence trick. "This is a story of deception, intrigue, and double-crosses," Nightfreeze wrote, in his own account of the scam. "It is a story of liars, bandits, and greed. This is the story of my life in EVE Online." EVE Online was Nightfreeze's passion. He spent more time navigating the EVE universe than navigating his campus hallways. Bored and restless, he and his best friend, Trazir, decided to form a partnership. Another trader, HardHead, lent them three million ISK. They bought a colossal ship, poured their cash into computers, and within three hours had doubled their money. They were in business—and at first, their business was legitimate, at least within EVE Online's accepted rules of space piracy. Their only obstacles were pirates. Every trade run, privateers homed in on their lumbering ship and demanded payment. When they refused, the pirates lasered their ship to ashes. With hardly any firepower, all they could do was run—so they learned to run in style, using expensive engines, microwarp drives (MWDs), which could rocket their ship to safety. The pirates ate exhaust fumes. Within two weeks, Nightfreeze was worth close to eighty-five million ISK. At this point, nothing untoward was taking place—in EVE Online, this kind of arms race between pirates and traders was par for the course. But then the universe changed the rules. One morning, two months into his lucrative new career, Nightfreeze baited the pirates as usual, waited until they closed in, then activated his drives. It didn't work. The enraged pirates destroyed his ship—thirty-five million ISK worth of hardware and forty million in cargo. In revenge for his insults, they shot up his escape pod, too. The pirates, unhappy with the MWDs, had complained to the gods—the developers—and the gods had listened. Suddenly, the drives barely worked. But nobody had told Nightfreeze. His fledgling career—and two months of his life—was in ashes. He was about to log off permanently in disgust, but then had a better idea. The rules didn't care for him; why should he care for the rules? He made a call to his friend, who agreed. They would perpetrate the biggest scam the universe had ever seen. To establish their con, they paid twenty new players ten thousand credits each to join their "corporation," named ZZZBest (after an infamously fraudulent carpet cleaning firm). In-world, on notice boards and in instant messages to all their trading partners, the pair announced their mission: to acquire the blueprints for an Apocalypse battleship, the most powerful in the game. These cost 1.2 billion ISK; by combining their purchase power, they claimed, they would offer the same blueprint to each investor for just one hundred million. Slowly, their offer began to attract potential partners. They populated bulletin boards with fake investors, and arranged a fake chat room "investor conference." One investor, the largest, insisted on speaking with Nightfreeze in person. Nightfreeze gave the number of his local library pay phone, and sprinted to catch the call. The investor said yes. By nine the next morning, Nightfreeze's account held 480 million credits (worth nearly three thousand dollars in real life). He transferred the money to a dummy character. Then, with one click of his mouse, he deleted his account. After gloating in reply to a few instant-message (IM) death threats, he canceled his IM accounts, too. It was the perfect crime—the criminal no longer existed. But what now? His half of the money belonged to a new character without pilot skills; he had hundreds of millions, but nothing to buy. He toyed with a few passing ships, and was instantly killed. Somehow, it barely seemed worth it. Nightfreeze hailed a passing player, Frosttt, in a beginner ship, and asked, "What would you say if I were to offer you 300 million ISK?" "I'd say pretty cool," said Frosttt. Nightfreeze wired all his credits over and logged off. He never logged in again.

After it became clear there would be no payback for Nightfreeze, the EVE Online bulletin boards erupted in fury. That's how virtual worlds affect us: Once the borders of the real world are threatened, we feel threatened, too. Only one level-headed commentator, on the message boards of the website Something Awful, pointed out the double standards: "You can be a pirate in this game, but you can't be a white-collar criminal?"

Virtual worlds, with their heady combination of experience without attendant risk, were starting to get real. Greed, corruption, and human weakness threatened to turn paradise into a lawless frontier world. Thomas Czerniawski, who conducted the "Pearl Harbor"–style attack on another EVE Online corporation, had a moral stance, too. Although his virtual property would fetch $34,000 on the open market, he refused to sell, or move into other virtual worlds where his actions could be more profitable. For those who profited from virtual worlds such as Second Life, he had only scorn. "If I want to make money, I'll buy my stockbroker a bottle of good cognac and watch the magic," he said. "Not try to peddle real estate and virtual pornography to some dancing cretin in a CGI raccoon suit."

In the real world it was heading toward the autumn of 2005, and everybody was anxious. The Geneva Conventions, a protection against the return of our savage history, had been replaced by a new global doctrine of preemptive war. In my hometown, London, subway trains and buses had exploded. The actions of my government—involving us in a war the majority of the population did not want—hung like a pall over everyone I knew. It made sense then that I wanted more time in my virtual shoes. As I walked the gray streets of London, I daydreamed about Second Life. I longed for escape. I wanted to rise above the gray roofs and bare winter trees, to free myself from gravity, to push up off the ground and fly.

Virtual worlds seemed far away from the chaos: a safer place than the real world. There was no pollution, no global warming, and—at least as I believed it then—no terrorism. I heard rumors, though, that more clear-cut virtual crime had found its way into Second Life. Some Second Life residents (including that world's richest, Anshe Chung—real name Ailin Graef—who reportedly made more than $200,000 a year from virtual land sales inside Second Life) had complained of underhanded attempts to force land sales at deflated prices. In one case, Anshe claimed, a group known as the W-Hats had intimidated potential buyers, erected unpleasant or intimidating billboards—anti-Anshe posters, and tasteless and angry images that included real-world photos of a naked man with children's toys over his groin—on small, cheap parcels of adjacent land, and built towering structures so complex that they slowed down all avatar movement on her own real estate to a crawl, all in an attempt to obtain her virtual property at below-market rates. (Another resident, Bakuzelas, who approached Anshe to buy the land on behalf of the W-Hats, claimed they had offered a fair market rate.) Others also complained that groups like the W-Hats had used similar tactics with them. The CEO of a corporation inside Second Life claimed the W-Hats had built towers so high he couldn't even enter his own property. There was more at stake, too. Like the real universe, virtual worlds were expanding. When I first entered Second Life, the land covered 120 virtual acres, with twenty-five thousand residents; in six months, this virtual world inflated to more than three hundred acres, and nearly one hundred thousand residents. More people meant more profit: In May 2005 alone, Second Life residents traded $1.47 million worth of virtual property. And now a seedier side of the virtual world had moved in for a cut.

"These are basically blackmail and mafia methods," Anshe said of the intimidation.

I wanted to do more than hear about virtual crime, however. I wanted to take part. After his raid on Ubiqua Seraph, Istvaan stole another battleship, worth three billion ISK ($1,800) but since then—despite his claim to have secret operatives planted inside every major EVE Online corporation—Thomas Czerniawski had hung up his space-pirate hook. His virtual self had taken a backseat to his real life. Similarly, Noah, the forging gnome, still hoped for another opportunity to bend the rules of virtual worlds and make a killing, but as yet he had found nothing—instead, he told me, he was considering a how-to book to help people discover similar exploits and make money themselves.

A different, more organized kind of crime was emerging in virtual worlds. Not long before, one resident of There, a Web-based virtual world with four hundred thousand members, put up a For Sale sign in front of a virtual home he didn't own. Many new players didn't know how the property system worked; he sold the house many times over, and pocketed the virtual cash. Now, I discovered, the same kind of fraud had taken root in Second Life. "Do I need to get in this game and bust some heads together?" wrote one J. C. Soprano in the comments section of an interview with Anshe about her harassment, on the Second Life newsletter site Dragon's Cove Herald. Soprano included a link to his website, the Sims Mafia, where he advertised his services. For the right virtual price, the mafia would assault another Second Life resident. (Because physical violence in virtual worlds is mostly harmless, in practice the assault included a barrage of instant messages, harassing them with scripted objects, and bad ratings that can affect everything from a character's virtual reputation to their virtual credit.) They would blackmail, bribe, or collect debts from one's virtual enemies.

It was time to return to Second Life, to talk with the Sims Mafia. Embarrassed by my previous difficulties, I considered creating a new virtual self, with a different computer and someone else's credit card. Linden Lab would never know. (However, when I had visited their offices, Robin Harper hinted they had ways to track the real people who inhabited their virtual residents. They were secretive about how they did this, but they seemed confident they could; a mixture of IP addresses, unique to most Internet connections; credit card data; and financial transactions between in-world residents would make most identities clear.) Unfortunately, it seemed that accountability and reputation were intrinsic to these worlds. Moreover, I didn't have another credit card. Errol Mysterio would live on.

When I logged in again, I reappeared on Wilde's island. Things had changed. They had built a platform over the ocean, to house a shiny blue virtual Spitfire. Across the bay I could see they had neighbors: two new islands, one tinier and deserted, the other mountainous. There were wood huts, palm trees, a blue avant-garde bubble-domed apartment. Everything was covered in drifts of virtual snow. It was nearly Christmas. To my left, a choir of snowmen, hymn books open in their mittened hands, were frozen in mid-carol. I walked the island looking for Wilde, but they weren't logged on. My avatar left crisp footprints in the fresh virtual snow.

5

VIRTUAL MAFIA

My life as a foot soldier

When I met J. C. Soprano, the virtual mafia don, he tried to hustle me, too.

In the real world, Soprano was Jeremy Chase, a twenty-eight-year-old customer service manager and IT specialist at a Sacramento, California, financial company, with hair spiked down across his forehead, a thin-line goatee, and tattoos on each arm. Chase (no relation to David Chase, the creator of another mafia mythology in *The Sopranos*) began his life of virtual crime in 2001, in the virtual world called The Sims Online. "Behind every fortune, there is a crime," reads a traditional Sicilian saying. This implies a basic balance in the universe—a great wealth, which upsets the order, demands a great act of violence. The phrase, which Mario Puzo used as a preface to his novel *The Godfather*, was originally coined as an argument *for* the mafia: a warning against the ruling principalities in feudal Italy. Under the restrictive and capricious martial law of ruling powers, which changed with the seasons, Italians grew to distrust those who ruled over them. When disagreements or vendettas arose, rather than turn to the latest despot who wouldn't understand their plight, some people chose to mete out their own rough kind of justice. Out of this tradition arose the twentieth-century mafia (the Cosa Nostra—"this thing of ours"). What the mafia taught the world was that sometimes, when the powers that be don't have your best interests at heart, strength and security have to be forged by the people.

Chase believed this was true for virtual worlds, too. Even the basic in-game laws, known as the "terms of service"—which generally included basic rules such as don't swear at other characters and don't cheat them out of virtual currency—relied on players to lodge complaints, and seemed to Chase poorly enforced.

This absence of virtual law enforcement led Chase, a longtime mafia movie fan, to set up his own alternative: The Sims Mafia. He named his virtual self J. C. Soprano—J. C. from his initials, and Soprano from the HBO crime family series. Players could hire Chase and his virtual employees to protect their virtual interests. The Sims Mafia used its virtual muscle to perform all the services you might expect from a bona fide crime family. The Sims Online, though, was never a runaway success. In late 2004, Chase's mafia family moved. In the same way Vito Corleone shifted his crime family from New York to Las Vegas in *The Godfather*, Chase decided to move the operation to another virtual world. He tried Star Wars Galaxies, but that disappointed. ("The most you could do was kill someone," he told me. "There was no way to gamble or extort like we had in The Sims Online.")

Next, in April 2005, Chase sold his J. C. Soprano Sims Online self on eBay, and moved to Second Life. When he joined Second Life, the surname Soprano wasn't available, but Wallace was; he named his Second Life self Marsellus Wallace, from a character in the movie *Pulp Fiction.*

In Second Life, for the right amount of virtual currency, Chase's family offered all the services they used to offer in The Sims Online, and then some. There they used to hire virtual escorts, but Chase— who once ran a porn site in his spare time—closed down the prostitution rackets because there was too great a risk of underage players hiring virtual hookers. In Second Life, however, where all the other residents are over eighteen, hiring a virtual escort is as easy, and about as expensive, as buying a pair of shoes.

"Essentially, I look at myself, in a way, as like Gotti," Chase told a Second Life website, the Second Life Herald. "He fought the law, like I do with Electronic Arts and other groups. And he was very respected . . . he gave to the community. Sure, he was violent and ruthless. I am not saying these guys are saints. But they do some good in the community. That's all. With the bad, there is always some good."

Inside Second Life, I ran a search for Marsellus Wallace. "This is who I am and what I do," his profile read. "My basic philosophy is don't start none, won't be none. Show some respect! Even if you don't like someone, they should never know it. Get them when they least expect it. I'm the face of online Mafias and the real-life press calls me the Boss of Bosses. Deal with it."

I contacted him via Second Life instant messaging, and, after a long, suspicious exchange, I finally managed to meet Marsellus. He received me in his virtual marble-floored mansion. He was broad and well-dressed in a virtual tailored suit, and sprawled on a virtual leather sofa. (His mafia family had already built up a reputation in Second Life; an interior designer, eager to curry favor, furnished his mansion for free.) "Currently, I have myself, the consigliere, the underboss, three capos, and several soldiers who work under the capos," Marsellus told me. "In total, with the foot soldiers, about 15 people."

Marsellus explained how he makes his virtual profit. He offered no-questions loans, at 25 percent interest. For a price, he offered mediation (a "sit-down") to settle a virtual beef. For "a very high price," he said, you could hire him to do what he called a "Moe Green": a virtual hit, which removed a virtual character from the game completely. I asked how they did that: "You'll see," he told me. As well as the paid services, which accounted for about 35 percent of his revenue, Marsellus also ran sports spread betting, and backdoor craps games in VIP casinos, with the virtual equivalent of about four dollars as the minimum bet. "We are working on a new gambling operation that's not up yet. We hope that to be our cash cow. I have a game here no one else has. I also am doing a website hosting and design business soon that accepts cash and Lindens: 2L Hosting. That's my legit side. My not so legit side consists of various scams—mainly real estate extortion (very small money in this though), protection, bribes (I can't go into details on this one but I have many, many connections with top players). We dabbled in prostitution here for a bit, but I prefer to stay out of the sex stuff. Too much competition anyway." Virtual war occasionally broke out with the other online mafia crime families, Chase explained, until both sides incurred enough losses that they were forced to sit down and make peace. Sometimes, to build their reputation, wannabe mafiosi took shots at Chase. (He invited me to search for "Marsellus" in the directory of Second Life residents. Other players with a vendetta had created alternate selves with first names like "MarsellusWallaceThe," and last names like "Prat.")

Marsellus told me about his latest virtual strong-arm move. An associate, "Drax Lemieux," who owned a Second Life establishment called the Red Dragon casino, had asked Marsellus to go into business. Marsellus operated a profitable virtual dice game, and Drax wanted to share his expertise. Drax paid Marsellus five thousand Linden Dollars (about $150), and agreed to pay another 19,500 Linden Dollars ($150) when the dice games were making a profit. The two grew close; Drax even acted as groomsman for Marsellus's virtual wedding.

Marsellus's Second Life bride, Mackenzie Draper, was played by Chase's real-world girlfriend, whom he'd introduced to Second Life. Mackenzie, a pretty redhead, worked inside Second Life as a virtual photographer. As Marsellus and I talked, she strolled over to say hi. Marsellus had mentioned she didn't like his being "in the life"; I asked Mackenzie how she felt, being married to the mob. "Well, he's right, I don't approve," she said. "But that's his thing."

"She's my voice of reason," Marsellus said.

After the wedding, Marsellus and Drax planned to split the casino dice game's virtual profits. According to Drax, though, the casino began to show a loss. Drax refused to make the second payment of 19,500 Linden Dollars. Marsellus then sneaked in and installed himself as a dealer; his table made money. Drax had been lying, it seemed, and even though Drax had been a groomsman at his virtual wedding, Marsellus couldn't let the disrespect stand.

Drax's casino was famous in Second Life for its unique façade: a huge sculpted red dragon, with the casino door in place of the mouth. After a "heated discussion" in which Drax refused to pay up, Marsellus chose his revenge. He persuaded Drax he needed to move the dice games around to make them more profitable. Drax made Marsellus an "officer" of his group, which automatically gave him the ability to alter his virtual property. Marsellus gave Drax one more chance to follow through with their deal. Drax passed, and Marsellus went into action. He deleted a partition wall, just to let Drax know what was coming. Drax panicked, and fumbled with his windows to try to change the casino, piece by piece, so Marsellus couldn't delete it. Marsellus sent him a message to keep him busy typing, then, while Drax was writing his reply, Marsellus did the virtual equivalent of torching the place. With two mouse clicks he deleted the casino's huge red dragon façade.

In the real world, time is money, but in the virtual world, money is time. Drax had lost the months it took him to construct the casino and its reputation, but he had no recourse for its loss: His virtual den of iniquity had no real-world legal value. Still, when I met Marsellus, the two had put their history aside. They were in talks to go back into business. "We have rules very similar to real mafia," Marsellus told me. "Our goal is to make money. All that other crap just gets in the way of business."

In the real world, Chase's mafia activities would be against the law, but in Second Life, the rules of conduct are less clear. Chase seemed to make little attempt to hide his virtual crime family. After all, in Second Life, every character's name and group is displayed for all to see. Chase's second self walked around with a sign above his head: "Marsellus Wallace. Sim Mafia Boss." Chase was known to Linden Lab—he applied, ironically, for a Second Life community liaison job—and had become a minor celebrity within some virtual circles. "EA [Electronic Arts] Games and me didn't get along," he explained. "Second Life seems to embrace it." His only worry, he explained, was that through some confusion between the real world and the virtual world, he would get himself into real trouble.

Chase admitted to me privately that he was worried about the possible consequences of his virtual crimes. "The money in this game is worth real money," he explained. "[Linden Lab] say[s] so. In Sims Online, EA said it was not legally protected. However, in Second Life I am worried that somehow my gaming could result in legal action. Even if I keep it in game."

Chase planned to consult a lawyer, he told me, "just to cover my ass. Because a game is not worth jail time." He even called up Linden Lab to speak with their legal specialist, who advised him to be careful.

Despite his anxieties, Chase modeled his virtual mafia carefully on the real thing. A week after we met, he e-mailed me. "If you can make it, we will be swearing in a new member tonight." The ceremony was to take place at 7 P.M. his time, or 3 A.M. London time. I hurried home from a night out to witness a virtual mafia member being made.

As soon as I logged on, Marsellus e-mailed me. The rules of the ceremony were his greeting. "1—Inductees may not talk until prompted to do so or the ceremony is over. 2—Only members of management and those getting made may attend the ceremony. (Making an exception for you.) 3—No one repeats what is said or done during the ceremony. (Once again, you're the exception.) 4—All in attendance of a ceremony must dress in a nice suit. [I hoped my white tux waiter suit would suffice.] 5—No pictures may be taken except by pre-authorized existing members. 6—No guns are allowed to be displayed unless security requires it."

When I arrived at the site of the ceremony—a concrete basement—Marsellus introduced me to his underboss, Tony Caligari.
Tony had been in online mafias, he told me, including under Marsellus, for three years. Suddenly the subject of the ceremony, Shadow
Tokhes, appeared beside us. Forgetting my commitment to remain
quiet, I asked what he had done to "make his bones." "He will be our
consigliere," Marsellus said. "He whacked the last one. Which is how
he earned his stripes to get in."

The hit went down in classic mafia style. "I called the guy over to
our casino and said that the family needed some money," Marsellus
said. "I took all his money with the promise of it being returned, and
he sent me a screenshot to show he had nothing." (Later, Marsellus
would demand the same thing of me.) "Then I walked him outside
where Shadow was waiting—under the dock." (Of course under the
dock.)

"I took out my gun and shot him," Shadow told me. "After, I told
him what the boss said, which was, 'Next time you take an oath, make
sure you fulfill it."

(It all sounded authentic enough. The only distraction for me was
the former consigliere's name: Gandalf.)

Before Shadow could be made, there was a little stagecraft. In Second Life, objects need to be prompted into action. Marsellus had prepared a ceremony, but it needed a push to get going. "Shadow, see
that circle by your feet? Choose the ceremony option." Shadow shuf-
fled into place.

"All right, you all know why we're here," Marsellus continued. "So
if you got any doubts or reservations, now is the time to say so. No one
will think any less of you. Because once you enter this family, there's
no getting out. This family comes before everything else . . .

"Everything. Before your wife and your children and your mother
and your father. It's a thing of honor. And, God forbid, if you get sick,
suspended, or something happens and you can't earn, we'll take care
of you. That's part of it."

"If you got a problem, you just gotta let somebody know," Tony, the underboss, chimed in. "This man right here." He pointed to Marsellus. "He's like your father. It doesn't matter if it's with some-body here or on the outside. You bring it to him, he'll solve it."

"You stay within the family," Marsellus said.

Shadow raised his hand, and in it appeared a playing card.

"That is St. Patrick, our family saint," Marsellus said. "He is the Saint of Sacramento, where I am from, and New York, where the heart of the mafia lies . . .

"Ignite," Marsellus said, for the card's benefit. The card burst into flames.

"Those flames represent the flames of hell. Now, as that card burns, so may your soul burn if you betray your friends in the family . . .

"Now, repeat after me. May I burn in hell."

"May I burn in hell," Shadow said.

"If I betray my family," Marsellus intoned.

"If I betray my family," Shadow echoed.

"Congratulations, you may step off the ceremony stand as a Made Man," Marsellus said.

"Thank you," Shadow said.

"Welcome to the family," Tony said.

"Now no one can touch you," Marsellus continued. "But that don't mean go around starting nuttin', either. Don't start none, won't be none. This is still a business. Now, Tony has some things he wants to cover real quick."

"You're a made guy now," Tony said. "It's your turn to make some real money, and I get to relax a little. Your only problem in life now is you give me 25 points of your take every settle-up day. Other than that, you got no problem. My only problem in life? I gotta kick my points to that man over there. And onward goes this thing of ours."

Slowly, Marsellus drew me into his mafia world. Even in the super-market, he found a way to reach me. The morning after the ceremony, Marsellus sent me a message inside Second Life, which was forwarded to my e-mail account, which was forwarded to my telephone. I received it in the frozen foods aisle. "Ahh the life," Marsellus wrote.

Over these weeks, my virtual life had already begun to blur into my real one. I had met Istvaan, the EVE universe's most feared warlord, who showed me his prize battleship's laser cannons; I had met Noah, the virtual world's richest gnome; and I had met the virtual Godfather, sprawled in virtual luxury. My diary was full of appointments with people called Eight Bar Masher Algernon Spackler and Biscuit Carrol. I felt the kind of dizzy head induced by too much travel, only this time it wasn't a whirlwind of airports, it was a whirlwind of worlds. Which universe was I in? One evening, I had to meet Marsellus, but I also had to cook dinner; my girlfriend sat at my laptop and pretended to be me. I had told her he was part of an online mafia; while I fried the fish she tapped at the keys nervously, imagining a different kind of fish nailed to our door.

Over time, Marsellus began to make me nervous, too. He scolded me for missed appointments, although he skipped his fair share—a boss's prerogative. "Just as in real life, intimidation is our biggest weapon," he had told me—and I suspected he was trying the weapon on me. He had told how, at his virtual wedding, a Second Life resident had disrespected some guests. As Marsellus, he strolled over to the resident's property and claimed the resident owed him money. The resident didn't owe him anything, and said as much, but after a few visits from mafia foot soldiers, their virtual guns drawn, he paid. Now Chase began to try some of the same tactics on me. When I asked him again to let me work for him, he asked what was in it for him—"Writers must get Bank!" he said. Later, after a documentary team borrowed my virtual self for a TV short, the director mailed me an update. "Marsellus came and had a few words," he said. "We told him we weren't you and we were making a film with you in it—and he started asking for money!"

There were surreal moments, too. I asked permission to take virtual photos of Marsellus and his mafia. They agreed, and gathered in a basement, dressed in dark suits (bought from "a friend of ours" at a Second Life store called Made Men) and posed—with and without guns—for the virtual camera. I took up various positions around them, framed them on my screen, and saved image files of my view to my laptop. It was awkward and disorganized, like a real-world photo shoot. I found myself saying things like "Candy, can you move in a bit?" and "Getting some great shots here. Marsellus, keep looking at me please."

I began a campaign to persuade Marsellus to hire me. I wanted in on a virtual mafia job, to see what was involved, and what effect Marsellus could actually have on his enemies. He dodged the issue.

Then, just when I thought I was out, they pulled me back in. Marsellus contacted me. He had overcome his objections, and decided to let me to do a job. We met in his new virtual home, a palatial development that had yet to be furnished. It turned out Marsellus had a network of characters designed to give the impression of an entire mafia family. He logged on as another virtual persona, Raymond Polonsky—who, in his black suit and jewelry, looked more than a little like Marsellus. Raymond was Chase's "legit" character, he explained, a lawyer "with a few mafia ties." (In Second Life, you can click on a character for more information. I clicked on Raymond. "I am your virtual legal representation," his description read. "IM [instant message] me if you need contracts written up and notarized, or if you need representation in-game for a crime you did not commit!")

"So, you want in and want to do some things," Polonksy told me. "First . . . you got any questions? Now is the time to ask them, because once I agree to this, if I don't like you, you will be part of the house foundation in-game." I nodded. "Let's step inside," Polonksy said. "Less ears there."

I followed him in. There was another concrete floor. "OK first a couple of ground rules. Common sense shit, but necessary.

"First off, watch what you say in-game. Never refer to avatar names, initials, description, things like that. If you have to, name a name, but once you say it, don't say it again. Refer to them as the guy or the girl or whatever."

"I'll keep my mouth shut," I said.

"Although it cannot be proven, I believe the Double L Mafia has the ability to monitor conversations, and does."

When I visited Linden Lab (the target of Chase's oblique reference), Philip Rosedale had explained that it was possible to record everything that happened. Technically, as the entire world was computer-modeled, they could record every single movement, gesture, and interaction that took place. In practice, though, Philip told me the amount of data storage required to record everything was far beyond their capability. What they did record, though, were a set of "logs," which included a record of every word, and every transaction.

I knew they could read the logs if there were any dispute, and I imagined it would be easy to monitor troublesome characters—or writers—should they become concerned their community was threatened. The United Kingdom, where I logged on from, has the highest public closed-circuit TV coverage in the world. In January 2004, there were over 4,285,000 closed-circuit cameras in the United Kingdom—about one for every four households, and the Metropolitan Police had ordered a trial of head-mounted digital video cameras. The average Londoner, me included, was caught on camera three hundred times a day. The heightened potential for surveillance in virtual worlds made me nervous. It felt strange to exist within a world where someone could watch not just most of but in fact *everything* you did.

Raymond Polonsky led me down to the basement. "Another thing. You are going to do some odds and ends shit at first," he said. "Just for a week or two. We've gotta get you used to the slang, introduce you to a few people. After that things will pick up, I'll get you running a crew, or part of a crew, depending on what we determine your specialty is."

I had to be willing to do anything, Raymond said, even if it seemed dangerous. "The Double L Mafia may try to eliminate you, in other words." We agreed I would remain incognito. To the rest of the virtual mafia, I would be just another foot soldier.

Then it was time to talk cash. "How much money do you have?" Raymond asked. When I had originally logged on to Second Life, Linden Lab gave me a small weekly stipend, which they did for any premium account at the time. I had bought some of my own currency, and over the year I had hardly spent any, so virtual cash had accumulated in my account. I had 61,590 Linden Dollars—worth, at IGE.com, about two hundred real dollars.

"Give it to me," Polonsky said. I thought for a moment, then, because I hadn't earned the money, and I wanted Chase to trust me, I handed him the cash.

"OK thanks for your money. Have a nice day!" Polonsky said. Then he laughed. "Just kidding. A little mafia humor."

As it turned out, though, he did keep most of it. He explained how, just as in the real mafia, new members paid for the privilege. "Normally, if no one is vouching for you, we require you to buy your way in. That is 25,000 Lindens alone. Normally most guys make it back over a period of time. A decent earner can pull in 5,000 to 10,000 Lindens a week. Now, before you decide, there are some perks you need to be aware of."

He gestured to my clothes. I still wore my white waiter's tuxedo. First—"no offense"—I had to get a new suit. "I will contact a tailor. Basically you go pick out some suits and I'll get you a discount. We get a lot of discounts." He told me to get some jewelry, too, although not too flashy. "Please don't gangsta yourself out."

I told him I planned to set up an office in Second Life. "Go to Home Depoz," he told me, referring to one of the largest virtual su-

perstore furniture chains. "Make a shopping list. Anything and everything you need. Give it to me, I'll make it happen. No cost."

"So. You getting nervous you ain't got the money back yet?" Polonsky said. I nodded, and he paid me back the difference. I was in. I
would have to pay the "vig." This last was from Yiddish slang, *vigorish*,
for "winnings," used in Mafia films to refer to interest on a loan and
used by Marsellus, it seemed, to refer to money I should just pay him
regularly: 2,500 Linden Dollars (about seven dollars real) a week,
come virtual rain or virtual shine. I asked what kind of work he had in
mind. "Police department for wiseguys, all we are," he said. "Most
bosses come to us to handle disputes." His upcoming jobs included a
little corporate espionage. "For example, this one guy who runs a very
popular business. In fact, he was recently in *BusinessWeek*. He turned
to us to spy on a rival business, see if they were competition. Paid
30,000 Linden Dollars—that's for a few days of work." First, though,
he had a bigger job in mind. "I already have your first real mafia job
lined up. A warning message to someone." He didn't want to say too
much, in case Linden Lab was listening. He told me he would describe the job now, then name names at another time. It was like having a conversation with a real mafia member, taking routine
precautions against phone taps. "The guy's name is Tommy Fitzsimmons. Just remember that."

The coming weekend was his girlfriend's birthday, and Chase was
heading out to Vegas. In true mafia style, he would coordinate the job
while he was out of town. He gave me some homework, too. As well
as order a new suit and get some gold, Chase told me to watch *Goodfellas*, *Godfather I* and *II*, and "*Donnie Brasco* for sure. It teaches the
structure and rules."

"Just remember one thing, Errol," he said, as we parted. "Don't
fuck me over."

With that he disappeared. I stood in his concrete basement, feeling more than a little paranoid. I wondered if I could trust Polonsky.
Was he trying to set me up, get me banned from Second Life? Did he
really charge that much to new mafia members? I hadn't earned most

of the money I had given to Polonsky—it had come free into my account from Linden Lab—but it still felt like a real loss. Was he
double-crossing me? Still, these anxieties of trust seemed suitable for
a new mafia member.

Afterward, I couldn't sleep. What would my other virtual friends
think of this? Who was the person, the target of the job? In real life,
were they vulnerable? Would I cause real pain? It was OK, right, because this was all a game? I logged back on and looked up some information on Tommy Fitzsimmons. A Google search brought a
couple of results: an ad for a poker game (run at the "Eiffel Tower
casino" by Tommy, and someone called Salvatore Muromachi); the
next result was an ad for the grand opening of the Il Calabrese Casino
("Free prizes and other fun!"). Tommy's Second Life profile included
information on his company, Platini & Co. "Want to create your
dream company, but don't know how to get started? Our crack team
of businessmen will meet your needs no matter what you need done,
be it a casino, club or something else." That "something else"
sounded ominous. His profile had links to more people with intimi-
dating names: Tommaso Ludovico, Carlo Platini. What was I stepping into?

It even crossed my mind that Chase himself might be Tommy
Fitzsimmons. A few months before, a friend, Matt D'arcy, had logged
on to Second Life. I took him to a strip bar, and a stranger asked him
to join his club; my friend agreed, and the name of his new group was
attached to his virtual name, which followed above his head at all
times: "Jimmy DeFarge, Hardcore Lover." Within minutes, he was
approached by another resident, a complete stranger. "You can't fool
me!" the resident said.

My friend looked at me. "What?!?"

"I know who you are," the resident said. He had mistaken Matt for
another resident, who he believed was trying to sneak back into the
group. "You're banned!" Jimmy DeFarge was a Hardcore Lover no
more.

I had had my own share of this confusion, too, after a TV company borrowed my virtual self for a documentary. I logged back on to find myself, as if after a virtual binge-drinking blackout, in an Ikea-style furniture store, wearing unfamiliar clothes, with no memory of how I got there.

A few weeks after my laptop was stolen, I suddenly realized that were the burglar to start up Second Life, my automatically saved password would allow them to walk in my virtual shoes. Unnerved by the possibility, I changed my password. In the virtual world, there is no easy way to tell if someone is who you think they are. (When I called Linden Lab to confirm my password change, to verify my identity, they asked me which magazines I wrote for. The information they had on file for me was out of date, but it showed the importance they placed on verifying the real people behind their virtual selves.)

The next morning, my worries were gone. After all, Chase wasn't in the real mafia—"I love Mafia movies and books and it's a culture that fascinates me," Marsellus had told me that first night in his mafia mansion. But it's something he admitted he will never get to be a part of in the real world. The morning after our meeting, an e-mail arrived from Chase with more details of the job. It was a big one, a "Moe Green": a hit.

"Errol: Good afternoon. You already have the target name. Hopefully you have not forgotten it. From this point on, refer to the target as 'young buck.' This avatar is going to be hopefully whacked by yourself. We use the term *whack* to define getting an avatar removed from the game. It is something we rarely do as it is hard to pull off most of the time, and we believe it is an extreme measure. No hacking is involved, just using the games Community Standards and Terms of Service in our favor." So the virtual equivalent of a mafia hit was to get a resident removed permanently from the game. It made sense. My job was to somehow talk "young buck" into breaking the rules of the game, or admitting something that showed he shouldn't be inside Second Life. He could then be reported, and banned from reentering.

Marsellus had some leads as to how the job could be done. "At some point an informant came to me and advised me that this young buck was just that . . . young. He was only 14 or 15 and should not be playing on the main grid, which is for adults only." (Linden Lab's separate Second Life Teen Grid was tightly controlled. Through various forms of age identification, including credit card details, Linden Lab worked hard to ensure those who played the main Second Life world were over eighteen. In some cases—as with this hit, Tommy Fitzsimmons—they failed.) Marsellus explained: I was to persuade Tommy to admit he was underage. Then, armed with a copy of the conversation, I was to report this infraction to Linden Lab. "You are going to use his age against him and file an abuse report once he confesses this to you. I'll set up a meeting between you two. You will have to use your own finesse at that point to get him to confess."

The e-mail also contained some background information on the target. "The young buck was at one point a friend of the organization. He came to us one day and asked permission to use our name as a reference for a deal he was doing. In exchange for this he would pay us part of what he earns. He wouldn't give us many details. We have mutual friends and have known each other for a while so it was reluctantly agreed he could use us as a reference and we got our Lindens. That is how all this started.

"It turns out his version of using us as a reference was using our name as a weapon. Basically, trying to intimidate avatars by saying he knows us. That is something we do not condone. He was warned nicely and told not to do it again. He then mistakenly sent me a screenshot of him talking to another mafioso trying to stir shit up."

Talking out of order in the mafia world was obviously a bigger deal than I would have thought. "This screenshot almost caused our organization to go to the mattresses with this other organization," Marsellus said. "Someone was talking out of school and it was the young buck."

As always, Marsellus gave me ominous warnings. "DO NOT CONTACT anyone in the organization about the completion of the job until 24 hours after it has been completed. We believe in warnings, in working things out diplomatically. We use these types of retributions as a last resort. If you mess this up, it will probably be the last time you participate in this type of job." He signed the e-mail "Marsellus Wallace, Boss, The Sim Mafia." Since our last chat, though, Chase's real-world anxieties had moved him into action. He had added a new signature to the bottom of his e-mail: "DISCLAIMER: This email is only part of a game and does not represent any real-life illegal activity even if it seems so. It is for a game called Second Life and we role-play mafioso. Please do not interpret otherwise."

Chase was out of town for the weekend, but he promised to arrange a sit-down with the target soon. I had some time to think about the ethics—even the legality—of the job. If the target really was fourteen, that seemed to make him vulnerable. Also, was this typical of Marsellus's mafia life? The virtual mafia don liked to brag ("I am now pretty much the second most famous gamer in the world, next to Fatal1ty," he wrote me in an e-mail—whoever "Fatal1ty" was) but when it came down to it, his first mission was for me to rat out a fourteen-year-old loudmouth. Marsellus had turned out to be a rather theatrical mafioso.

Still, he had already made a real hundred dollars off me. Maybe he knew what he was doing, and maybe there was more to this than met the eye. I decided to take the job—but I wouldn't see it through. I wouldn't report the boy to Linden Lab. Instead, I would play him against Marsellus, who seemed a much more robust target. I had done my homework, and watched *Godfather I* and *II*. I had learned that it is good to have a war every now and then. It clears the air, gets rid of bad blood.

In the meantime, though, more serious crime had come to virtual worlds. A series of attacks from inside Second Life were apparently designed to damage the infrastructure of the world itself. Terrorism had come to virtual worlds, and it seemed that Marsellus hadn't been entirely paranoid in his worries about real-world law enforcement. This time, Linden Lab called in the real-world FBI.

6

CYBER-TERRORISTS

Attacking thought

When I visited Linden Lab, Philip Rosedale had told me he couldn't help but admire the ingenuity of people who cause trouble—known as "griefers"—in his virtual world. "Everyone at Linden Lab is in awe of the residents. When a 'griefer' with many alternate characters causes trouble, we try to control him. Our overarching priority is to support the culture of our community—still, at the same time, we also think, 'Isn't it amazing? What this dude did?'" But, since my visit, their stance had hardened.

In early December 2005, at a virtual Christmas celebration inside Second Life, Philip Linden made an announcement. They had tried banning a few culprits—rumored to be members of the W-Hats—but the attacks continued. Each time their servers were shut down it cost them money, and they regarded this as a real crime. Dressed in a virtual Santa's hat, Philip Linden announced their harder line: "This seems about as good a time as any to tell you that I am turning over names to the FBI." On the night of December 23, Linden Lab made an official announcement: "In the last month there have been several attacks in which users of Second Life have intentionally released objects or taken actions intended to disrupt activity in the Second Life grid. These attacks result in substantial real-world economic harm, and Linden Lab intends to protect its interests using all legal means."

Part of Second Life's flexibility as a virtual world stems from residents' freedom to create. When someone designs an object in Second Life, they can choose how it appears, but they can also sculpt what it does. Any object can be "scripted" to interact with itself and other objects and people. The W-Hats had discovered how to create something simple but devastatingly effective: a kind of virtual bomb. They had built an object that looked like an orb, with a picture of a character from the popular computer game Half Life on it, and that was scripted, when triggered, to copy itself. So each copy made a copy, and soon the world filled with copies. The world overflowed, the Second Life servers crashed, and every resident was ejected.

Anyone who possessed one of these objects could crash the world at any time. Linden Lab developed a virtual firebreak, an impassable virtual barrier that contained outbreaks to certain areas of the map. But the attacks were repeated. Some days, over the last few months of 2005, it was hard to log in to Second Life at all. The group had refined their scripts into a device shaped like a block of C-4 plastic explosives. Just as in a real terrorist attack, when the virtual bomb went off, the world went dark.

Between October and December 2005, a group of Second Life residents—who cannot be named here for legal reasons—persisted in these "global attacks." In Linden Lab's eyes this was a step too far. The attacks cost money and time. U.S. law is clear: U.S. Criminal Code Title 18, section 1030, drafted to outlaw denial-of-service attacks (in which Web servers are taken out by a barrage of requests for information), says, in effect, that if you knowingly transmit information to a computer involved in interstate communication, and cause at least five thousand dollars in damage, you will be liable for a crime that may be punished by a fine, imprisonment of up to ten years, or both.

"These attacks affect the ability of our servers to provide a service for which people are paying us money," Linden Lab's legal counsel, Ginsu Yoon, told me. Yoon was eager to play down the virtual nature of the crimes and focus instead on the real-world effects. "I don't think of these denial-of-service attacks as taking place *within* the virtual world. These attacks affect the ability of our servers, which are physical and located in the real world, from providing a service for which people are paying us money. It doesn't really matter to me what the attack looks like in the virtual world. What matters is that the effect denies access to our service." Yoon said Linden Lab had warned the perpetrators prior to calling in the feds, although he stressed they were under no obligation to do so. "If a burglar breaks into your house, do you warn them that you will be calling the police?

In Linden Lab's eyes, at least, planting a virtual bomb was a real crime.

In the real world, terrorism aims to attack thought as well as property, occupying our mind with fears and shifting the dialogue toward the violent mind-set of the terrorist. In virtual worlds, the same appeared to be true. Instinctively, Linden Lab's step seemed to me an overreaction. The zeal I had felt firsthand on my visit to their offices was now being turned on a few troublemaking residents. On the other hand, I could see the events from Linden Lab's point of view: They had tried to stop the attacks, and warned those involved, who really were threatening the stability of their world.

One group was repeatedly mentioned in connection with the attacks: the W-Hats, the same group accused by the world's richest resident, Anshe Chung, of trying to intimidate her into selling virtual land. In a world where the politeness and positivity sometimes grew cloying, the W-Hats were determinedly perverse. I'd read about their exploits: They had built a communist-red van, with hammer and sickle, and the slogan, "W-Hats: Cyber Terrorists since 2004"; littered some areas of virtual land with swastikas and giant virtual penises; and built a scale model of the 9/11 attacks, complete with flames and crashing planes. Their website was full of pictures of Second Life avatars, including Transformer robots with penises, called "Optimus Dong."

The W-Hats, and a splinter group called Voted 5, were closely linked to the scripting attacks. The W-Hats publicly insisted that their scripted objects were only intended to annoy other residents, not to crash Linden Lab's servers. In September 2006, Linden Lab announced they had banned sixty accounts associated with Voted 5. Since then, the W-Hats had adopted a new, less confrontational tactic—more Dada than Weathermen—which I had witnessed myself: They followed people around and mocked them with virtual hand-puppets.

Plastic Duck, a former member of W-Hats—and onetime target of the wrath of Catherine Smith, Linden Lab's community manager—seemed central to the story. Smith, in her e-mail to CBC reporter Lindsay Michael about W-Hat member Plastic Duck, listed his infractions as follows:

- Stolen scripts and republished them on the Web
- Hired residents to negative rate other residents
- Dropped the infamous Goatse image [a notorious sexually explicit photo] all over Second Life
- Harassed the furry community
- Sexually harassed female residents
- Spammed others with penis images
- Was part of the group that re-created a flaming World Trade Center in Second Life with a smashed plane and falling bodies.

W-Hat headquarters was inside Second Life; I went to take a look. They lived in an area of Second Life called Satyr, which seemed to fit their priapic ethos. When I visited, there was a giant statue of what looked like a hatless Hamburglar with a penis attached. There were fan club areas for classic computer games. There was a terminal for W-Hat applicants: "Welcome New Goons!" In the sky, written in giant, flamingo-pink letters, was the word *FAGS!* Inside their warehouse-style headquarters was an auditorium, two rows of chairs and a giant bone throne. ("Like being inside the mind of a crazy person," another W-Hat tourist, here to check out the view, told me.) In one oddly psychedelic corner of their workshop, everything I said fell out of my mouth to roll around on the floor.

I waited around on their property. A few tourists, who had heard about the W-Hats by reputation, dropped by to take a look, then moved on. Finally, a W-Hat member arrived. It turned out to be an avatar called Masakazu Kojima, a short woman, dressed up like a Japanese *otaku* anime cartoon fan, with a pink off-the-shoulder top, jeans with heart and star prints, pink pigtails, and a bright yellow cat-themed cap. Kojima, it turned out, was co-founder of the W-Hats. She wanted to make it clear that she hadn't encouraged the global attacks, or any of the other troublesome behavior perpetrated by her members. "W-Hat is the non-griefing 'SA Goon' group in Second Life," she said, referring to Something Awful ("The Internet Makes You Stupid"), a prank-based Internet forum. "Although I always want to put 'non-griefing' in quotes. It's more of a goal than a reality."

Kojima admitted that some W-Hat members had been behind a few of the recent attacks, but she insisted they were no longer members. She told me the latest trend among her troublemaking members was to find shared objects, which could be altered by anyone in the right group, and set them to copy themselves and destroy the world. That way, it was harder to track down the culprit.

I asked if Plastic Duck was behind some of the recent attacks. "He would probably deny it," Kojima told me, "but yeah. He can put you in touch with the other grid crashers, too. Most of them hate me, quite a lot, for kicking them out of W-Hat.

"Crashing the grid is not quite in line with our ideas," she told me.

Kojima gave me instructions on how to find Plastic Duck. "Just keep in mind that he likes to mess with people," Kojima said.

Kojima also told me about an obscure chat channel dedicated to reconstructing the Second Life client outside the reach of Linden Lab's control—so users could alter it. Here the notorious former W-Hat Plastic Duck lingered under the name GeneR. It was my best shot at getting a straight answer, Kojima told me; in more public areas, she said, "he's more likely to just mess with you." I lurked in the chat channel for two days before Plastic Duck replied, although once we had exchanged e-mails, I found him very willing to talk.

Plastic Duck turned out to be Patrick Sapinski, a nineteen-year-old high school student from Ajax, Ontario. Patrick first logged on to Second Life in January 2005. He was seventeen, and constantly ill with the symptoms of a disease that had yet to be diagnosed, when he saw an interview with Philip Rosedale on the cable gaming channel TechTV. Then Second Life became a topic of conversation on one of his favorite websites, Something Awful. Patrick had enjoyed playing with level designers—software for creating small, shared online areas people could download and plug into existing combat games—but he was frustrated by the weeks it took to release a design, spread the word, and get people's comments. He saw the more flexible Second Life as a place to build and try things out immediately. Soon he was spending all day either in bed or playing Second Life. "I'll admit that a lot of the time I wasn't sick enough that I couldn't go to school, but I preferred staying at home and logging in," he told me.

It took doctors a year to figure out Patrick's illness. "It turned out to be Crohn's disease," he told me. "At that point it had gotten so bad that I pretty much didn't have a life outside of my room. Crohn's disease is an immune disorder where your immune system attacks your bowels. The pains are often compared to those of birthing pains, but constant throughout the day. It was pretty bad, but looking back, I wouldn't have changed a thing."

After a long post on Something Awful about Second Life, the "goons, " as the website's regulars called themselves, created virtual selves and began to enact the jokes they had talked about online for so long.

"One of the first organized projects was when we took a Something Awful real-life idea called a 'fauxtest' into Second Life," Patrick told me. "A fauxtest is basically a fake protest. Some goons organize these in real life and, for example, on a rainy day make signs to protest the rain, silly stuff like that." As an early virtual prank, Patrick's friends organized a "fauxtest" in Second Life, where they dressed in black mime outfits and made blank signs, then stood around in the welcome area doing absolutely nothing.

Not everyone enjoyed it. "This absolutely enraged the Second Life community," Patrick told me. "It was never done before and wasn't normal, people didn't like the change. Since its inception, Second Life has mostly consisted of people who generally treat it much like real life. They build homes, buy clothes, and hang out with friends. They take things like virtual guns very seriously and don't take kindly to anything that wouldn't normally belong in real life."

And Second Life residents weren't afraid to report people who offended them. (At the time I visited Linden Lab, about 6.5 percent of logged-in residents had filed one or more abuse reports. By the end of 2006, Linden Lab was receiving close to two thousand abuse reports a day.) Virtual residents who were jostled by the mock-protesting mimes reported them to Linden Lab. "You can bet that every single one of them was reported repeatedly," Patrick told me. Within weeks of joining, many W-Hats were banned from Second Life.

Those who survived, or came back under a different name, began to make new kinds of virtual mischief. "We had fun," Patrick said. "A W-Hat member would randomly stumble upon a couple having virtual sex." In Second Life, as in many virtual worlds, avatars can have sex. Later, I would learn more about how this worked, but for now, Patrick told me to picture pixellated, interactive pornography, accompanied by basic text sex chat.

"They'd attach a chimney avatar and sit on the couple's house, then they'd mention the fact that they are doing this in the W-Hat group chat. Soon enough a goon would show up soliciting Bible sales, or dressed as a fire hydrant. To us, it was silly fun; to others, it was horrible griefing."

W-Hat members posted videos of these pranks to YouTube, under the title "Second Life Safari." Predictably, the victims were incensed.

Across virtual worlds, other residents were testing the line between one person's fun and another's suffering. To retain the attention of their residents, virtual worlds such as World of Warcraft often hold special events—Fourth of July fireworks, fancy-dress nights at Halloween. In these more themed worlds, events are mostly under the control of the companies who make the universe, though players craft their own fun, sometimes at the expense of others. In February 2006, the real woman behind a popular World of Warcraft troll, Fayejin, died. On March 4, her online friends decided to hold a virtual wake; they gathered by a snowy virtual lake, the Frostfire Hot Springs in Winterspring, "because she loved to fish in the game," her funeral announcement read. "She liked the sound of the water, it was calming for her, and she loved snow." Her virtual friends lined up by the lake to pay their respects to the dead woman's virtual self, who was controlled by a real-world friend. As a mark of respect, they decided to attend without weapons. "$10 on somebody fucking with it," World of Warcraft resident Stanos wrote, under the funeral announcement. He would have won the bet. An opposing band of players, ironically named "Serenity Now," decided to take advantage of the vulnerable moment. They stampeded through a cavernous tunnel and attacked the ceremony, their weapons drawn, and killed everyone there. The first virtual resident to be killed was the dead woman's virtual self. Serenity Now posted a YouTube video of the attack for "recruitment."

By March 2005, when I traveled to Boston to meet Wilde in person, Patrick was forging a virtual reputation as Plastic Duck. Among his already mischievous W-Hat peers, he stood out. "I participated in a large majority of these outings, which is likely why people even know of my existence. In early 2005, I was known to actively play Second Life at least ten hours a day. I would show up as a lost robot, Oompa-Loompa, or something equally silly. The name was also easy to remember. People didn't remember Operating Thetan, Louis Neutra, or Dave Eisenberg; half the time, when listing suspected griefers, people listed completely wrong last names, but they always got Plastic Duck right."

His antics came to the attention of Linden Lab, and Plastic Duck began to accumulate the first of his eventual double-digit rap sheet of suspensions. "I recall that one of my first suspensions involved me following a woman around the welcome area who was trying to get away from my avatar, an Oompa-Loompa from *Charlie and the Chocolate Factory*, because she claimed it was ugly," Patrick said. He thought the Second Life community too sensitive about the W-Hats' playful attitude. "It's hard for non–Second Lifers to realize the severity of these 'crimes.' I can guarantee you that if I did the same thing in real life, I could likely get a laugh out of anyone who saw it. But in Second Life, people are living a very sheltered life. They can't stand the smallest change."

Despite Patrick's insistence that the W-Hats were just out to have fun, their antics did stray into offensive and damaging activities. W-Hat member Ol Fitzcarraldo liked to change his virtual shape into what he called his "black" avatar: a racial stereotype, complete with watermelon slice, bucket of chicken, and Afro. I asked Patrick about these. "There are goons whose intent is to harass," he told me. "That's against the Second Life rules, and those goons get kicked out and come back on new accounts. Then there are those, which I guess I sort of fall into, that like to have fun, and sometimes get a kick making fun of some really weird people and communities out there. On my Plastic Duck account, I pushed the boundaries and rules, but I rarely if ever broke them. Almost all of my suspensions were for disturbing the peace—words most goons have seen many times. If you get reported enough in Second Life, no matter how innocent you are, you'll eventually get a suspension for disturbing the peace."

I asked whether the W-Hats, including the provocative "Cyber Terrorist" slogan on their van, were out to destroy Second Life. "Someone on the Second Life forums made a claim that W-Hat are cyber-terrorists because of what we do," Patrick told me. "The group found this rather funny. The 'W-Hats: Cyber Terrorists since 2004' moniker is a complete parody. Not a single person in the group believes they are really cyber-terrorists."

Patrick then told me the W-Hat side of what he called "the drama with Anshe Chung"—the incident where Anshe had publicly complained that avatars were pressuring her to sell land in an area of Second Life called Baku, at below-market rates.

"When Baku was put online, I believe half the land was first land, which consists of small parcels made available to Second Life newbies," Patrick said. "The other half was purchased by land baron Anshe Chung, who divided it up into small chunks to resell for profit. A number of goons bought up the first land parcels and joined them together to be used for the W-Hat land, and added to that were a few Anshe parcels we purchased."

"Anyway, W-Hat as a group did what they did," Patrick said. "The land was very colorful, with random 'newbies' leaving all kinds of offensive crap around, swastikas, penises, bombs, etc." ("It's a common joke that in Second Life, *Star Wars* fans build their first lightsaber; goons build their first penis," Patrick had told me.) "That'll lower the value of any land around it.

"I'd bet that more than a few new goons tried to extort Anshe, no doubt about that. But their perception of Second Life," Patrick said, quoting the Linden Lab slogan, " 'Your world, your imagination,' made this acceptable."

I enjoyed the stories of some of the W-Hat pranks, but some—Ol Fitzcarraldo's "black" avatar, the intentional grid attacks—seemed genuinely offensive. In the real world, terrorism attacks thought, and cyber-terror also disrupts dialogue. Still, as a group the "terrorists" seemed to have a place in the virtual world. They were the anti-Lindens, the amoral shadow of the crusade for community and calm.

"A lot of people want to live perfect lives in Second Life, but I don't think those people could stand it if Linden Lab did somehow manage to rid the grid of any drama or griefing incidents. They may not like it, but in the end, it's a part of the world."

At this point, Patrick had to take a break; it was time to travel to his clinic for a treatment for his Crohn's disease. When he returned, our chat continued.

Over time, Patrick told me, the bans added momentum to W-Hat's more disruptive side. "Usually when a clean account got banned I'd be left with nothing, no land and none of the content I created," Patrick said. "This pissed me off, so in turn I would make throwaway accounts which I would just mess around on. Squat on other people's land, and build stuff that I didn't really care if I lost."

I asked if this was when the attacks against the whole world began. "I remember the first grid crash like it was yesterday," Patrick told me. "We were doing a top hat, monocle, and suit theme at the time. It happened in October 2005. Ol Fitzcarraldo, a member of W-Hat and a W-Hat splinter group, was working on objects called 'griefspheres,' which were balls that randomly flew around and tried to place themselves at the location of an avatar, in effect swarming and surrounding unsuspecting players." The griefspheres, a meter across, were painted with a picture of an evil character from the video game Half Life 2, grinning maniacally. Another W-Hat brought up the idea of making them replicate. After some reluctance, Patrick told me, Ol Fitzcarraldo altered the griefspheres so they copied themselves. According to Patrick, Ol didn't want his new invention to spiral out of control. He built a self-destruct command, the letter *d*. The first time he released the new, improved griefspheres, they quickly filled the room. "They were replicating pretty fast," Patrick said, "so Ol flew around shouting 'd.' After a few minutes, he got rid of all the griefspheres around the area. He thought he was safe."

About ten minutes later, another W-Hat sent a message: "Hey Ol, What the fuck are these griefspheres? CLEAN THIS SHIT UP." Patrick checked the map; that particular W-Hat was on the opposite side of the world. "That was when we realized the severity of what was going on."

Linden Lab had built Second Life to be easily expandable, so that at first, every geographic area, about sixteen acres of virtual soil, was supported by a single piece of hardware, a server box, at its San Francisco server farm. Later this relationship between virtual soil and real hardware became more flexible, but the nickname for these servers, "sims"—short for *simulator*—stuck, so that each Second Life sixteen-acre area became known as a "sim." According to Patrick, these Second Life servers, interconnected on a grid, are surrounded by a buffer zone, the "space server." "When something crosses into the space server," Patrick said, "it is deleted and sent back to your inventory. Now, all these self-replicating griefspheres overloaded and crashed the space server. Because of this, any object that left the grid would warp to the next closest 'sim' as it never made it to the space server. This caused just about every single sim in Second Life to be packed full of griefspheres." (Some reports put the total number of griefspheres at 5.4 billion.)

"Within about half an hour," Patrick said, "the space server had crashed, and so had about half of the other servers. So while others may believe it was a planned attack, the first griefsphere incident was definitely an accident, one that the creator attempted to clean up but had managed to get out of his control.

"There have been many grid attacks since, maybe around five to eight that appeared well thought out and planned, and were often successful, and about twenty that appeared to be spur of the moment: Hey, we made this big fetus object, let's make it attack people! Or more, let's see how five hundred of these spinning around flying at people will look!" (One of the "Second Life Safari" showed this kind of grief: In a Second Life nightclub, a W-Hat filled the dance floor with body-popping gremlins.) "I recall a few of the smaller random 'attacks' were sometimes color-changing cubes called 'lolcubes' and a few times a brown fetus object was used called 'chocolate fetus.' I recall a specific chocolate incident where one of the Live Help goons was sending us chat logs from Live Help. One resident complained that he was being 'hugged by big brown bears.' A Linden employee told this resident to restart their computer as a means of fixing the problem. Most of us found this reply rather funny."

Attacks that actually shut down the grid were rare, Patrick claimed. "Only a few of them caused any actual crashes." He told me that a hard core of five "vengeful goons" was responsible for most of the grid attacks—and in fact only two or three times was Second Life brought down when they couldn't work out who was responsible.

"I know most of the grid attackers pretty well," Patrick told me. "Most of them were former W-Hat members."

In the end, bored by his regular bans, Patrick told me he decided to return to the straight and narrow. As his new character, Gene Replacement, he had even earned bounties—ten thousand Lindens, about thirty dollars a time—from Linden Lab for reporting possible exploits: mistakes in the world that other residents might have used to cause trouble. "On one occasion I had a chat with Philip Rosedale himself," Patrick told me, "where he personally thanked me for turning in a pretty big exploit, one that let you generate unlimited and untraceable amounts of Linden Dollar currency."

After he told Linden Lab about the exploits, Patrick said, a Linden Lab manager even considered hiring him as a security consultant. "I was put in contact with some management, and we discussed a possible consultation contract for about a month or so, to see how things go." The idea wasn't received well with some other Linden staff. "From what I gather, the other management just shot the idea down as soon as they found out who he was talking to," Patrick said.

I asked about the e-mail Catherine Smith had allegedly sent to

CBC reporter Lindsay Michael, listing Plastic Duck's infractions. "Some of them are partly true; overall everything is exaggerated," Patrick said. "For example, I might have sent the Goatse image [the notorious sexually explicit photo] to a few people, but they were friends within W-Hat, not all over Second Life. Anyone can be guilty of being in a group with another griefer in it. Most Second Life groups are public. It's sad that Catherine would stoop to that level, and stupid of her to actually think that such an e-mail would change Lindsay's mind." (In the end, Patrick was interviewed on CBC. He showed them a model he was working on, a virtual Mac-10 subma-chine gun. He read out his notice-of-termination e-mail from Linden Lab. "Apparently they seem to think when I make fun of someone I'm causing them intense mental anguish," he said. "I don't believe that. It's a video game.")

Despite his attempts to stay clean, Patrick's new virtual self, Gene Replacement, was dragged down by his friends. "In the end, I was banned for associating with a grid crasher, including about sixty other people banned for the same reason. There were one, maybe two peo-ple involved in the grid attacks. In an effort to make it look like Lin-den Lab was working on the problem, they pinned the blame on a group of sixty goons and banned them all. Then they reclaimed our entire land, which they resold on the open market."

When we spoke, Patrick still had a few Second Life accounts, which he and friends had created when they discovered a simple loophole in the registration system. (In 2005, Second Life accounts cost $9.95; banned W-Hats would just pay a friend to set up an account for them. Later, first accounts were free, but you needed to establish your identity with a credit card, PayPal, or cellphone authorization. A Something Awful goon discovered you could just click on the form button twice to register an account without any authorization. "The Second Life client does use various unique parts of your computer to identify you," Patrick told me. "However, those are easy to get around once you know what you're looking for.")

But it wasn't the same. All his friends had been banned. By the time we spoke, he was spending less time in his virtual shoes. He wrote a Web posting for his friends, called "I miss Second Life." "I miss it all," Patrick wrote. "It was silly, it was pointless, we didn't really accomplish much, but we had fun.

"The sexual deviants, the builders, the scripters, the thinkers, you, my friends, your friends, everyone. I miss all of you."

"I definitely made a connection with these people, and I still care for them very much," Patrick told me. "We've mostly lost contact, outside of a few who still idle in our Ventrilo server and one person who I often visit in real life. It's a shame that Linden Lab had to ruin that for us."

"The whole thing was like being back on the grade school playground for me," one of the banned Voted 5 members, "fiddy"—one of Patrick's closest friends from Second Life—wrote on Patrick's website. "Just being a total inner child and doing ridiculous silly things and having our own immature little wars and drama. It was also kinda like being at the kids' table at a big family Thanksgiving or something. A few yards away everyone is trying to be real mature and stuff, then you have a bunch of kids flinging food around and making fart jokes. It was the most fun and best laughs I've ever had on the Internet. I guess the big adults finally had enough though, and sent us all to our rooms."

"I know the real people behind a lot of the anonymous accounts used for grid attacks," Patrick told me. "I would consider a lot of them friends. No one is really afraid of the FBI threats. We've had Lindens tell us anonymously that the FBI threats were fake. There's really no reason to believe that the FBI is even remotely interested to hear LL's cries for help."

Patrick saw the FBI announcement as "a bad PR move." "I doubt there are more than a few people in SL crazy enough to want the FBI investigating grid crashes instead of real crimes relating to national security," he said.

Earlier, Masakazu Kojima had backed up Patrick's comments. "As far as calling in the Feds," Kojima had told me, "I can tell you for sure that the Big Bad Guys have yet to hear from anyone."

Linden Lab had hoped a real-world prosecution would intimidate others tempted by similar trespasses against their universe. A Linden Lab contact told me the FBI had in fact visited Linden Lab three times. (After the first two visits, the FBI apparently had trouble grasping whether a crime had taken place. The third time, after Linden Lab gave them a list of the credit cards involved, they returned to report the credit card numbers were stolen, and there was little more they could do.) Linden Lab had at least pushed its security to the point where it required breaking a real-world law—in this case, credit card theft—to persistently disrupt their universe. But the lack of real-world consequences for these disruptive activities made me wonder how the virtual community might handle these infractions themselves. Virtual worlds like Second Life were now full of crimes and misdemeanors. Linden Lab published a weekly "police blotter"—lists of offenses committed by residents. In the real world, many of these crimes would have led to a jail sentence; in the virtual world, where stakes were lower, they mostly led to warnings or a short-term suspension. In one day, June 14, 2006, two residents logged in to other residents' accounts and stole their virtual cash; Linden suspended each for seven days. On September 21, 2006, one resident was warned for wearing a giant penis attachment in a PG—for "Parental Guidance," akin to a cinematic rating suitable for kids—area. Another was warned for harming a virtual pet, and a third suspended for seven days for wearing a KKK outfit, yelling "Sieg Heil!" and waving a Confederate flag.

When I visited the Linden Lab San Francisco offices, I had broached this subject. "We always thought that there would be a lot of disputes," Robin Harper said. As part of her work as vice president of community development, Harper tried to encourage Second Life residents to get along. "We believed that part of complexity was intrigue. Part of why we like the world is because it is complicated. The explicit feature set of Second Life is so open, there's always going to be people defining what making you miserable means in different ways. I think we expected to get asked to resolve disputes." Linden Lab employees told me, though, that with just thirty of them, they did not have the resources to handle every argument, and they hoped the watchful eyes of the virtual community would begin to police them-selves, "to delegate that responsibly, wherever we can, to the people who live there," in Robin Harper's words. With the aim of fostering community spirit, Philip Linden held a weekly "town hall" event in which he discussed Linden Lab plans and opened the floor to ques-tions from concerned residents. But for some residents, those who wanted freedom but didn't want the attendant responsibility, Linden Lab wasn't doing enough. "Some people are very unhappy that we haven't put a system of governance in place," Harper said. "And we keep saying governance will come when it's ready. There is one small community, called Neu Altenburg, that does have a system of self-governing. I'd say you will probably start to see more of these local ju-risdictions in Second Life. A group of all the landowners in a large area, saying, 'Hey look, if you don't play by the rules, guess what, you'll never come to this place again, you'll be exiled from that part of the world.' I can see that being a very powerful motive. If you go against that and lose you might have interests there, that would be very serious, that would be nearly the same as death."

To build any society, you need a pillar, a foundation for the struc-ture to come: a constitution, a senate, a guru. Linden Lab sees its "terms of service" and "community standards," both of which new residents have to read and agree to, as equivalent to a basic constitu-tion, designed to foster a cooperative culture based on mediation rather than arbitration. "Basically we have three rules," Harper said. "One is the golden rule: Do unto others. Then growing out of that is the second rule, which is that we support and promote tolerance and so we don't allow any hate speech. The last rule is that we don't allow you to reveal other people's real life information." By March 2005,

Robin Harper told me, they had only ever needed to ban twenty people, many for credit card fraud. But the idea of emergent arbitration seemed to excite them. "In a decentralized way, local governance is all that makes sense. Sometimes that's a bit painful and chaotic but far more fundamentally right."

"Where there's no law, there's no bread," Benjamin Franklin wrote. The converse is also true: Where there's bread, there's law. And where there's law, there's disagreement. Now that people made actual bread in virtual worlds, the ways in which those worlds were policed seemed increasingly important. Virtual residents knew, though, that real-world courts rarely offered recourse for virtual damages. Even in Korea, where the phenomenon of mass population of virtual worlds had reached its peak, real-world cases rarely extended beyond violence caused by games. There, the Seoul Police Cyber-Terror Unit, which polices real-world crimes related to online gaming, told me that virtual objects had no legal value. If you paid someone for a virtual sword and they didn't deliver, it was fraud—after all, you had lost money. If you delivered a virtual sword and they didn't pay, well, that was just a disagreement inside a game.

So what options did virtual residents have when they felt they had been the victim of a virtual offense? How were the rules enforced among those who played? Virtual worlds liberate us from our bodies, but not from one another. In Second Life, to take two actual examples, a sniper who took potshots through a school window was a mild nuisance; someone who skinny-dipped in a PG area was considered far more problematic. The usual path of action for disagreement in virtual worlds was to plead with the game developers, usually via a Games Master (the virtual equivalent of the local councilor), in the hope that the gods—the world's makers—would intervene. (Often, they didn't. Spokesman Jeff Brown of Electronic Arts, developers of the virtual world The Sims Online, admitted that, in their world, the rules "are enforced about as well as the rules are enforced on the

Massachusetts Turnpike.") When I visited Linden Lab, Robin Harper cited some examples. A resident who threw a firebomb at a wedding, she said, might get a few points against his or her record, whereas someone writing a self-replicating, heavily scripted object that caused a whole section of Second Life to crash—a kind of terrorist attack against the infrastructure of the world—would be suspended. (Later, their stance against this kind of attack toughened considerably.) The community-focused Linden Lab said it took the decision to ban someone seriously. Residents who committed more serious infractions would have their accounts put on hold while a randomly selected jury of twelve residents reviewed the anonymous facts of the case; those convicted by their virtual peers would have their Second Life selves permanently banned. But what about more subtle forms of disagreement? What if your neighbor builds a huge high-rise and puts your virtual garden in the shade? Who can you turn to?

"Do what thou wilt shall be the whole of the law," Aleister Crowley wrote. In virtual worlds, to some extent, this was true. Still, there was an inherent contradiction. What if people wilt make laws? In September 2005, two law school students, Judge Mason and Judge Churchill, took it upon themselves to solve this problem: They built a virtual courtroom and opened the Second Life Superior Court. Residents could take their arguments, large or small, to the court. The judges would, with reference to the Linden Lab Community Standards, and their own knowledge of real-world law, resolve the disputes. The court followed basic legal procedure, including brief and counterbrief, and any decision by the court was intended to be final. (It was the formation of this court that led Marsellus Wallace to create Raymond Polonsky, his virtual legal counsel.)

Not all Second Life residents agreed the court was a good idea. "What a mind-numbingly futile exercise," resident Tony Walsh wrote on the Second Life Herald website. "So now we have yet another level of tedious bureaucracy to Second Life, one administered by self-appointed 'officials' with no recognized real-world powers, let alone make-believe ones. I'm in contempt of this kangaroo court." Others wondered whether the court would have teeth to back up its judgment, or even what would happen if a Linden employee were the target of a case. "Perhaps even the Lindens themselves will take action to stop this," wrote another resident, Dygash Talamasca.

In fact, Linden Lab did step in. Not to stop the court, but to request the pair change their organization's name, so as not to confuse residents about the court's authority. It was renamed "The Metaverse Superior Court," but the lack of authority did cause problems, and it never heard a case. Others were exploring possible solutions to the lack of virtual law. Second Life resident Zarf Vantongerloo realized that most legal agreements are founded on signed documents. Using cryptographic keys and secure communication with a server outside of Second Life, Zarf designed a notary service, providing signed, untamperable documents, for virtual agreements and business deals.

The legal status of virtual trespass has yet to be established. At real-world conferences like the one on State of Play: Law, Games and Virtual Worlds, which convened in 2005, real-world lawyers have begun to examine the new legal frontier. As yet, although virtual items have real value, those with virtual income do not pay real-world tax, unless they convert their virtual earnings into real currency. Most virtual world developers try to stem this problem by banning the sale of virtual items through eBay: Sony Online Entertainment, which owns EverQuest and EverQuest II, insists that all the content of its virtual worlds, including items and even avatars, remain its property. All new residents must agree to the terms and conditions, which state as much. The terms and conditions of Ultima Online, another massive fantasy-themed virtual world, state: "You acknowledge and agree that all characters created, and items acquired and developed as a result of game play are part of the Software and Service and are the sole property of EA.com." Lawyers, though, are not convinced these disclaimers will hold forever. For legal and copyright purposes, European and American legal systems equate lines of computer code with narrative prose; this stance implies ownership remains with the companies that own the worlds, although once creative input takes place on behalf of the player, it isn't always clear who has made the content, and therefore who owns the virtual self. Virtual worlds have created a whole new nexus of legal debate; copyright laws, laws of identity, and, in the case of well-known virtual selves, rights of publicity, are all arguably relevant, and each branch of the law reaches a different conclusion about who owns what in the specific universe.

Virtual worlds give us an opportunity to observe the development of society again, from basic tenets. ("In Second Life, we are free of everything but the need for community and novelty," Philip Linden told me.) In medieval times, banishment from your community was the worst possible punishment; it cut you off from your collective self, which held both your earthly and heavenly connections. It was a fate worse than death. Ever since, police, moral philosophers, and criminals themselves have all wrestled with the thorny problem of what to do with those who break society's moral codes and repeatedly hurt others. In the real world, our attitudes to punishment evolved. When banishment stopped being seen as worse than death, we switched to using death—now the most extreme exclusion. Later, the British tried banishment en masse, sending convicts across the world to Australia. In the modern world, social conditions have changed; we are no longer tied into the body of our local community, so to be removed from it is no longer to be cut from your heart. Now we exclude people "humanely"—in prisons, detention centers, reformatories—inside the world, but outside society. Murderers get imprisoned or deported. Ghosts get sucked up by Bill Murray and kept inside a toaster. Whoever you are, society's greatest punishment is still removal.

As a rule, though, in virtual worlds the medieval approach prevails: Those who break the rules of the game are banned. (In December 2005, Blizzard banned eighteen thousand residents for trading virtual gold for real money.) And for those who identify primarily as their virtual selves, nothing could be worse than a ban. To be cut off from Second Life or World of Warcraft is to be exiled into the purgatory of the real world.

———

Some virtual worlds, I discovered, were working to make the punishment fit the crime. The Egyptian-themed world A Tale in the Desert has a player-run legal system, modeled on the ancient Egyptian one, that allows residents to vote on the banning of another player. In other virtual worlds, the punishments play a dramatic role in the stories of the worlds themselves.

Cynewulf, a barbarian and resident of a new online game set in Roman Britain, A.D. 180, called Roma Victor (developed in the United Kingdom by virtual world company RedBedlam), is perhaps the only living American to survive crucifixion. In our real world, Cynewulf was a twenty-seven-year-old electrical engineer from Flint, Michigan; in the virtual world, he was a bloodthirsty barbarian. Throughout the summer of 2005, Cynewulf raided the areas where new residents, and residents who had been killed, rejoined the virtual world. These defenseless young Romans, fresh to their virtual sandals, were easy prey, and other residents complained. Finally, the rulers of the virtual empire decided enough was enough. As punishment, the world's gods (RedBedlam) decided Cynewulf would spend seven days nailed to the cross.

"I was raised in a fairly religious upbringing, but I don't view this game or this method of punishment as an insult against Christians," Cynewulf told me, of his virtual crucifixion. "In fact, the era being represented is rife with possibilities for Christian gamers to role-play. A Christian player could decide to be another Perpetua and face lions rather than renounce her faith, or be an early church father and reenact with other Christians the debates that formed the various sects of Christianity—this could actually be a great opportunity for religious players wanting to relive that rather momentous time in their history. My chosen preference, however, is just to step away from the modern world and pretend to be a Woden-worshipping Germanic warrior. It's just a game, after all."

Cynewulf's punishment was untested, and there were a few

glitches. The sinning barbarian should have been firmly nailed to the cross, unable to speak or move, but as a crowd watched the cross being pulled erect, Cynewulf raised an arm and waved.

Still, Cynewulf told me, being nailed to a virtual cross for a week wasn't as painless as he had thought it would be. "It was surprisingly agonizing for just being a game," he told me. As the virtual crucifix was raised, a fellow barbarian ran from the crowd and attacked the guards in a rage. Cynewulf watched helplessly as his compatriot was put to death. "Being jeered at by the Romans while immobilized is not much fun. Particularly since they are all weaklings who deserve to die by my sword."

When I visited Linden Lab, they had hinted at their hopes for new forms of punishment. ("It's a really interesting area," Philip Rosedale had told me. "I don't know yet, do you go to jail or do you go to virtual jail? I love that.") A year after my visit, they tested a new approach, designed to rehabilitate, rather than just punish, offenders. Also, their solution was designed to amuse. Early in January 2006, Second Life resident Nimrod Yaffle broke the Second Life terms of service by hacking into the Second Life code to steal items from a virtual store. Instead of a suspension, Yaffle was the first resident to be sent to "the cornfield." Every time he logged in to Second Life, where there once was a whole world, suddenly all he could see were endless rows of corn. (The scenery was inspired by a classic episode of the TV series *The Twilight Zone* in which an omnipotent child rules a town in terror. Anyone who offends his infantile sense of right and wrong is banished to the "cornfield," never to be seen again.) Yaffle walked the rows for what seemed like days, under a full moon that never waned. No one else came. He found a tractor, but the tractor was "insanely slow. " He found a TV, but all it ever played was a cautionary 1940s film about a troubled teenager trying to avoid a life of crime. Nimrod's crime wasn't too serious, nor was his punishment. ("The cornfield is not used often," Catherine Smith told *Discover* magazine, "and it is only for white-collar crimes. It is supposed to be funny more than anything.") Nimrod knew he would be seen again. He was temporarily cut off from his heavenly connections, but he still had his earthly ones. (He posted pictures of the cornfield on Second Life bulletin boards.) Nimrod even tried, unsuccessfully, to create a scripted object that would crash the world—an echo of the crime that had him teleported into the cornfield in the first place. Nimrod was being asked to consider the effect of his actions, but mostly what he did, he said, was drive the tractor, keeping half an eye out for the virtual Children of the Corn.

7

VIRTUAL RICHES

Where there's money, there's an addiction

My time in the lawless virtual underworld had made me conscious of my own safety. When I met Wilde in person, I told them I planned to set up a virtual office. "Make sure it's burglar-proof!" June-Marie had joked, and the group had laughed.

As it turned out, even in the virtual world, home security was a concern.

In the real world, my housing situation was turbulent. I had read stories of homeless people in New York City scraping up change to maintain their virtual mansion, but I no longer believed these tales. I was having enough trouble building my own virtual life, on the short security of six-month tenancy agreements. To build virtual stability, I had discovered, you needed real stability. You needed to have something before you could want to escape it. Over the last ten years of living in London, property prices already among the world's most expensive had tripled in value. The pressure on young people to rent or buy their own accommodation was phenomenal. I wanted a place in the city, large and full of light. At the same time, I longed for a place in the country, away from everything and everyone. My day-dreams were of penthouses with views of the metropolis, or quiet places by the sea: homes above or outside the crowd.

I made a few small steps in these directions. On a trip to Brazil, a friend and I seriously considered putting down twenty thousand dol-lars for a plot of land overlooking the ocean. A local hotel owner led us over the brow of a hill, still thick with near-jungle, and we paced out the plots (lots one to eight had been snapped up by French in-vestors; nine, ten, and eleven were still available). We could build homes there, we thought—share an Internet connection, and live our real lives in a tropical paradise. I knew enough about paradises, though, to know things would be hard there, too—and besides, nei-ther of us had the money. Closer to home, I considered moving to the British seaside. I visited a lighthouse keeper's cottage in Dungeness; it was a low-rent, single-story building with little insulation and no heating. The view from what would have been my office was a long, low, shingled beach, gray stones and sea and endless sky, broken only by the boxy silhouettes of the two Dungeness nuclear reactors. But London was three hours away, and here again there was no Internet connection; I would have had to end my virtual life and settle exclu-sively on the real. I wasn't ready to make the sacrifice.

I realized that we hadn't just chosen to live in virtual worlds; we had also been driven there, in the same way American colonists were driven to leave Europe. The pioneers headed west to find a new free-dom of religion and expression, and people seemed to be heading for virtual worlds to find a similar kind of relief, in this case from the pres-sure to live apart. In the real world, people were living alone because they chose to do so—for so long we had wanted to be free, and, we found, part of being free was being alone—but we also lived sepa-rately because our "free market" system had pushed us away from one another. We had been divided by the forces that profit from our sepa-ration—the companies that made the washing machines, that prof-ited when they sold more cars and other things to people who lived alone. The separation resulting from these kinds of pressures has helped drive people to live in cyberspace—the place William Gibson called "the city of lights."

In the real world, we are surrounded by glamour, but our access to such glamour is restricted. We need money and influence to reach those spaces. In our commercial culture, the big lie is that money and success bring happiness. Even the wealthy struggle; even the famous are unhappy. In virtual worlds, we can live out our material hopes much faster, experience an echo of the hollowness without spending a lifetime to achieve it. Even those who are wealthy in the real world suffer from the attendant separation: Money creates access to space but erodes our access to one another. We want one another, and we don't want one another. Virtual worlds are a kind of solution to that tension, between self and other, a way to be together when we feel so alone. We can come together but also keep one another at a safe distance.

(Given this real-world economy that underpins our virtual worlds I've wondered if our new frontier is in some sense a gated community of privilege. After all, I invested $1,800 for a personal computer that helped me spend time in virtual worlds; for real-world residents from poorer nations, that would be a significant barrier to virtual lives. However, in November 2006, the charity One Laptop Per Child announced that its first twenty-one thousand laptops—designed to cost just one hundred dollars, and subsidized by bulk orders from the governments of Argentina, Brazil, Libya, Nigeria, and Thailand—had rolled off a Shanghai production line. The laptop, designed to promote IT education for the world's poor, ran Doom, a classic 3-D video game. It shouldn't be long before virtual world technology will be able to transport many in the third world, too.)

When my mother and her friends decided to set up a commune, to build their own solution to the problem of how to live, their zeal for a better world drove them to buy Herringswell Manor, a mock-Tudor house on fourteen acres of Suffolk countryside. They knocked down walls and filled the space with dormitories, meditation rooms, and communal dining halls. Coincidentally, the week I visited the countryside looking for my own space, a Herringswell resident who knew about the commune sent me a brochure. In a "sympathetic refurbishment," the manor, our old commune, had been converted into luxury apartments. Walls had been rebuilt so the new residents could shore themselves up against one another. When my mother and her lover went to the Suffolk real estate agent to sign for the commune property, they carried a cashier's check, the pooled money of hundreds of fellow devotees, for the entire purchase price. At the time, that money bought a home for four hundred adults and thirty children. Now, the cheapest one-bedroom apartment was being sold for exactly the same price.

In the society where I lived, status was indicated by the amount of space you were able to put between yourself and others. I wanted some of the space for myself, but space, above everything, was at a premium. Along with almost everyone I knew my own age, I was priced out of the market. Instead, I would build a temporary solution to these problems of space and need. My own real-world life was beginning to be more stable. I had abandoned my dreams of both Brazilian beach life and London penthouse living for a more practical solution. With a new girlfriend, I had found a new home, a two-bedroom apartment in northwest London. But the place, already small, was further crowded with our stuff (OK, my stuff). To find space, I would have to go online.

I had the beginnings of a real-world home. It was time to build a virtual home, too.

Getting a seaside home in a virtual world wasn't as easy as I had imagined. For a start, there was so much choice. I began by logging on to Second Life. Each time a resident enters, while the world loads, a "tip" message appears. This might be a reminder about a town meeting, or a useful but little-known feature. This time, coincidentally, the log-in message was a warning about castles in the air. "If you build a castle in the air, be sure to buy the land below it. If someone else buys the land, they can delete your castle."

I considered a whole island, but with an initial purchase price of $1,250 in actual U.S. dollars, plus a monthly fee of $175—about what you'd pay for a car loan—they were beyond my budget. (Within a month, prices would rise to $1,675 per island; residents, of course, complained—suddenly every message board was full of people who had been "about to buy an island." That same day, I read that mogul Richard Branson had bought an entire island, shaped like Great Britain, in Dubai's man-made, as-yet-unfinished Earth Archipelago—a different kind of virtual landscape, laid out as a faux earth atlas—for around $6.7 million.) I browsed through the in-world classified ads. One caught my eye: "Private sims, tropical island views: $39.50 U.S. a month." But the price seemed high. I looked at a mountaintop retreat, above a private bay resort (17,600 Linden Dollars, plus fifteen U.S. dollars a week to Linden Lab). Some ads claimed to be selling land a stone's throw from the ocean, but it seemed that in virtual worlds, apparently, you could throw stones a lot farther. Not all the ads were placed by Linden Lab. In fact, most were from other residents: private property speculators who had bought desirable land—a snowy cliff, a sandy beach—in order to resell at higher prices.

It was a business model, I knew, that extended across other virtual worlds. For example, in 2004, David Storey, a twenty-two-year-old graduate student who lived in Sydney, Australia, bought a virtual island in a game called Project Entropia for $24,000—not for fun, but for profit. Every month, for the next twelve months, he could sell five plots of land on his island, which he hoped might net him as much as $80,000. There were people in Second Life already making even more than that. The classifieds for virtual land I had seen included many ads from Anshe Chung, Inc. (When I later met Anshe, her current account balance—that day's virtual turnover—was 1.6 million

Linden Dollars: about $5,500 in the real world. That would put her annual turnover at just over two million real dollars a year.)

In the end, I fell in love with a new development: a series of hill-side plots similar to the ones I had looked at in Brazil although the landscape was more autumnal. On each plot, the virtual developer had built cantilevered glass-and-concrete homes, clearly influenced by Frank Lloyd Wright's Fallingwater, and each one had a sea view. I clicked on the For Sale signs to learn more. A property here would cost me 14,000 Linden Dollars—about $45 real dollars—plus $15 per month, charged to my credit card. Even after Marsellus had cleaned me out, the price fit my budget. A passing resident swooped down out of the virtual sky to ask if I was interested. I nodded. He began to show me around the homes. It was like being taken around by a real-world real estate agent. ("This one has a lovely terrace," he told me.) It became clear, though, that he himself was another kind of profiteer. Spotting a smart investment, he had bought half the properties from the developer and was offering them for rent. But I wanted a home of my own. He told me numbers seven, eight, ten, and twelve were still available; I chose ten, a modest split-level with room for an office and a lounge upstairs.

I clicked "buy," and paid 14,000 Linden Dollars to someone called Rocky Rutabaga. (His profile showed a buff man in jeans and nothing else. According to the accompanying text, he was a member of 3 Feet Under Scuba Divers, Busy Ben's Vehicle Lot, and the Bareback Woodsmen Gay Club.)

I was now the owner of a new virtual home. I could ban people, charge people money to access my land, play loud music. But first I needed some virtual furniture.

As it happens, that evening my girlfriend had persuaded me to go to the exhausting Swedish furniture superstore Ikea to choose kitchen chairs for our real apartment. I cut a deal: I would go if she would help me choose virtual furniture for my virtual office.

We went first to Home Depoz, the virtual superstore—"Define Your Space!" It was the place Marsellus had directed me to in my mafia phase. These days, though, Marsellus seemed barely available—perhaps he was in the avatar protection program—but it seemed a good place to start. For 300 Linden Dollars, or one real dollar, we picked out a pair of easy chairs that you could customize with the click of a mouse. At another store, Belle Belle furniture—"Everything you need to make your Second House beautiful"—a virtual resident was earning a tiny wage (150 Linden Dollars, about fifty cents, an hour) to stand on a ladder and go through the motions of dusting. The cleaning had no use (in virtual worlds we have conquered housework as well as taxes and death) but the motion gave the place some authenticity, and to the virtual storeowner the ambience was worth the money. In the end, we picked up a pair of Louis XV chairs, a daybed, a private-eye-style desk and chair, a laptop, and an ashtray with smoking cigarette for effect.

In this world, land seemed more plentiful, and therefore relatively cheaper, than furnishings. My house and land had cost forty-five dollars; all my furniture together cost almost a quarter of that.

Then it was time to shop for real. The roads surrounding the west London Ikea are a masterpiece of hard work to navigate, in the center of a vast industrial area: factories, businesses, and warehouses, split by an almost impassable main road. From the car on the way, we saw the angular jumble of warehouses and business parks in great gray blocks, some with bright neon blue and red logos: It looked to me like Second Life, only uglier. This was the landscape of urban consumption after hours, empty of promise. In our virtual worlds, we had already replicated this landscape; perhaps soon we would replace it. When we arrived, Ikea itself didn't seem too different from Home Depoz, except that it took twice as long—and, in the real world, there was a lot more arguing about the route.

When we arrived back in our real home, we watched a BBC-TV

arts show, *Imagine*, about J. M. Barrie. Barrie's own life was full of loss. ("To be born is to be shipwrecked on an island," he once wrote. I thought of Wilde, who had been shipwrecked their whole lives, only to be washed up, whole again, on their virtual shore.) Barrie, the author of *Peter Pan*, conceived of Neverland as his refuge, "a place where people never die," a place—along with the real-world children who inspired it—that became Barrie's hard-won consolation.

Later that night, after we unwrapped our new kitchen chairs, I set up my furniture in my new virtual apartment. It felt sparse, but adequate. I turned on my new virtual TV, and watched *StrangerHood*, a piece of "machinima"—machine-made cinema—filmed with a virtual cast inside The Sims 2. In it, the characters wake up in their new virtual neighborhood, with no memory of how they arrived. I watched and laughed. I was sitting in a virtual world, watching a virtual TV show made in another virtual world. Almost nothing here was real.

At my Second Life desk, I could stare into space—just as I did at my real desk, only, in the real world, my view was of our garden wall; in the virtual one, I got an autumnal landscape, orange leaves, the sea, and a view of the rising full moon, blood-red against the night sky. (Faded discreetly into the moon was the Linden Lab logo.) I had bought a virtual cigarette, for show; I placed it in my virtual lips. Virtual cigarettes couldn't be addictive, but this one made me want a real smoke. I put it out. The air was quiet. I turned the TV off. Around me I could hear the virtual world: the faint wind, the flutter of a nearby flag, the first few spots of coming rain.

But I had forgotten Wilde's advice. My virtual home was not yet burglar-proof. Right then, behind me, my automatic door—a logical descendant of the *Star Trek*–style door Philip Rosedale built in his childhood bedroom—slid open and a passerby strolled in. My house had come without a manual, and it turned out I had forgotten to lock the virtual door.

———

From the beginning, Linden Lab decided to encourage ownership and trade of virtual items. Second Life was the first world to grant intellectual copyright to residents for the items they created in-world. (In 2005, one Second Life resident, Kermitt Quirk, sold the real-world rights to his popular in-world game, Tringo, a combination of Tetris and bingo, to a cellular provider, for delivery on cellphones.) Linden Lab makes most of its money through taxes on virtual land. A newcomer who buys a half-acre plot of virtual land pays one Linden Dollar per square meter, plus a monthly land fee, depending on how much they own, to Linden Lab. Just as in the real world, once property has been developed, it increases in value; then whenever it's sold, Linden Lab charges sales tax. The company also encourages trading in Linden Dollars. When I first visited, Second Life saw $250,000 worth of real-life currency conversion per month, and now people are exchanging $250,000 into Linden Dollars *every day*. A healthy economy is crucial, so to protect its investment, Linden Lab has to monitor for inflation. (When I spoke with Philip Rosedale, he told me Linden Lab was hoping to recruit its own "Alan Greenspan," but until that happened, they planned to handle the economy in-house.) So those who wanted to profit from the unprecedented mania for nonexistent things (young, urban professionals, who would laugh at the suggestion of a job in a real-world shoe factory, would, it turned out, spend hours making a virtual boot) had to turn to third-party item brokers and risk being banned for breaking the rules.

From the start, Linden Lab had taken a more risky, but potentially more rewarding stance: The entire copyright of a Second Life virtual creation remained with the resident who created it. Encouraged by this vested interest, Second Life residents drove a huge growth in their economy. In November 2006, virtual currency was changing hands inside Second Life to the equivalent of half a million U.S. dollars a day. ("The U.S. has had a GDP growth over the last century of like two percent per year," Philip Rosedale told me. "Ours is more like two percent per week.") I wondered exactly who was creating and trading this much imaginary property.

When we met, Philip had used the example of Second Life fashions to illustrate the entrepreneurial side of his virtual worlds (the top fashion designers earned in the region of 75,000 real dollars a year from their creations). I knew that some residents made a living from organizing events—there were even Second Life tour guides, who charged a real-world hourly wage—but the most obvious way to earn money in virtual worlds was by making virtual things.

I had experimented with building myself. In Second Life, building objects is like sketching in three dimensions; with a few clicks you can create basic shapes; stretch, push, and rotate them; and join things together to make something new. To help people learn the process, Linden Lab provides a "Sandbox," a vast empty area where you can build as much as you like, without paying land charges. (The name is metaphorical; there is no sand. You create things out of thin air, by clicking to make a shape appear, and dragging the mouse until the shape is the size you want. Then you can edit that shape in any way you choose.) Like a 3-D Etch A Sketch, every night the Sandbox is wiped clean. When I visited to try my hand, the Sandbox was a vast, dusty plane, overgrown with a forest of oddball creations. Blue-square whirlwinds, ridable yellow griffins, oblongs, two wooden cubes a quarter-mile square. A pink pig surrounded by a pink force field. A jumble of random vehicles piled together, like a child's Matchbox collection: a Ferrari, a Batmobile. A flying shark. Pegasus. A Chevy Malibu. A colossal blue marble bowl, like an Anish Kapoor installation, tilted toward the sun. Here and there, more professional builders were honing their skills, preparing developments for paying clients: In one corner of the Sandbox was a meticulous re-creation of palatial Roman gardens, a high jet of water at the center; the illusion was punctuated only by the three bright red motorcycles parked against the fountain.

Although the act of building is easier than in the real world, virtual worlds can't help with the inspiration. I found an empty spot, created a huge wooden triangle, and sat on the top.

It seemed that building virtual objects was easy, but not that easy. I decided to go shopping.

All good reporters need a Dictaphone. I searched on a Second Life website, SLBoutique, "Second Life's Premier Web Shopping Site." (When I visited, the top-selling items included a cherry tree, a wrist computer, and a device to follow other people around and record their conversations.) Payment was a complicated procedure; to verify my Second Life identity, I had to sign up on the website, then visit a virtual terminal inside Second Life. After some confusion, I bought the Dictaphone for 250 Linden Dollars. As far as I could tell, the terms and conditions stated that anything I bought could disappear at any time, and no one would be liable. I wondered how far a real-world retail outlet would get with a disclaimer like that. (In fact, an hour or so later I discovered what claimed to be an ATM, which seemed to work a little differently from the ones I knew in the real world. I put some money in. "Thank you," it said.) I opened my inventory, selected the Dictaphone, and clicked "wear"; what looked like a cardboard box appeared on my wrist, and did nothing.

Not all virtual purchases were so complex, or so unrewarding. Earlier, on my second visit to Second Life, in January 2004, shopping had been an easier experience. I had wandered the virtual malls. I bought a Panama hat, then a roll-up cigarette, which, when placed in my virtual mouth, looked like a cartoon joint. I tried to play automated poker, but the table told me it was broken. I had been warned by the tailor of the Panama hat that there were few places to buy clothes for men, but I wanted something writerly: a scarf and tweed coat—or maybe, for my mafia missions, some bling. Still, everywhere I looked, almost everything for sale was lingerie.

Eventually, I found a showroom, run by Thai Greenacre, that catered to the "discerning gentleman." For twenty Linden Dollars (prices were lower then) I bought a pair of "Black Brushed Oxford Lace-ups." In some cases, the virtual manufacturers had made no bones about the brands they were copying. For another twenty Linden Dollars, I bought a purple pair of "Converse" lace-up sneakers. In other cases, the designers copied brand names in the same oddly transparent attempt to avoid prosecution as the Devi-Krauss jeans you find at a Thai market stall: In a virtual electronics showroom, I found a wall of "Sono" televisions.

In Greenacre's store, I ran my virtual hands along the rails. Fifteen Linden Dollars got me two pairs of boxer shorts (I passed on the penguin and polar bears, and bought the tropic print). I skipped the thongs, the bowling shirts, and the pajamas (I didn't even own a bed yet). I did decide to splash out on a smart suit, my white, cruise-ship-steward tuxedo.

As I walked through, the shop seemed to slow down, from the pressure of so many objects on the servers, perhaps, or the pressure of so much consumerism on Errol Mysterio.

Near the clothes shop was a sign: "Monkey Mafia Gun Store." I clicked, and found myself teleported to an iron fortress. I clicked on the portcullis, and a claw dropped a ball to open the cantilevered gate. As I entered the castle, I saw a record sleeve on the wall; I clicked it, and death metal—the kind of music I imagined trench-coated kids cleaning guns listened to—filled the main hall. I browsed through the shelves: a paintball gun, a skateboard (at one hundred Linden Dollars I couldn't resist, although when I put it on it just stuck to my feet, and wobbled a little as I walked around). One wall was covered in blades: "A Sword," "A Big Sword." Under the swords was a butterfly knife, just like those carried by the kids in the high school up my road. The butterfly knife seemed expensive, the same price as the sword. Deeper into the store, the weapons became more outlandish: an automatic turret gun, designed to shoot people who trespass on your land; a belt to make you fly faster; land mines. In one corner was a "nearly" free sales bin: handguns for a reduced price of one Linden Dollar.

None of these weapons could hurt other residents, although in certain, "damage-enabled" areas, you could mock-fight; those attacked might crumple to the floor, but they would wake up immediately in a nearby safe place.

Upstairs—the music still playing, sounding now like the noise that came out of Sigourney Weaver's fridge in *Ghostbusters*—there were more weapons: a flamethrower, a sniper rifle, assault weapons, shotguns, a missile launcher, a remote-controlled "Predator" armed drone. Who wants these kinds of things in their ideal world? I thought.

Years later, prices had risen. After furnishing my virtual office, as an offering to tempt my (real-world) girlfriend to take another look into Second Life, I decided to buy her some virtual shoes. I searched on the Second Life classified ads, and teleported to a smart virtual store called Shiny Things, run by a resident called Fallingwater Cellardoor. There, a shiny green pair of sling-back heels cost me three hundred Linden Dollars.

Those shoes were made by a resident, but Second Life fashion wasn't just about people building their own clothes. In January 2004, a British company called Rivers Run Red had brought the first real-world designer label into Second Life. Mrs. Jones, famous for designing Kylie Minogue's dress in her video for the single "Can't Get You Out of My Head," designed an exclusive virtual collection. Since then, virtual fashion had become big business. In July 2006, when American Apparel launched their virtual store, 40 percent of items traded in Second Life were clothing. (The most popular items were shoes.) I wanted to talk to a virtual fashion designer, to see what kind of work, and profit, was involved.

Fallingwater Cellardoor—in real life, forty-two-year-old Alayne Wartell—first joined Second Life in October 2003. Her stall, Shiny Things, sold fashion, mainly for women—shoes, handbags, cocktail dresses—that she had designed inside Second Life. After I bought a pair of her heels, Alayne visited my virtual office. ("Ah, cool, you bought from Szabo," Alayne—or rather Fallingwater—said, eyeing my virtual furniture with a professional eye. "He's good, and he's a friend of mine.") By then, October 2006, Alayne made her real-world living solely from Fallingwater's Second Life store. She had been a computer programmer, but although she had no background in fashion, or 3-D design—just some Web design experience—she began to feel her way and found she enjoyed designing clothes. "I was programming for twenty years," she said, "and at times, it was very fulfilling. But I was a bit burned out. This is fulfilling because I get to be creative in a different way from programming, and I love being my own boss, making my own decisions about what to do, not having set hours. And, honestly, the feedback I get from my customers—such nice things they say. It's an ego boost."

At first, working days and sometimes nights, she earned a hundred bucks or so a week. "It took a year before I could say I was making a real income," she said. "I remember early on I was making about 5,000 Linden Dollars [then about $20] a day—calculating how much would constitute a living wage, and wondering how on earth I'd ever get there. I couldn't even imagine how I'd manage 10,000 Lindens a day."

She didn't advertise, relying instead on word of mouth and a few virtual fashion shows—and business grew. By the time Fallingwater and I met, in October 2006, her sales of nonexistent clothes and accessories earned her an average of a thousand real dollars a week.

In the real world, space for others to meet and fabricate objects costs; you need both money and the will to risk losing it. In virtual worlds, venues—to reside in, to meet in, to work in—cost almost nothing. The material costs are literally zero. With no barrier to entry, any resident can set up a shop and begin to sell the things he or she has made. For Alayne, the liberation from the physical meant she could turn a profit. "I started my businesses here because I loved building and was good at it. I didn't need anything more than that. That's not possible in the real world."

Fashion design is creative work, though, and sometimes she struggled for ideas. "I run dry sometimes," she told me. "Nothing works, or I'm trying too hard, or something."

When we met, she was working on a messenger bag. She had finished the woman's version and was now customizing it for men. That didn't take too long, she said, although she had spent up to five days crafting a single pair of virtual shoes. (Once the design is complete, she can sell as many as she wants; in Second Life, there are no production costs, apart from her labor as a designer.) I asked about her sales. "It varies a lot; some things hit big, others don't," she said. "I just make what I like and see what happens." I showed her the shoes I had bought my girlfriend. "Ah, the lady sling-backs!" she said when she spotted them. "Those are one of my proudest creations." A product like the sling-backs might sell at the rate of 150 pairs a month, at the Linden equivalent of one real dollar per pair—all through automated sales at her virtual store. (Although her accountant barely understands how she makes her money, she does pay her taxes.)

She gave me a freebie: a recent creation, a pair of brown leather shoes. They didn't quite fit, but, like a real pair of shoes, I couldn't change the size. "If your feet are too big, you'll have to modify those," she said. I laughed, and adjusted the size of my feet to fit the shoes.

To promote her virtual wares, Fallingwater had tried a few ads on SecondStyle, a Second Life fashion website, with little effect on sales. "As Second Life grows, using that stuff as brand awareness becomes more important. I may actually hire a marketing consultant, someone I know here with that background."

When I began my journey into virtual worlds, the idea of hiring a marketing consultant to help sell virtual things would have seemed bizarre. But by that point, in October 2006, it wasn't so outlandish. A new class of virtual professionals, the land baron, was making more serious money, and apparently it wouldn't be long before a whole professional class emerged to serve them.

I visited another virtual world, to speak with a virtual land developer. Project Entropia, later renamed the Entropia Universe, is a world somewhere between EverQuest and the more free-form worlds such as Second Life. (In Project Entropia, you can buy EverQuest-like role-playing items such as Kobold Thigh-Guards, but you can also buy investment rental property.) The Entropia universe was constructed specifically to tap into the global mania for virtual funds. With the Entropia Universe Cash Card, residents can even visit real-world cash machines in the United States, or post office counters in the United Kingdom, and withdraw real-world currency, at a fixed exchange rate, directly from their virtual Entropia account. In October 2006, over half a million people called Entropia Universe their virtual home, and in 2005 their in-world turnover—the amount of virtual currency that had traded hands between Entropia residents— was reportedly 1.6 billion Project Entropia dollars ($160 million in the real world). I spoke with David Storey, the young Australian doctoral student who, for 265,000 Entropa dollars (about $24,000), had bought Treasure Island, about four square miles of land, with three human settlements.

Storey's virtual self, Zachurm "Deathifier" Emegen, was a dapper, crisp-suited man in a button-down shirt and shades. As the owner, landlord, and host of Treasure Island, Storey offered spaceflights and, in his island mansion and bar, regular full moon parties with music and competitions.

Storey staked out some areas of the island for virtual residents to hunt in, sold mining rights to other areas—part of his income comes from a 4 percent tax on any hunting bounty or mining rights—and developed the rest as estates, including "Lake View," "perfectly suited for those looking for a nice home or place of business close to a teleporter." Residents rented these areas to establish virtual shops, in the hope of turning a profit. Storey told me the island earned him around a hundred real dollars a month. "Right now the island is the only thing that really earns money," Storey told me. He hadn't expected to make so much, but he credited his island's success to the development work he had done: When he bought it, he told me, Treasure Island was "a few fairly standard creatures scattered amongst lots of trees and grass, and mineral resources that bordered on nonexistent."

"Initially its income was to be through estate sales," he said. However, over time that's transitioned to tax income from people hunting and mining on the island. This transition also brought with it extra costs as hunters want to hunt cool creatures, and finding the DNA materials to create said cool creatures is somewhat expensive, ranging from a few hundred to thousands of U.S. dollars." Since his success, others have offered unique properties for sale; when we spoke, an Entropia Universe space station was on sale for $100,000.

Second Life, I knew, had land barons, too. When I met Philip Linden, he had shown me a list of the world's richest residents. At the top was Anshe Chung, the woman who had been financially harassed by the W-Hats. In the years since, I had heard more about Anshe. Anshe Chung, real name Ailin Graef, was a thirty-three-year-old Chinese woman living in Germany. Anshe began her Second Life life in March 2004, after time as a powerful player in other virtual worlds, including Shadowbane, an apocalyptic fantasy-themed universe. Anshe didn't think Second Life would hold her attention for more than an hour, but she was intrigued by the possibility of residents owning copyright to their virtual creations. She stayed. At first, Anshe supported herself by teaching languages, both in the real and virtual world (she speaks German, English, and Chinese). She supplemented the virtual side of her operations with another business: virtual escort work. Anshe's escort ad described her as "a material girl with a money fetish," and for a thousand Linden Dollars (then about four real dollars) an hour, she offered "exotic massage." Anshe also taught people, for a fee, how to have better online sex, and she sold virtual animations to accompany her lessons. In July 2004, Ailin's husband, Guntram Graef, joined Second Life as Guni Greenstein; together they began to buy and sell virtual land. "Somehow I ended up sending money to my parents in China," Ailin later told me. "I also helped one boy in one poor country. Suddenly the SL economy become very real." (Through a German charity, Anshe donated some of her virtual profits, translated into real cash, to a Singapore boy, to support his family until they found work.) Anshe's business model was simple: She bought large plots of newly available land, separated the areas into lots, and sold or rented the property at a profit.

In November 2006, I joined a press tour of Anshe's latest virtual developments, built by her team of twenty-five employees in Wuhan, China, which included three ex-architects. We followed Anshe, a medium-height, Chinese-looking virtual self with straight black hair, a smart pantsuit, and a dragon tattoo on her back. She strolled through a huge white-latticework nightclub, elevated over a pastoral field, and a crisply clean mall with water features and old-world clock towers—like a mall, only cleaner. (There, the virtual press corps moved slowly, as if we were flying through treacle. I quite liked the effect, although Anshe said it was a technical problem. "This sim need reboot badly," she said.) Anshe said she was already working to provide virtual developments to real-world corporations. "Last night we rented twelve sims to one major TV station, for example," she said. "We also have several universities as clients and other companies, small and large." Anshe told me she had had a number of super-rich (in the real world) clients live on her islands, but they preferred to remain anonymous.

Next on the tour was her in-world headquarters, still a construction site: a sci-fi office tower block surrounded by domed gardens. (Because the site was still under construction, I got pinned by the elevator. "All systems online," a calm, robotic voice stated over and over, although, as I struggled to escape the elevator shaft, I felt less than calm.) The futuristic tower was designed to be Anshe's business center for meetings and press conferences. In London, where property prices were among the most expensive in the world, I had grown used to seeing towers rise up slowly for six months; Anshe's headquarters would take just two weeks to complete.

In a desert development, a Second Life prostitute in a short plaid skirt, bright red heels, and a silver necklace that said "Slut" (her job was clear: written above her head was her group name, "Peaches Escort") flew down, sucked a lollipop, and listened in. Even the virtual ho was business-minded. "Really too bad I hooked in this late!" she said. (She told me she had just been passing by, and she had recognized Anshe Chung's name; she had read about Anshe in *BusinessWeek*.)

I had toured a few of Anshe's properties when I was looking for my own land. She bought land in bulk—by late 2006, her territory, christened DreamLand, covered fourteen square miles, about 10 percent of the total land area of Second Life—and she leased her property to residents for real-world dollars. Anshe's rates varied, depending on location and the kind of development she included in the price, but even her most expensive land was only twenty Linden Dollars (about eight cents) per square meter. Her revenues were small-margin and high-volume. ("We move very, very huge volumes, so that is how relatively small margins help us grow fast," Anshe later told me.) By June 2006, *BusinessWeek*, which had put her on its cover, estimated her land holdings at $270,000; Anshe Chung Studios, her company, put the figure for 2006 at close to $2.5 million. ("I'm like Wal-Mart," Anshe told *BusinessWeek*. "The margins are small, but the volume isn't." Rocky Rutabaga, the developer of my virtual office, called her "Anshe Cha-Ching.") Dreamland had become a kind of democratic fiefdom, something akin to Robin Harper's vision of a self-policing community. In November 2006, after consultation with her residents (she polled each one using an in-world vote), Anshe banned from all her Second Life land any organization new to the virtual world that claimed to be "the first"—the first radio station, the first tabloid—at anything residents had already been doing for years.

Those like Anshe Chung and David Storey who made their living from virtual actions were in a relative minority. When I visited Linden Lab in 2005, Philip Rosedale told me twenty or so residents worked exclusively inside Second Life. At the time there were 25,000 residents, which meant this number was less than 0.08 percent. By October 2006, Linden Lab estimated that more than 13,000—1.3 percent—made a profit in their world.

Sociologist Ivan Illich observed that in a consumer society, "There are two kinds of slaves: the prisoners of addiction and the prisoners of envy." Computer games, which offer a favorable ratio of reward to effort, have always presented the problem of the first. But now our virtual worlds also offer us the chance to become enslaved with envy. Virtual worlds play to our longing to be accepted, to be a success, to overcome all obstacles. The story that some residents made money had become a Second Life selling point—but once again, the reality was less rosy than the dream. Rocky Rutabaga told me he couldn't see how Anshe made her money. The margins are too small, he said. He had never managed to turn a virtual profit. Outside of the worlds, though, a whole breed of virtual service providers was making a different kind of killing. In 2004, after Sony Online Entertainment petitioned eBay to ban the sale of EverQuest accounts—which were, according to the terms of service, Sony's property—a whole raft of third-party websites sprang up to fulfill residents' desire to buy and sell virtual things.

These were the third-party dealers to whom moneymaking gnome Noah Burn turned after raking in virtual platinum from his forgery trick. Noah had explained to me how his experience with some virtual currency dealers taught him a few lessons about trust. On one occasion, he sold five thousand real dollars' worth of EverQuest II currency to a dealer; once the virtual platinum arrived in the dealer's account, the dealer reversed the real-world payment, then claimed its account had been hacked. The next day, though, the same dealer had a large amount of EverQuest II currency for sale. Noah was convinced he had been ripped off, but he had no recourse—and anyway, he was too busy churning out virtual money to worry about one bad deal. But another company, Noah told me, had been honorable and efficient in all its dealings: the largest,

IGE.com. Noah was a big fan of the operation. "They are so fast at handling things, I can't even explain how much of a breeze it was to work with them compared to just selling person to person."

I had had some experience with IGE myself. In my days as a resident of Star Wars Galaxies, I paid them ten real dollars, for which I received ten million Star Wars credits—enough to buy a fast landspeeder, with plenty of change. I paid my money by credit card through the IGE website and received my virtual currency in a clandestine virtual meeting, with a fish-faced alien IGE courier who met me by a virtual bank machine in the city of Coronet, on the far-flung planet of Corellia—where Han Solo was born. After he handed me my credits, I tried to talk with him, without much luck; whoever operated the courier was either too busy to talk, or English wasn't his first language. Noah Burn had told me he suspected that many IGE employees worked in China, at so-called virtual sweatshops, where low-wage workers made a better living online than they would have in a real-world factory. (When he contacted them to complete deals, he said, "they barely spoke English.") In virtual worlds, these Chinese workers were now an everyday reality. Known as "gold-farmers," they were recognizable by their broken English and their tendency to lurk around the most profitable spots while trying to attach themselves to any group that passed. They would join groups to kill the biggest monsters, playing the game as fast as they could to loot the most gold, which was then sold via brokers to Western buyers. In some circles, their commercially oriented play was discriminated against; Blizzard, the makers of World of Warcraft, had banned tens of thousands of accounts for "gold-farming," and in the West, some groups of players asked all new members to type a few sentences in English before they could join. (Chinese World of Warcraft residents who played for fun had begun to complain about what they saw as racism.) In Korea, Lineage II players teamed up to butcher those players they believed were farming gold.

At the age of twelve, Brock Pierce was a child actor. He debuted big, with a starring role in 1992 as Gordon, the ten-year-old lead of *The Mighty Ducks*, but by 1995 the roles (notably a bit part in the TV movie *Problem Child 3: Junior in Love*) were less prestigious. He collected trading cards as a hobby but always had trouble finding the last one or two he needed. So, in his late teens, to augment his income, he set up a business bulk-buying trading cards and selling them individually to people keen to complete their collection. After the bottom fell out of the trading card market, Brock cast around for another idea. He had always been a keen online gamer, and, in 2001, after a chance meeting with Alan Debonneville (a Hong Kong–based former Warcraft II champion), Brock and Alan co-founded Internet Gaming Entertainment (IGE) to help online gamers buy and sell the virtual objects they most desired. (One survey showed that one in five virtual world residents had bought gold at a third-party website such as IGE, spending an average total of 135 real-world dollars each.)

At IGE, residents could even buy and sell their virtual selves. On one day in 2006, you could buy an EverQuest II account that included three characters: a paladin, a warrior, and a priest, "with excellent gear and skills!"—with horses, for $663. Once payment was complete, the seller e-mailed his or her virtual username and password, and the buyer inherited the virtual self, property, clothes— even friends, who had no way of knowing the transfer had taken place. (There was a glass ceiling in the virtual world, too: On average, one study showed, woman selves changed hands for 10 percent less.)

In January 2004, IGE, already the biggest player in the virtual goods market, bought its closest competitor, Yantis Enterprises, for upwards of $10 million. By August 2004, demand for its nonexistent product was so high that IGE hired five new people every week. On a single day in April 2007, for $200 IGE would have sold you virtual currency from one of sixteen nonexistent places. For Lineage II, your money would have bought you around 100 million Adena (the Lineage II currency), which would buy enough swords and armor for any budding elf. Or, in Second Life, you could have visited another website and bought 59,000 Linden Dollars to fritter away in a spree at the virtual malls, or invest in a thousand or so virtual square yards of oceanfront land. (At IGE.com, while trading currency, you could also click on the charity banner—"Virtual Worlds, Virtuous Hearts"—to donate some of your virtual cash to the Mercy Corps, which works to alleviate real-world poverty.)

In October 2004, I spoke with Brock Pierce, then twenty-one, who was at his office in Dearborn, Michigan. Brock told me his company bought items and currency from suppliers across the real world. Some were American kids who played games on evenings and weekends. Others owned cyber-cafés in Europe and the Middle East; they let people play for free, as long as each player donated half of his or her virtual booty to the café. IGE also worked with Hong Kong partners who subcontracted the work to mainland Chinese suppliers. There, people were employed to play the games nine to five, hunting virtual beasts, fashioning virtual items from their loot, and selling them via IGE. I mentioned the idea of virtual sweatshops to Brock. He was quick to interrupt. "They can earn up to one hundred dollars a day," he said. "That's a higher wage than almost any career opportunity available in rural China." (Other sources put earnings at virtual sweatshops between $75 and $250 a month, still a relatively high wage.)

I wasn't earning anything from my time spent in virtual worlds, but I was conducting some business there—I invited a few residents in for interviews, a more convenient way to meet than traveling in real life. Moreover, I liked having virtual guests. I felt proud of my new office and wanted to show it to my real-world friends (although, when I asked them to log on and visit, many rolled their eyes and pleaded a prior engagement).

My new home was a new place, like the communes my mother and her friends had built, but it didn't replace my old life. I didn't have to move away from my own home to inhabit it. My virtual life was an overlay, like a membrane over the real; it extended my life but didn't inhibit it. I wondered if I was finding the right balance between the real and virtual after all.

I began to smoke less. The comfort of my virtual home, a kind of security blanket against real-world anxiety, was making my life better. At the same time, in real life, I was slowly settling into our new apartment. Perhaps the calm of a home helped me to stop smoking. Either way, the real and the virtual were reflecting—and perhaps complementing—each other.

Instead of stepping outside for a cigarette in the morning, I would step into my office and log in to Second Life. I found myself longing for it. Halfway through one dinner party, I abandoned the table to sneak moments at my PC. I lounged in my virtual office, chatting with my virtual friends, when I should have been in my real apartment entertaining my real friends. My actual apartment seemed needy; keeping it clean demanded constant attention. But my virtual office was free of entropy, and required no maintenance at all. In my real life, I rented my apartment. In my virtual life, I already owned land, with a beautiful view of the sea. During the day, I began to see as much of my virtual desk as my real one. The virtual world was often the more interesting one; my real apartment, which I saw mainly on trips to the kitchen for coffee, began to feel more like a backdrop to my other life.

Inside my virtual home, my real-world worries about rent, the struggle of living in a big city, seemed to fade. Virtual worlds had become wish fulfillment, and I was addicted—as surely as I was addicted to nicotine.

Then, as always, in my paradise, trouble emerged.

Plot 11, the next one down toward the sea from me, had been sold. My neighbor, Wayne Nohkan, sent me a message saying "Hi." The next time I logged in, there he was; we hovered in the air between our properties—the virtual equivalent of chatting over the boundary fence. Someone else had bought the plot behind mine, Wayne said, and had already erected a sign: "SL Travels and Tours—office opening soon."

The next day, a Second Life message from Wayne was forwarded to my e-mail. "Let me know if my trees block your view out front," he wrote. "I'm trying to block out that crap next door." I logged in to see. The travel agency, which hoped to profit from the growing interest in Second Life by charging for themed tours, was under construction, and it didn't look pretty. As protection against nearby development, I had already bought the lot next to mine, for three thousand Lindens (about ten real dollars); I told Wayne, and he bought the three farther down. "Not sure what I am going to do yet," he told me, "but that will give us some buffer from development."

Then, the next day, our local land baron, Rocky Rutabaga, sold more property in the area. He had planned to build an undersea theme park, Wayne told me, but must have given that up. The whole bay was for sale. In Second Life, you can not only build, but also re-shape any land—literally. They had even marketed the feature with a hip allusion to Jimi Hendrix: "Now, when you're standing next to a mountain, you really can chop it down with the edge of your hand." The new buyers of the ocean floor could develop their land any way they liked. Soon my view of the sea might become a view of a building site.

"I've been considering moving to an island and renting," Wayne told me. "Someplace with a controlled theme. I don't like zoning in the real world, but it's a bit out of control in Second Life."

In my real life, too, I didn't stay calm for long. During the week I smoked less, but during the weekend I smoked more. On frequent nights out with friends, we searched the urban landscape—in all the wrong places—for the excitement our everyday life lacked. Mostly we ended up drinking in bars.

And as I worked alone, my solitude seemed only to increase the tension: my body, like an animal, driven to anxiety by separation from the herd. The anxiety was of course a fear of loss, ultimately a fear of death. My mind, eager to ease the pressure, sought distraction. Also, I was a young man. I wanted what young men want. I wanted what cigarettes and alcohol and coffee and nightclubs gave me — but I wanted more. I wanted movement, adrenaline, risk. I wanted to fight.

I wasn't alone.

8

VIRTUAL WAR

Join up and see the imaginary world

In our virtual worlds, we were fighting—but this kind of virtual conflict had a history. People, me included, had been fighting in imaginary places for years.

One afternoon in the winter of 2001, I went with a friend, Chris Lahr, to a gaming café, where he had heard about a new way to kill time. There, in a labyrinthine cellar in the West End of London, kids were gathering to play games, not alone, but with one another. These weren't massive virtual worlds, but more localized computer-generated places, dedicated entirely to armed combat.

I had played games like these before. In 1996, fresh out of college, I ended up working for a new media firm in a converted old mansion house near Arundel, a country town a long commute from my Brighton home. The office stood alone, among fields, by a run-down divided highway; at lunchtime there was no real-world destination except the local gas station, where the sandwiches were wrapped in what looked like medical gauze. So, instead, to take a break and to remove ourselves from our workaday surroundings, a friend and I would spend our lunches logging into the company network to play

Quake, a 3-D futuristic combat game where we hunted each other through gray, computer-generated industrial corridors, armed with machine guns, grenades, and—if you were lucky and got there first—a rocket launcher.

By 2001, though, Quake was old news. In the West End basement, my friend and I sat at PC consoles, our heads brushing the damp brick ceiling, and asked the kid running the place what game we should play. "Counterstrike," he said, without hesitation.

Counterstrike—as I write, still the most popular online war game—is a terrorism and counterterrorism simulation. Played in first person, as if you are looking through the eyes of your virtual SAS soldier—or terrorist—you buy weapons, then you struggle to kill or save hostages, and plant or defuse packages of C-4 explosive at strategic locations. The battlefields of Counterstrike are complex, 3-D, convincing. The sounds are real, sampled from real-life gun models. As in real life, one or two shots can kill you, so you are vulnerable; you *need* your teammates if you are to survive. Many afternoons, when we should have been elsewhere, we descended into the basement to become warriors: We crouched, our eyes darted into every nook; we inched our way around corners, our fingers poised above the mouse button to fire. Our opponents were real people, their virtual conflict skills honed by many hours inside Counterstrike. They shot us, and we died, and over time we learned to shoot them back in turn. We became addicted.

In August 2001, a full month before the 9/11 attacks briefly made *terrorism* the world's number-one website search term, Counterstrike was by far the world's most popular online war game. Twenty-four hours a day, wherever there was electricity and Internet access, upwards of two million people gathered in virtual dust-strewn battlegrounds to shoot terrorists, marines, and SAS men. There was never any moral preference for one side or the other; after all, nothing was at stake except our time. We competed to throw concussion grenades, or to save or destroy well-known landmarks. We fought the same battles over and over again, destroyed each other with the same guns, scrambled over the same rubble, fought under the same sky. At any time, there were an average of one hundred thousand Counterstrike players online (in total, I later discovered, those gamers fought virtual wars for over seventy-five million hours every month); whatever time, day or night, worldwide, someone wanted to fight. We had the company of strangers, and each other, and, while it lasted, it was enough. Counterstrike tapped into a primal desire to compete, but also a basic need to transcend our everyday concerns—after all, when you're fighting a war, how can you worry about doing laundry? We couldn't play Counterstrike all day, but we played for as long as possible, hunched over the PC, wide-eyed, munching snacks while the game loaded, until it seemed our only natural place was scrambling over rubble with a gun.

Then, when we finally left to go home, we rose from the basement, climbed up the stairs to street level, and blinked in the fading light, to find that we had achieved nothing. We were virtual war veterans, back in the world and alone again, with not even a scar to show. We separated and headed off alone to trace the urban gauntlet of other addictions to our empty homes.

We didn't know it, of course, but our new distraction had its roots directly in real-world conflict.

On Sunday, June 27, 1976, aboard Air France 139 from Tel Aviv via Athens to Paris, two Palestinian members of the Popular Front for the Liberation of Palestine and two members of the radical German militant group Revolutionare Zellen ("Revolutionary Cells") produced automatic pistols and insisted the pilot divert the flight to Africa. After a seven-hour refuel at Benghazi, Libya, the flight landed on an airstrip in Entebbe, Uganda, where dictator Idi Amin had agreed to give them safe haven. There, three more Palestinians joined the hijackers, and all non-Israeli passengers were released. (The entire French crew, also offered freedom, elected to stay on the plane.) One hundred and five Israelis remained on the plane. In exchange for the

hostages, the hijackers demanded the release of forty Palestinian prisoners. In forty-eight hours, they announced, executions would begin.
At midnight on July 3 an Israeli strike force hit the airport. Two Boe-
ing 707s and a C-130 Hercules transport, their cargo bays already
open as they landed, unloaded twenty-nine Israeli Defense Forces
"Sayeret Matkal" commandos in Land Rovers and a black Mercedes—an exact replica of Idi Amin's personal limo and escort. Idi
Amin's Mercedes had recently been painted silver, but within minutes the only guards who knew that fact were dead. Just over an hour
later, thirty Ugandan troops and all seven hijackers had been killed.
To prevent a chase, eleven Ugandan Army Air Force fighter jets were
destroyed on the ground. The hostages were on a military flight back
to Israel. Just one Israeli soldier and three hostages lost their lives.

From the Israeli perspective, "Operation Thunderbolt" was the
most successful hostage rescue strike in human history. The U.S. military was so impressed that they tasked the Defense Advanced Research Projects Agency (DARPA) to develop ways for U.S. soldiers to
get the same kind of training. In the Israeli training, it turned out that
Entebbe airport had been built by an Israeli contractor. After the hi-
jacking, he produced the plans, and, on Israeli military property in
the Negev desert, helped build a full-scale partial model of the
airstrip. For days Israeli commandos practiced landing on the airstrip
and assaulting the passenger terminal where the hostages were held.
When they arrived at the real airport, they had won the attack many
times before.

DARPA was fascinated, but flummoxed. There was no way to
build scale models of every possible battlefield and hostage situation.
That would mean creating a scale model of the whole planet. However, that year, Nicholas Negroponte, founder of MIT's Media Laboratory, was contracted to the Department of Defense and suggested
exactly that. DARPA approached him for advice, and he proposed a
simple solution: They would build technology that simulated various
battlefield situations, in which soldiers could practice as if in the real
world. At the time, computer technology had barely evolved from

room-sized mainframes, so they began with video editing. The project was so successful, the U.S. military began to make video simulation models of every airport in the Middle East. That program evolved into the U.S. military's simulation arm, which among other things bought up Atari's futuristic Battlezone tank game en masse, and, in 1996, converted the PC game Doom, which portrayed a futuristic marine hunting demons on Mars, into "Marine Doom," which showed soldiers with realistic guns.

Nearly thirty years after Israel's Operation Thunderbolt, virtual simulations of battlefield and hostage situations have become a core component of U.S. military training. In June 2003, the U.S. Army commissioned NovaLogic, makers of PC war games including Delta Force, to build notoriously complex new equipment, such as their "Land Warrior" technically assisted battle suit, into new versions of the game so the military could use it to train their soldiers. The Marine Corps asked Bohemia Interactive, who developed the modern PC war game Operation Flashpoint, to build a custom marine version. In most ways, because the virtual body could not be harmed, virtual worlds circumvented physical violence. In other ways, though, they began to encourage it.

The trend begun by Negroponte resulted in multimillion-dollar efforts to model every aspect of the military experience. The U.S. Army's Modeling, Virtual Environment, and Simulation Institute at the Naval Postgraduate School, with the help of virtual world developers Lucasfilm, spent between six million and eight million dollars to develop America's Army—an online war game like many others, except in this case also a free advertisement for serving the country. Commissioned in 1999, when army recruitment was at its lowest in thirty years, and launched in 2002, America's Army simulated the experience of war, from boot camp to front-line action. A player who "fragged" (i.e., internationally blew up) his sergeant materialized immediately in a jail cell. What many people didn't know was that America's Army was also an intentional and cost-effective recruiting tool. In 2003, 19 percent of U.S. Military Academy freshmen had played the game, and that year the army met its recruitment quota. ("We want the whole world to know how great the US Army is," the game's website anonymously declared. "In elementary school, kids learn about the actions of the Continental Army that won our freedoms under George Washington and the army's role in ending Hitler's oppression. Today they need to know that the army is engaged around the world to defeat terrorist forces bent on the destruction of America and our freedoms." To complement the positive message, they sanitized the game; America's Army developers admitted that the bloodiness in the game was purposely toned down.)

The value of games in the struggle for cultural dominance hasn't gone unnoticed by those countries America declares as its enemies. The Syrian-developed game Al-Quraysh shows the history of civilization from an Arab perspective. Under Siege, developed by the same company, portrays the Palestinian struggle from an Arab viewpoint, with Palestinians trying to protect their villages and olive groves, and re-creates notorious Israeli attacks, such as Baruch Goldstein's 1994 machine-gunning of twenty-seven worshippers at a Hebron mosque. (In Under Siege, the hero, Ahmed, must help an ambulance reach the mosque; killing civilians, either Israeli or Arab, leads to in-game penalties.)

America's Army also has a more practical recruitment value. A website monitors the statistics of each virtual battle. When a player turns up at a recruitment office, the U.S. Army can access these online records to gauge immediately the recruit's fighting potential.

By 2004, the military project that began at Entebbe airport had matured into a plan to rebuild the planet. To further their stated aim of "Full Spectrum Dominance"—military superiority in every sphere, from information technology to orbital satellites—the U.S. military decided to build a scale model of the whole planet after all. However, they planned to build it online. Dr. Michael Macedonia, a West Point graduate and Gulf War veteran (and on 9/11, he was in Corridor 5 of the Pentagon), then headed the U.S. Army's Executive Office for Simulation, Training, and Instrumentation, where he oversaw the development of virtual war zones. Macedonia was part of the team that commissioned the developers of There, a massive online virtual world, to build an Asymmetric Warfare Environment (AWE) to run on the army's own network, the largest private Internet portal in the world. A large, free-form world like Second Life, There had hundreds of thousands of players, except the world was constructed by the world's developers. Players could create something new for the There world, but any new object needed to be approved by the There team before it could be used in-world. There became more of a social world, populated by Californian beach hunks and babes, bouncing around in dune buggies and chatting in tiki bars. In AWE—which was the There world with the bathing trunks and bikinis changed into military uniforms, the dune buggies replaced with military jeeps, and the text chat adapted into voice communication—soldiers would be able to train and reexamine battles in an environment that allowed for social as well as violent interaction.

Beginning with the army's 101st Airborne Division, soldiers based anywhere in the world could train for warfare in any environment. It wasn't a game—it was a "tactical decision aid." Plans were discussed to bring college kids, well-versed in online games, to play the enemy. They started with one square mile of Baghdad, complete with palm trees and Arabic road signs, and within four years, according to some reports, they planned to model the entire planet, a virtual carbon copy of the real one.

"The reason we started funding the development of these games was to teach soldiers," Macedonia told the website Gamespot. "That was our audience—not civilians or kids in high school, but soldiers." To Macedonia, the AWE wasn't a game at all. "Our thing is not making people shoot better; it's making people think better." It was the role-playing, not just the point-and-shoot features, that made the There game engine so appealing to the U.S. Army. "What's a soldier's experience in Iraq or Afghanistan? Who's the enemy? How do I get these people to not necessarily like me, but to relate to me? How can I keep a riot from starting when the food runs out?" Macedonia said.

"America's Army says it's a first-person shooter. Our games have moved way beyond that. My particular concern is ensuring that that young sergeant, who's going to go lead soldiers in combat, is not confronted with that situation for the first time while in combat."

In 2002, There, the Silicon Valley–based game developer who made the game the same name, launched a new company, Forterra, to handle commercial applications of their virtual world. In November 2006, I spoke with Robert Gehorsam, president of Forterra, to see how plans had developed four years down the line. ("One thing I can tell you about working with the army? It's slower!" he said.)

Robert told me their simulation was never about combat. "Soldiers have plenty of ways to learn how to fire a weapon. Except in technology like ours, they have no opportunity to learn about the kinds of decisions in different cultures that lead them to decide whether to fire a weapon or talk. Imagine a typical soldier, in their early or mid-twenties, from the midwestern United States, for whom Iraq is some abstract thing. How do you build the kind of cultural sensitivity that lets them make the right decision? Realizing that you could essentially role-play in this kind of environment was very powerful.

"Obviously the Middle East, especially Iraq, is of particular interest," Robert told me, referring to Forterra's continuing work in military virtual worlds. "It's ground conflict, it's urban conflict, and it's counterinsurgency. And all of the training work, and all of the simulation, that has been going on in the military for decades, has been about massive tank conflict in East Germany, against the Soviet Union. There haven't been effective simulations for the kinds of scenarios where the interaction of the soldiers with the local population becomes really important."

Robert gave me more detail about their first training session, in 2002, with a National Guard group from Illinois. "They were an artillery unit that was being deployed to Iraq to become military police," he said. "When you're artillery, you're about ten or fifteen miles away from the action. When you're military police, you're ten or fifteen *inches* away from the action."

To help the young artillerymen adapt to close contact with Iraqi people, Forterra built a virtual checkpoint. They set up fifteen PCs in the conference room of a Moline, Illinois, Holiday Inn. Over four days, the unit, many of whom were gamers, rehearsed various checkpoint situations, with army researchers and Forterra employees playing Iraqi civilians and insurgents. Forterra varied the scenario each time, with insurgents in different places, and in some cases no insurgents at all. "In a typical training scenario, you know exactly how it's going to be scripted," Robert said. "In this case, we didn't tell them. So they had to figure out if that family in that car approaching the checkpoint was a bunch of insurgents, or if it was actually just a family. Sometimes they made mistakes—but they weren't real bullets."

At one point during the training, Robert closed his eyes and listened. "One guy says, 'There's a car approaching.' Another guy says, 'What's their behavior? How does it look? What do you think?' And you could hear them gain confidence.

"We took them through these scenarios, and they said, 'Wow. We didn't even know what we didn't know.' " After being deployed, some soldiers e-mailed their gratitude. "They wrote us later after they got to Iraq, and said they really appreciated just those couple of days."

The 101st Airborne combat division had a chance to practice in the virtual world only after a tour of duty in Iraq. "Some of them actually said, 'If we'd had a tool like this before we went over, more of us would have come back,' " Gehorsam told me.

When I spoke with Gehorsam, he was excited about the assessment features Forterra was building into its virtual worlds. "The core of the army are the sergeants and the captains," he said. "They're the junior leaders, so their skill is critical. We've done some leadership training, which is really exciting." The virtual war world has proved popular with the troops. In 2005, another group of National Guard soldiers were preparing to visit Iraq to liaise with local police to set up security procedures: of their two-week training period for that year, they chose to work with Forterra for four days.

As well as potentially saving lives, Gehorsam argued that virtual war training also saves money. Over four years, the army had invested around four million dollars in the AWE. "To train one brigade, for three weeks, at Fort Polk, Louisiana, costs about eight million dollars. Of which something like seventy-five percent of the cost is getting their equipment there. So what if you didn't have to get their equipment there?"

When we spoke, Forterra's current, more modest, plans were to extend its virtual world on a slower scale, using the army's vast databases of real-world terrain data. "So if you need to populate your scenario with four thousand civilians, or a couple of old Soviet fighters because that's what Iran has, or something like that, you can now do that.

"The technology can handle any amount of people you want," Robert told me. "Once a year, twice a year, the joint forces run exercises that involve ten or fifteen thousand people, that use a whole federation of simulations. We're certainly prepared to do that."

The technology is adaptable to other fields. For example, Forterra is also working on a commercial project, with a budget of between one million and two million dollars, funded by the Army Medical Command, to develop a virtual world to train medical first responders for mass-casualty events, such as terrorist attacks or hurricanes. ("We work at the extremes of life and death, I guess.") Here medical workers can practice separating the worst casualties, and treating them in the hospital. They've simulated a sarin gas attack and are working on dirty bomb scenarios.

Forterra has also customized its virtual world, in partnership with the Federation of American Scientists and the Fire Department of New York, to train fire chiefs and captains in high-rise fire response. "High-rise fires are the rarest, and the hardest to train for, because typically firemen don't see the fire they are trying to control." (The fire chiefs were not as computer-literate as the young soldiers. "They'd stab at the keyboard with one finger," Robert told me. "They're not gamers.")

"There doesn't seem to be any limit to the sorts of situations it's useful for," Robert says. They're working, for example, on projects that involve the flow of people through proposed building designs, like hospitals, examining whether carts reach the emergency rooms in time.

Robert was an editor at Simon & Schuster, and after working in its electronic publishing arm he directed the original EverQuest team as an executive at Sony. Now he was thrilled by the opportunity to save lives. "To come out of the game industry, which is anything but life and death, to something where literally the same code is being applied to something so vital . . ."

Sometimes, simulations offer another kind of therapeutic hope. In July 2005, Forterra was asked to demonstrate its virtual world to Dr. Francis Harvey, then the U.S. Army secretary. (To show how easy virtual worlds are to navigate, Robert roped in his ten-year-old son to demonstrate EverQuest.) "The scenario we did was what's called a 'cordon and search.' This was an army squad that was looking for a high-value target, like a lieutenant of Zarqawi's, or someone like that. One of the 'playing cards.' In the scenario, they had intelligence that this person was hiding in a family's house, in a well-to-do neighborhood of Baghdad. With an interpreter, they knock on the door and ask permission to search the house. As they're searching the house, the bad guy takes a hostage, a family member. There's a confrontation; the bad guy happens to be killed, but the hostage is rescued. A soldier is wounded." They used a cast of forty, including real soldiers returned from Iraq, who logged on from all over the U.S., and Iraqi Americans acting as the Iraqi civilians.

A retired general who helped establish the modern army's training program witnessed the virtual hostage rescue. In the ten-minute scenario, the general spotted a dozen important—and possibly lifesaving—training opportunities. "Decision points, techniques, things like that," Robert said. "How do you stack a patrol along the wall before you enter the house? What's the proper way to ask permission to enter a house in the Middle East? How do you do a hostage rescue?

"We found a navy corpsman, which is the navy's version of a medic," Robert went on. "Let me tell you what happened to him. He had been patrolling with the marines in Fallujah. He had been walking down the street, and a car bomb went off. He came to a second later, and he noticed his leg was lying in the middle of the street. He crawled out from behind shelter, to retrieve his leg, and was shot six more times. He lived. He lost his other leg. He was recuperating six months later when we found him, at Walter Reed Medical Center. He asked if he could play the role of the medic in the scenario. So now you had a guy who really was there, who could suddenly run around in the virtual world with legs he didn't have in real life."

The corpsman corrected Forterra's simulation, explaining that if the medic entered the house in the way they had planned, he would have been killed instantly. "You saw him run in, you saw him call for the medevac: He got to live again."

Ironically, the first antiwar protest in a virtual world took place in the original incarnation of There: On February 15, 2003, as part of a co-ordinated global protest against the imminent invasion of Iraq, a group of one hundred There residents gathered for the "Polygons for Peace" demonstration. That day, along with a million others, I marched down Trafalgar Square in the middle of a British winter to register my displeasure at the erosion of international law, and the people who would soon be killed. The There residents did so, too, but they marched at sunset, on a perfect beach, under palm trees.

Elsewhere, virtual military conflict was intruding into the real in other ways, too. In World War II, famously, only 10 percent of soldiers shot to kill; fifty years later, in the first Iraq war, 90 percent did so. And, as David Bartlett, former chief of operations at the Defense Department's Defense Modeling and Simulation Office, told *The Washington Post* of his new recruits, "[Their] experience leading up to that time, through on-the-ground training and playing Halo [a futuristic first-person war game] and whatever else, enabled [them] to execute."

Since America's Army was created, other commercially available war games have been pressed into military service. The Department of Defense uses Tom Clancy's Rainbow Six: Rogue Spear, a PC game, to train personnel in urban combat. This blurring between real-world fact and virtual fantasy brings to mind Jean Baudrillard's famous proclamation, "The Gulf War did not take place," by which he meant that the video news piped home to us seemed like footage from a video game. In the more recent Iraq war, the soldiers themselves made the comparison. "I have seen innocent people being killed. IEDs go off and you just zap any farmer that is close to you . . . hit him with the 50 [heavy machine gun] or the M-16 [rifle]," veteran Jody Casey told Iraq Veterans Against the War. "Overall there was just the total disregard—they basically jam into your head: This is Hajji [an Islamic honorific that can also be an ethnic slur]. This is Hajji. You totally take the human beings out of it and make them into a video game."

"All I saw was the street where the RPG [rocket-propelled grenade] came from, and I just fired in that direction, maybe twenty rounds at most," twenty-two-year-old Sergeant Sean Crippen told The Washington Post, of an Iraq gun battle. "It felt like I was playing Ghost Recon at home."

Technology has long trickled from the military-industrial complex into entertainment. Talking dolls have their root in "talking cockpit" projects from the U.S. Air Force, and in 2004, war-keen children could covet George W. Bush action figures, with a complementary "Mission Accomplished" banner—or even a "Talking Uday," a model of Saddam Hussein's son with a badly wounded face. (When you pull his talking string, the doll yelled, in a mock-Arab accent, "Someone must help me. I am still alive, only I am very badly burned. Anyone! Can someone call my father? I am in a lot of pain, I am very badly burned so if you could just . . . You shot me! Why did you . . . ?" followed by the sound of three final gunshots.) With virtual worlds, the process had turned around: The CIA has an entertainment industry liaison, and Hollywood talent, such as *Star Wars* production designer Ron Cobb, was consulted for the army's development of its virtual wars.

Most virtual war games are pure fantasy: There's no pain, no loss, and no "collateral damage." (In Counterstrike, you can shoot a hostage, but you can't bomb a wedding.) Even your virtual comrades' dead bodies, after a respectful minute or so, disappear. In response to these games, where meticulously illustrated 3-D violence is run-of-the-mill, Joseph DeLappe, a professor at the University of Nevada, Reno, set up the "dead-in-Iraq" project. Each day, DeLappe logs in to the servers of America's Army and broadcasts the names of America's war dead. He logs in, he types, he gets shot, and he keeps typing.

"I enter the game using as my login name, 'dead-in-Iraq,' and proceed to type the names," his website reads. "I am a neutral visitor as I do not participate in the proscribed mayhem. Rather, I stand in position and type until I am killed. Upon being re-incarnated I continue to type. I intend to keep doing so until the end of this war."

"I became interested in memorials soon after the online publication of a website that presented the thousands of proposals for a 9/11 memorial on the World Trade Center site," DeLappe told me in May 2006. "This gave rise to thoughts of a memorial for the thousands of civilian deaths in Iraq."

DeLappe's words offended some players more than the simulated experience of being shot in the head. Transcripts of his time inside America's Army show the confused and sometimes hostile responses of the virtual soldiers.

>MICHAEL VANN JOHNSON JR. 25, NAVY, MAR 25 2003
>dead in iraq, are you enlisted? reserve? Have you been to iraq?

>ARMONDO ARIEL GONZALEZ, 25, MARINE, APR 14 2003
>dead in iraq, shut the **** up!

Many players ended up banning DeLappe from their servers. "I am looked upon as an obnoxious interloper bringing real-world content into the magic circle," he told me. "Other players get angry, ask me questions, to which I do not reply. I doggedly continue typing the names."

DeLappe had previously reenacted presidential debates in The Sims Online and Star Wars Galaxies, and he had also logged in to a small-scale Star Trek virtual combat world called Elite Force: Voyager, as "Allen Ginsberg," and typed out *Howl* line by line (it took him six hours). "The other works were for the most part enjoyable to create," he told me. "This one is not—it is depressing and weighs heavily upon my conscience."

DeLappe, who at age eighteen had come close to signing up, told me he found the use of America's Army as a recruiting tool "problematic in the extreme. If one tries to imagine the U.S. Army creating a TV show or a film that purely exists to recruit young, impressionable ones to join up, we might find this questionable, no?"

More than 3,800 U.S. service personnel have died in Iraq. November 12, 2006, DeLappe had been typing names for a few hours a week, for over seven months; he was only halfway through.

In my own real-life quest for stability, virtual war cropped up in the unlikeliest of places. In a meeting about how to handle my mounting debt, my bank manager told me he was a regular player of VASSAL Engine, an online medieval war game. I told him hopefully about the book I was working on; he laughed, but refused to give me a loan. Wagner James Au reported on a war veteran who lost a quarter of his kneecap to a mine in Afghanistan, and who used Second Life to help him get over the horrors of war—by establishing a property and gambling empire that earned him two to three thousand dollars a week. Au also reported on a U.S. Department of Homeland Security–funded virtual island in Second Life designed to simulate emergency response in the real world. (Even outside virtual worlds, imaginary selves were being used to support the U.S. war effort. The Maine Army National Guard had issued over one hundred full-size cardboard cutout replicas of service personnel. These virtual soldiers, or "flat daddies," were intended for families to sit at their kitchen table, take to ballgames, and place in the backseat of their cars to remind children of their absent fathers.

Cardboard cutouts are no replacement for real family, and ultimately the military's virtual worlds are no replacement for real conflict. Both Counterstrike and America's Army offer a limited field in which to relate; you can only shoot one another; teams are limited to twenty or so; the battlefields are restricted to an acre of virtual soil. And, of course, the bullets don't hurt. In our new, larger virtual worlds, this same kind of artifical, simulated conflict is also available, although on a larger scale. In many, such as Lineage and EverQuest, there are areas—called PVP zones, short for "player versus player"— where residents can pit themselves against one another. Usually, all that is at stake is honor, although sometimes the victor is allowed to loot one item from his opponent's virtual corpse.

For most residents, this kind of conflict is nostalgic—they're not training to cast spells in a real war, and, at least in most of Western society, people long ago put down their swords and began to fight one another with property. But of course this kind of economic struggle translated to virtual worlds as well. Virtual property now had value. My own boundary concerns—Wayne's worries about the travel agent; the possibility of new ocean development obscuring my view—were small versions of new arguments, over virtual and moral territory, that had begun to spring up everywhere virtual feet touched virtual soil.

9

US

Together in electric dreams

The new virtual conflicts weren't just between residents. Sometimes the inhabitants gathered together to register their displeasure with the world's makers. This was unique. Consumers don't usually rally against changes in products. When the Coca-Cola Company introduced New Coke, no one campaigned in the supermarket aisles. They just didn't buy it. But if Coca-Cola owned your whole world, and it wasn't just the taste of the drink they altered—it was your job, your house, or even your ability to walk—you might complain.

In virtual worlds, there is a history of protest against the ruling classes. In 1999, residents of the fantasy virtual world Ultima Online, angry at software problems that had lost them valuable virtual items, protested in a suitably medieval fashion: They stormed the castle, and murdered the king. (Their victim, "Lord British," was the online self of Richard Bartle, the man who had created the world).

In January 2005, World of Warcraft's developers, Blizzard, made some changes to the Warrior character class. Many warriors felt their virtual lives had been unfairly restricted. To highlight their plight, the players decided to hold an in-world demonstration. A hundred gnome warriors gathered en masse in the dwarven city Ironforge and stripped naked. It took some time for a game master to notice the bare gnomes, but when they did, the totalitarian boot came down. "ATTENTION: Gathering in a realm with intent to hinder game play is considered griefing, and will not be tolerated," the GM announced. "We appreciate your opinion, but protesting in-game is not a valid way to give us feedback." There were no water cannons in World of Warcraft for the GMs to turn on the crowd, but gnomes who persisted with their naked frolics, as well as a few innocent bystanders, had their accounts temporarily suspended.

The attendant joy of virtual worlds—the narcotic virtual world from which companies profit—is that, by removing our selves from our bodies, they allow us to escape reality. The attendant sorrow of virtual worlds is that we of course don't leave our problems behind: They simply reemerge in another form. In the real world, democracy didn't have an easy birth, and elsewhere, in other virtual worlds, the struggle of the people to be heard seemed to be mirroring our social struggle for representation.

In April 2000, when Sony Online Entertainment (SOE) negotiated with eBay to prevent EverQuest players from selling accounts or EverQuest items, eBay declared that Sony had applied to their Verified Rights Owners Program, designed to stop people from selling items for which they do not own the copyright. That meant, in effect, that if you identified primarily with your virtual self—as 20 percent of EverQuest players declared they did—then Sony owned you. In this light, worlds like EverQuest were totalitarian regimes, and virtual residents lived in a new kind of bonded slavery.

To Sony Online Entertainment, this was a selling point. "You're in Our World Now," they told every resident every time they entered the world. In these virtual worlds, society wasn't a democracy; the relationship was more like that between citizens and an occupying power, as was illustrated in August 2004, inside the virtual world Star Wars Galaxies. A group of players discovered a credit "dupe," like Noah Burn's forgery shortcut, with which they could generate as much virtual cash as they liked. The developers, understandably un-happy with this threat to the game balance—and their real-world rev-enue—decided to clamp down hard. They traced everyone who had come into contact with the hacked credits—44,800 residents—and, whether they knew about the dupe or not, the residents were banned. The wrath of SOE rained on the just and the unjust alike.

Although many successfully appealed the ban, those players who felt they had been banned unfairly decided to protest. They created new virtual selves and gathered together in a prearranged spot inside Star Wars Galaxies—outside the Theed Starport on Naboo, the home of Jar Jar Binks—to protest their innocence. Sony broadcast warnings to local residents to leave the area. Those who ignored the warnings found themselves scattered randomly across the Star Wars galaxy. (The cartoon website Penny Arcade satirized Sony's attitude: "Sir. We have reports of player protests on Naboo," a lieutenant re-ported. "I recommend we resolve this in a way that shows we respect our customers." In response, the emperor held up a crooked finger. "Teleport them into space.")

From Sony's perspective, the protesting residents were ruining the fun. From the residents' perspective, Sony was abusing its power. Ralph Koster, a lead designer on Star Wars Galaxies, told the Cana-dian Press, "If someone started walking around in the San Diego Zoo screaming profanity or handing out Nazi leaflets, the park would re-move them from the premises. We need to be able to do that also." But the Naboo protestors were also at the front line of an underlying moral struggle. In 2000, an EverQuest resident called Mystere, who played the game around twenty hours a week, published EverQuest fan fiction online, which included the (fictional) story of a virtual rape of a fourteen-year-old girl. Mystere was banned from EverQuest. "If we determine that one person's actions make EverQuest a game that other people do not want to play, based upon those actions, we will exercise our right to refuse service," Gordon Wrinn, EverQuest's Internet relations manager, explained. "The laws governing the use of copyrighted material . . . give us the exclusive right to permit or disallow the outside use of our intellectual property so that we can properly manage our business and nurture the EverQuest brand."

One place we gather, outside the reach of commerce, is in the church, and religion too has appeared in virtual worlds. The Anglican Church has set up an "i-church," with its own virtual pastor, to explore ways to worship online. At Saint Philip and Saint James's Church in Bath, England, the Reverend Alan Bain runs regular sermons streamed over the Web. Meanwhile, the Meenakshi Temple in Madurai, in India, offers "E-pujas" for people who can't make the real-world pilgrimage. One Second Life resident, OmegaX Zapata, conducted a Catholic Mass, dressed as a virtual priest, with his congregation of ten or so reading along from a virtual book. Another retired Episcopalian built a church and handed out virtual T-shirts that read, "Jesus had a Second Life, too."

On their website, the Christian organization Ship of Fools has built a tiny virtual world, Church of Fools, which you can inhabit, either as a *Simpsons'* Ned Flanders look-alike; a bearded, Gap-shirt-wearing teenager; a raver; or a smart black man in an Ozwald Boateng suit. You can wander among the other virtual parishioners, virtual pews, and virtual pillars—hung with rebellious Christian modern art, such as Albert Herbert's *Jesus Falls Under the Cross*—that turn transparent so you can watch yourself pass. There is no virtual collection plate, but, for a while, visitors could contribute funds from their mobile phones. As your virtual self, you can attend a sermon, talk, whisper, kneel in prayer, extend a hand, or raise both arms in rapture, all without leaving your living room. (One visitor arrived with her five-year-old son in her real-world lap. "Who's on my team?" he asked. "Which ones do I kill?") From May to August 2004, an average of eight thousand virtual people (the size of a cathedral congregation) visited each day. Even in the virtual church, though, trouble arrived. As Richard Chartres, the Anglican bishop of London, addressed the virtual church's opening congregation, some of his virtual flock wandered around, pointed at him, and swore. People arrived with racist names, or rubbed themselves against members of the female congregation. More than once, "Satan" himself logged in and climbed the pulpit.

Apparently, even religious apparitions had come to virtual worlds. In August 2006, one Second Life resident, Kali Zeluco, claimed to have had a virtual vision. Kali had created a "prim," a single block of Second Life wood material (in this case, virtual wood). With no modification of the block on her part, she claimed, an image of the Virgin Mary appeared. (Kali apparently considered donating the block to a local church, but instead decided to offer it for sale on the website SLExchange for 30,000 Linden Dollars—about $100. "People will flock from sims around to see this prim, to touch it, to be healed by its holy aura," she wrote in her sales pitch.)

In the meantime, inside Second Life, my personal struggles had taken on a new edge. Someone else had moved into the area; our new neighbor had a larger, more palatial home—and on his roof were two huge military helicopters and an Israeli flag. Further down the hill, my other neighbor, Wayne Nohkan, had decided to build around his home to preserve his view. But he had constructed a Japanese garden, complete with a shower of snow, which drifted sideways and somehow through the wall of my house; now, when I sprawled on my chaise longue to watch TV, a white cloud fell around me.

Virtual snow doesn't make you cold, and I didn't mind. It was a small hint, though, of the virtual boundary disputes that had sprung up all across Second Life. Residents who didn't get along sometimes descended into a war of ugly structures and billboards, which reminded me of the U.S.-Cuba "billboard war." In early 2006, the American mission in Havana erected an electronic billboard that translated freedom slogans from Martin Luther King, Jr. into Spanish including "I have a dream that one day this nation will rise up." Castro's government responded with a new billboard, emblazoned with images from Abu Ghraib prison in Iraq, along with the slogan

"Made in America." This symbolic struggle over territory seemed more common inside Second Life. As the development continued on the hillside above my office, a new structure sprung up: two stacks of cubes, each with a different theme, hanging unsupported in the air. One stack was plastered with G.I. Joe–style posable dolls in distinctly gay pinup positions. The other set was plastered with anti-Bush jokes: a Connecticut road sign, "Birthplace of George W. Bush," customized to include "We Apologize," and a photo of Bush and Dick Cheney photoshopped to look like Beavis and Butt-head, with the caption "Huh huh, you said Bush!" "Huh huh, you said Dick!"

These posters echoed an earlier conflict that had spread across Second Life. In December 2005, one resident, Lazarus Divine, bought up small plots of virtual land all across the world. This was common: a search of "land for sale" inside Second Life showed hundreds of small plots, a few square yards for sale—sometimes literally for pennies—and billed specifically as "Excellent Ad Lot." On each of his plots Lazarus placed a giant blue billboard that read: "Support Our Troops—end the illegal war in Iraq. Restore U.S. credibility— impeach Bush."

Many Second Life residents were unhappy at the real-world intrusion. (Some erected their own billboards: "Impeach Lazarus Divine.") In a straw poll conducted by Wagner James Au, over 70 percent of the world's residents had a strong opinion on the posters. Linden Lab brought up the issue in its weekly newsletter. "Over the past many months the Second Life landscape has been dotted with signs calling for the impeachment of President Bush. The ensuing debate has people on one side calling for the suspension of the sign creator for spamming the landscape, and on the other side championing his right to free speech. . . . Second Life is built on the twin values of tolerance and free expression: tolerance of other people's views and the right to follow one's own path. We believe that these two values combine to allow for the fullest emergence of innovative new experiences. Sometimes those experiences will be amazing and sometimes less so, but on balance the community gains when its Residents have the widest freedom possible."

There were hints, though, that some of those putting up anti-Bush posters had ulterior motives. The plot of land behind my office where the Bush cartoons hovered had a label attached to the land: "Got ugly neighbors? Buy the neighborhood!" The implication was that those who posted the pictures did so to encourage local residents to pay more money, just to clear the view.

The anti-Bush posters didn't bother me — in fact, I agreed with them — and I wasn't tempted to buy the land to remove them. But, without meaning to, I had entered into another kind of property conflict that hit closer to home.

Wagner James Au wrote to me. He had heard I was working on a book about virtual worlds, and he was working on one, too. He wanted to clarify the stories I would be covering. He asked for a broad outline of my book, which he could forward to his agent, to reassure publishers that our material wouldn't overlap. We met, in a Dr. Seuss candy land, to talk it over. I told him I would be writing about a range of virtual worlds, not just Second Life. He seemed pleased, and perhaps proprietary about Second Life.

Still, Wagner James Au had made an effort to be courteous about our potential territorial conflict, and I was grateful to him, as a guide to my early Second Life years. Others, though, weren't so polite.

When I first traveled to meet Wilde Cunningham, June-Marie told me she met someone who was working on a book with me. It was news to me. "Robbie something," she said.

I knew who it was. A month or so before, I'd met up with a photographer whose current project was taking portraits of real-world people, then exhibiting them alongside images of their virtual selves (a boy with multiple sclerosis, whose oxygen face mask strangely echoed his Star Wars Galaxies bounty hunter's boxy helmet; a fat player with a thin virtual self; a mother turned punk). We had exchanged stories, and I left confident that we could cooperate without competing.

After my visit to Wilde, I e-mailed the photographer and asked him to stop using my name in his book pitch without my permission. A few months later, I wrote a column about the photographer, and e-mailed him to ask for some details on a story he had told me about. He said he wasn't sure that would work for him. Instead, he suggested I write a longer piece about him. (I resisted the temptation.) A year later, after I had mentioned him in another article, he e-mailed me again. I called him, made some polite chat about his own book, and thought nothing of it. But a week later, he sent me another e-mail. I was using him to further my own agenda, he told me. I should have asked him to be the photographer for the piece. (I had, but the editor chose to run his own photos.) He accused me of showing a "lack of character." "Be careful how much you take," he wrote. "I'm not your mother," he added (in case there was any doubt).

The e-mail shook me. Was it true? Did I take too much? Was it time I gave something back to virtual worlds? Was I lazy, using others to further my own agenda? Then I settled down, realizing that I had simply been drawn into a different kind of territorial conflict, no less real than Wayne's anxieties about the encroaching travel agency. Cultural commentators are occupiers, too—we invade the story, tell it our way—and, in our new virtual gold rush, everything, even the story of the world itself, is up for grabs.

That night, aggrieved by the e-mails, fighting the urge to respond, I couldn't sleep. I lay in bed staring at the ceiling, until an old childhood dream, which used to help ease me into sleep, returned. I imagined myself able to fly, to become invisible, and to pass through walls. I left my body, got out of my bed, walked to the window. Liberated from my self, from gravity, and from the gaze of others, I drifted off above the streets of London, under the stars.

10

VIRTUAL SEX

Boys who are girls who like boys who are girls

As it turned out, the time I had slipped out of a real-world dinner party to hang out in my virtual office hadn't gone unnoticed. The next day, my girlfriend asked me, "Do *you* have a virtual girlfriend?"

Since their origin, virtual worlds have turned our heads away from our real-world relationships and toward the screen. Women who lost their boyfriends to video consoles had coined a name for themselves, "PlayStation widows." But, as well as pulling us apart, virtual worlds were also bringing couples together.

The games company Verant began building EverQuest in 1996; by 1999, when it launched, their expectations were modest. "When I joined the project, EQ was just an idea," senior game designer Bill Trost told me. "They wanted to create a graphical MUD, and had some idea about how it would look, but not many specifics."

"We came at the right time, with the right weirdly addictive design," the Sony executive in charge of EverQuest, Robert Gehorsam, told me. They had expected a fantasy-themed game, but found they had built a world.

During development, they had to constantly fight against Sony

Consumer Electronics, who, intent on the upcoming PlayStation 2 launch, didn't see how an online PC game fit their gaming strategy. Fortunately, Trost and his colleagues won their internal battle, and at the world's launch they planned for a few thousand subscribers. Within a year, they had half a million residents. Despite the explosive growth, it took the first EverQuest wedding to drive home the fact that what they had built was an entire world, rather than just a game. They heard about the wedding from a resident, and logged on to watch characters exchange rings and vows. It was nothing they could have predicted. "There was a GM, me, Brad McQuaid [EverQuest's executive producer] . . . and we saw a wedding in the game. It was awesome," John Smedley, who originally conceived EverQuest, told me in 2002.

It wasn't just the law that was struggling to catch up with the new possibilities inside virtual worlds. The fault lines were being redrawn in every area of human experience. Virtual worlds had become a place where people could act out their fantasies, and, in some cases, the relationships were as "out there" as the costumes.

One of the first stories to attract me to Second Life was a column by Wagner James Au about the virtual love affair of a Second Life resident named Torley Torgeson. Torgeson used to wear a neon-pink monk's robe with bright green gloves, to match his pink and green speedboat. An Asperger's sufferer, Torley took to virtual worlds quickly, moving into a custom-made Dumpster like a bright, energetic version of Oscar the Grouch. "For the first time, Torley believed he'd found somewhere he could truly call home," he wrote on his website, of his entry into Second Life. Linden Lab later hired Torley to work on bug testing and user interface; he was renamed Torley Linden. By the time I met Torley online, he wore a black dress, and he had breasts; he had become a woman. Sometime in November 2004, Torley wrote on his website, his male character "vanished into the space-time rift."

Meanwhile, somewhere across the virtual continent of Second Life, Jade Lily was born. Jade's owner was a man, but he chose to join

Second Life as a woman just to see what it felt like. (A 2006 study showed that as many British women as men spent time in virtual worlds. Another study, by Nick Yee, a Ph.D. graduate of Stanford University, showed that men across all virtual worlds chose to inhabit them as virtual women around a third of the time.) Jade's creator originally joined Second Life to have an online relationship with an ex-girlfriend, who now lived far away. The girlfriend joined as a man, and they tried a few virtual dates. "I thought it would be interesting to have a relationship with a guy in Second Life who was actually a girl in real life," Jade explained to Au. "It didn't work out." But Jade kept playing as a woman, and soon Jade and Torley met. "Jade's the type of person who I felt I 'knew' early on," Torley said. The two hit it off, and are now an inseparable virtual couple—even after they both confessed their real-world sex. "I am in love with Jade," Torley said. "Simply put, I am happy when I am with her."

"I'm not attracted to guys physically," Lily insisted. "In real life, I'm clearly attracted to women. In Second Life, it gets shady. I see my avatar, Jade, and I'm compelled to play a female role . . . because it's what she's supposed to do, I guess. Second Life has either taught me a lot about myself, or created more questions. Maybe both."

Torley and Jade, overwhelmed by their feelings for each other, even told James Au they hoped to meet in person. Their love was so pure, they thought, that perhaps their lack of homosexual feelings wouldn't matter. "Do I want to meet Jade in real life?" Torley told Au. "ABSOLUTELY, YES! She's such an exceptional person. Simple as that. There are certain things that can be faked online, but real personality shines through. And she shines so brightly." (Whether they actually met or not, I never discovered.)

A few weeks after Alayne Wartell had told me about her virtual fashion business, she made another visit to my virtual office to tell me how she met her husband, virtual name Eddie Escher.

Two years before I met Alayne, her younger brother, who had joined Second Life, persuaded her to become a resident. "He kept bugging me to try it," she said. "I was skeptical. I'd never been interested in MMORPGs"—by which she meant Massively Multiplayer Online Role-Playing Games, a hackneyed term for fantasy virtual worlds like EverQuest. "But I tried Second Life, and it hooked me. I made good friends and had fun with them. And, of course, not long after I joined, I met my husband."

Alayne, newly reborn as Fallingwater, had flown across the Second Life landscape searching for a place to settle. She spotted a building she liked, "a futuristic bubbly really nice pod thing." The nearby land was for sale, so she bought a plot, and began to build her own home.

After a few weeks, as neighbors do, Fallingwater and Eddie said hello. The pair began to socialize. (He had built a brain in a jar, which he had scripted to respond to nearby conversation. She would greet Eddie, then say hello to the brain.) Soon she found she felt shy when other Second Life residents were around; she looked forward to meeting Eddie alone. "I remember spending time chatting with him and maybe a couple other people in there, and I remember starting to hope I'd see him over there. And it turns out he felt the same—he'd hope to see me, and if I had visitors, he'd feel shy.

"You probably know or have heard how fast things can go here," Alayne told me. (I had noticed. In another survey by Nick Yee, one in five female EverQuest players said they had had a crush on or fallen in love with another player.) "It's like life intensified. It was maybe a couple or a few weeks later that he asked me out on a 'date.' "

For their first date, Eddie took Fallingwater, or really Alayne, to what was then that world's only private island. Linden Lab had given the island away as a prize in a contest, and the owner had turned it into a romantic getaway; he charged residents to bring dates to his island paradise. "They set a table with dinner for us," Fallingwater said, "which we both laughed about, because we think Second Life food is so dumb. And there was a little room with a fireplace and stuff, and it was all very sweet and nice."

Across the private island, Eddie had set up a trail of roses, each one with a clue to find the next. "How could I go wrong with a guy like that?"

I asked if they had fallen in love.

"We did!" Alayne said. "And it didn't feel weird."

The lack of physical reality, according to Alayne, made their romance smooth. "I think the distancing in a way lets us be more ourselves. You don't have any physical stuff getting in the way. It doesn't confuse things. You're getting to know the person, not the body.

"I was less nervous, the distancing of typing to each other, and not having to make real eye contact is very freeing. I was more nervous about our first phone call."

Eddie Escher—real name Chris Edwards—lived in Harrogate, North Yorkshire, England; Alayne lived on the outskirts of Philadelphia. But they spoke on the phone, and they enjoyed each other's virtual company. Two months later, over Christmas and New Year, Eddie flew out to visit Fallingwater. Chris and Alayne met for the first time. "I tried to keep in mind the fact that meeting face to face can be very different," Alayne told me. "But it didn't change how I felt, and I was very confident that we'd get along in real life.

"I met him at the airport gate. I wasn't even nervous until about an hour beforehand, when I was getting ready to drive to the airport. And then I started hyperventilating.

"I was waiting outside the gate, pacing and shaking. I saw him coming out and he has this bouncy walk. It's kinda funny. Then he walked up to me, and we kissed, and the world around us disappeared."

I asked if Chris resembled Eddie. "Well, he's an android, so, no!" Still, their time together was a real success. "We had a great time and my family loved him, too," Fallingwater said. "It was really hard to part.

"I started getting teary about it a couple days in advance. We both did."

A few days later, on the phone, they got engaged.

At least once, inside Second Life, the pair argued—still, they visited each other in the real world twice, and decided to live together. Chris ran his own games company, which seemed on the brink of bank-ruptcy. Alayne had a secure job. "I was working for Towers Perrin [a professional services firm], the biggest and most corporate place I'd ever worked. The corporate atmosphere sucked, but for a while the work was really fun." Chris made plans to move to Philadelphia. Then Alayne lost her job. "It was due to a total fuckup on my part. I think I really wasn't happy there, and was dealing with it in a passive way."

After missing a lot of work, Alayne was fired; at the same time, Chris was hired by a successful games company, Rockstar Games. So they switched; Alayne got on a plane to England. For Alayne, it was a relief. "I'm glad [our plans] reversed. I've gotten a new start, and it's terrible what's happening with U.S. politics these days." Within a month of her move, in a Yorkshire registry office, they married.

The couple never bothered with a Second Life wedding. "That wasn't important to us. Though we did have an engagement party that a friend really wanted to have for us."

After a few months of struggle with work-visa bureaucracy, Alayne began to design her virtual fashion label. "I love my job, I love my husband, and I'm enjoying living here.

"Second Life has improved my life vastly," she said.

By 2007, there had been an estimated five thousand virtual weddings in EverQuest. By the summer of 2006, according to Sony, twenty couples had married in the real world after meeting inside EverQuest. Funcom, the developers of the science fiction world Anarchy Online, claimed the same number of real-world marital successes.

Elsewhere in virtual worlds, romance had become part of the virtual money machine. For Valentine's Day, 2004, Chinese virtual world developer GinSoft sold special edition game vouchers that entitled residents to playing time as well as a one-time-only extra: a shower of virtual flowers, to help romance their virtual date.

Not all virtual worlds are as open as Second Life to the possibility of romance or sex. Star Wars Galaxies allows tame fan events, such as the Mrs. Galaxies Contest, a beauty pageant for residents' virtual selves, but in other worlds some forms of sexual expression are punished. In January 2006, Blizzard, the makers of World of Warcraft, banned guilds—groups of residents with similar interests—formed on the basis of homosexuality. (Their reasoning, in reference to their "Sexual Orientation Harassment Policy," was that such an advertisement would provoke others to harass the members of gay guilds. In this virtual world, being openly gay was forbidden, allegedly because it might incite intolerance.)

In 2000, Richard Bartle, one of the early founders of online MUD text worlds, spent a long year as head of online games for a start-up company. With a team of six and a budget of almost zero, Bartle decided to try to revive text-only worlds by giving them sex appeal. Players could enact or explore their sexuality by describing their actions, along with other consenting players. Room descriptions were sense-specific, so for example if you were blindfolded, your surroundings would be described in terms of sound or heat—"hmm, that feels like the heat from a branding iron"—and if you were, say, tied to a bed, your possible actions would be limited. No one else had worked with text worlds in this way, but after eight months the game was canceled.

The success of virtual worlds has led to smaller, sex-focused worlds dedicated to meeting niche needs. In Sociolotron residents can drug and rape one another. Naughty America offers a range of sex-focused virtual environments: public and private sex areas, cowboy rooms, make-your-own-porn rooms. SeduCity is a 2-D sex world that launched in 2001 and has fifteen hundred residents. Red Light Center, still in beta testing in 2007, allows people having virtual sex to talk to one another with headsets. Rapture Online, set to launch in 2007, is a 3-D sex world designed to be anatomically correct. Developer Kelly Rued hopes couples will use the world to connect when they are apart. It's big business, to the extent that in March 2006, California porn company Digital Playground trademarked the term *Virtual Sex.*

Games have been compared to pornography, and there are parallels, notably appearance without substance and experience without risk. In October 2006, an Oklahoma judge issued a preliminary injunction against a bill, passed the previous June, that would have made video games and pornography the same in the eyes of the law. (In September 2005, one porn company cashed in on this, releasing a series of videos with porn stars dressed up in face paint and pointy ears, called "Whores of Warcraft.") In the United States, the porn industry grosses between $10 billion and $14 billion a year; about on a par with the video games industry.

In virtual worlds, where we are liberated from the restrictions of our bodies, sexuality is often the first area in which people experiment. After all, many residents see in virtual worlds the seeds of a new kind of utopia: a world free from the dangers of pregnancy and disease, recapturing a postwar, pre-AIDS innocence.

But there is a dark side to virtual sexuality, too. In late 2003, Peter Ludlow, professor of philosophy and linguistics at the University of Michigan, began a series of articles for an online newspaper, *The Alphaville Herald.* He journeyed into the seedier side of Alphaville, The Sims Online's capital city. There, among that world's eighty thousand residents, he found scammers, a whole Sims neighborhood devoted to sadomasochism, and "Evangeline," a virtual madam who managed a stable of virtual prostitutes, exchanging cyber-sex for "simoleans" (Sims virtual currency).

Evangeline was openly racist: Ludlow once walked into her virtual property to see a dark-skinned avatar trapped by a fence, next to a sign reading "monkey for sale." She claimed to have set up the first Sims brothel, in October 2002, and that she had earned up to $50 per trick. "My girls worked hard," Evangeline told Ludlow, after her brothel had closed down. "I only hired real cyber-sex girls who talked dirty." Evangeline's girls charged 20,000 simoleans (then around $4.50) for a virtual blow job. Richer clients were catered to by Evangeline herself—who, she claimed, charged the equivalent of $40 or $50 per customer.

After publishing the interview, Ludlow put in some detective work and published the cyber-madam's true name on his website. "Evangeline," it turned out, was a seventeen-year-old boy from Florida, and some of his "girls" really were underage girls. His work as a virtual prostitute and madam was arguably a major felony. At the virtual frontier, though, real-world law has yet to catch up. Even after Ludlow's article, no prosecutions were brought. Still, his mother did reportedly cancel his Sims account. (Electronic Arts also canceled Ludlow's account, claiming he had advertised his website in-world; Ludlow insisted his ban was because he had embarrassed the company.)

Electronic Arts didn't like the seedy underside of its virtual world being exposed, but in the "Mature" areas of Second Life, I discovered, pretty much anything was permitted. There, an ongoing rivalry simmers between two fetish groups: the "Goreans," who favor master-slave relationships and sadomasochism (for a world without physical pain, S&M seemed oddly popular); and the "Furries," who dress up as animals for fun and sexual kicks. ("I hate the furries," Philip Rosedale had joked to me. "What's up with these people who want to dress up like animals?")

In the PG areas, though, Linden Lab keeps a tight control. One virtual sculptor, Stormy Roentgen, was upset after copies of one statue—a woman breast-feeding a baby—were removed from PG areas for revealing a nipple.

For much of Second Life's development, the twenty most popular places were almost all strip clubs. There, in clubs modeled on their real-world equivalents, naked avatars gyrated around chrome poles, and gaping men sat on barstools to watch. Virtual strip clubs occasionally depart from real-world standards; the naked virtual dancers sometimes breakdance; virtual men and women on the dance floor wave dildos. Some strippers have signs above their heads: "Want sex?

IM me." Many clubs feature upstairs rooms, where virtual sex is bought and sold. Prices for virtual sex vary between 500 ($1.60) and 3,000 ($10) Linden Dollars an hour; typically, the club takes 20 percent for every virtual trick. (In one posting on the Second Life Herald, a virtual bouncer complained he received a tenth of the wage of the escorts who worked in his club.)

Second Life escorts can also be hired privately, through the virtual classified ads. In October 2006, a search for "escorts" in Second Life's directory of users and places brought up 383 results. Each listing came with an image and a description. Broken Hearts was apparently "a dark, smoky strip club, the kind where the dancers break the rules"; the girls at Moist Escorts were "hotter than you!" Some were ludicrous: "Specialty pubes! Stop by to see my awesome collection of specialty pubic hair designs!"; "Free sex, free cocks, free clothes!" Some were barely literate: "Group of sexy horny women hear to pelase you! " Some escorts offered "anthro" services, a niche word implying virtual sex with a virtual animal (one escort traded under the name "Giant Horsefly"). Still more escort services were mafia connected: Carducci's Escorts was partnered with Carducci's Guns, Employment and Jobs, and Carducci's Horse Track. Would-be punters didn't have to fly blind; at websites such as SLescorts.com, residents could read reviews of virtual hookers.

In virtual worlds, we don't have to worry about disease, but there are other dangers. One Second Life resident I read about had entered into a virtual relationship that had spread offline, to the extent of sharing intimate photographs. But after a nasty breakup, his ex wreaked a uniquely virtual kind of revenge. She built a scripted object, designed to look like a desirable accessory: a red pair of wings, given away free to anyone who clicked on them. These wings, though, had a secret purpose: Anytime any resident put them on, they broadcast a compromising picture—an image of the victim's real-world self masturbating—to everyone nearby. The outbreak was small, perhaps the first virtual analogue of a sexually transmitted disease.

There were certain elements of Second Life's sex trade I wanted to steer very clear of. In September 2004, one Second Life resident, "Sasami Wishbringer," offered her services through a group called "The Edge Escorts" as a virtual eight-year-old sex slave. ("Small, petite appearance," her profile read, "though perky and in the blossom of physical maturity.") She also offered cartoon child porn, although Linden Lab quickly removed it. A year later, one scantily clad World of Warcraft Night Elf called "Jailbait_15" tried to sell one hour of her sexual services on eBay. "I have several sexy outfits I can wear for you and getting new ones every day. I love to dress up. You are welcome to take screenshots and make movies of our time together. I am very photogenic!" she wrote in the ad. In the end, no one met the minimum ten-dollar bid.

On the Second Life forums, Robin Harper, Linden Lab's vice president of community development and support, posted Linden Lab's response to the Sasami outcry. "There are people who are role-playing children engaged in sexual activities," Harper wrote. "While not a terms-of-service violation—no illegal activity—it could be argued that this behavior is broadly offensive and therefore violates the community standards." If they had evidence of any real-world child abuse, she wrote, they would notify the authorities, and close associated Second Life accounts. If residents engaged in inappropriate sexual activity in public areas, they would face similar consequences. There was little more Linden Lab could do. In the United States, an actual child has to be involved for child pornography charges to be brought; the Supreme Court ruled that computer-generated images depicting a fictitious "computer-generated" minor are constitutionally protected. However, in the U.K., even computer-generated sexual images of children are illegal. If Sasami Wishbringer or her clients were British, they would have risked jail time.

I found it hard to imagine what virtual sex really looked like. So—purely in the spirit of writerly research—I decided to rent myself a virtual escort. I chose Second Life, because that virtual world is only accessible to adults, so there was no risk of a real minor at the other end. Nonetheless, I still felt awkward about my first encounter with paid sex (not least because my girlfriend was asleep in the upstairs room). So I roped in a real-world friend to keep me company. Even though the sex would be virtual, embarrassment was still a real possibility. The person behind the escort might also be any of the people I had already met. The chances were slim, but, afraid for my virtual reputation, I created a new virtual self and logged in under a different name.

I sent an instant message to a madam, and within a minute received a reply: There were two escorts online. The price was 1,000 Linden Dollars (about $3) for an hour. I picked an escort at random, and within a minute received a teleport invite. I accepted, and rematerialized in what seemed to be upstairs from one of Second Life's many virtual strip clubs: a "VIP" room, decked out in virtual tiger-print wallpaper. Various odd items dotted the place: a ball, a bench, wall shackles. And there in front of me was my virtual lady of the night. I made my avatar gulp nervously. She laughed. Then she took off all her clothes.

As far as I knew, my new nubile sex worker could have been, in the real world, a middle-aged man from Texas. (The real-world selves behind Second Life residents are approximately 40 percent female, but, according to Linden Lab, female Second Life residents play longer, so each virtual self you meet is as likely to be a real-world woman as a real-world man.) "She" took me through a variety of poses. Following her directions, I clicked on button after button ("Male BJ"; "Male wall push-up"; "Male doggy"), and she did the same.

In The Sims Online, there were no sexual animations. Evangeline's girls simply offered dirty talk in a hot tub. In Second Life, I discovered, much more was on display. Some of Second Life's most profitable businesses revolved around avatar customization: dances, hugs, costumes, and avatars in various stages of undress. The default Second Life avatars have no genitalia, but my companion had clearly invested in an avatar "skin"—Second Life outfits that change your body shape, in this case, to a long-haired, buxom, beautiful blonde—

with all the detail filled in. She invited me to kiss her (which basically meant walking up close to her and typing "mmm" and "*kiss*"). Then she lay down on the floor and opened her legs.

In Second Life, for more anatomically accurate virtual sex, you had to visit shops like The Black Room Genital Shop to buy gynecologically realistic selves, and add-on genitalia. I hadn't bothered. She had genitals, but I didn't. My first virtual sexual experience looked oddly like a G.I. Joe getting it on with a red-light girl.

The escort I had hired didn't want to talk about her virtual life on the record so I searched the classified listings again. (This time I really was only after conversation, although I wondered how often the girls had heard that line.) During the search, I spotted an ad for Femme Fatale. "New Zealand's no.1 gentlemen's club has come to Second Life!" it read. The real professionals, it seemed, had stepped in for a cut of the virtual action.

Perhaps understandably, Aurora Walcott, manager of the virtual Femme Fatale, was the one resident I met who was reluctant to give her real-world name. "I live close to Cleveland, Ohio" was all she would tell me. There was no way to confirm her story, and there was also a theatrical feel to Aurora's language ("I must say your message ignites my curiosity. When are you typically available here in-world?") that caused me to further doubt her story. Still, even if she was a construct, she would be interesting to talk to. It might tell me something about the way we reinvent ourselves in virtual worlds. I invited her to talk in my virtual office.

When Aurora teleported into space a few feet above my desk, there was something wrong with her dress; all I could see was her body shape, with the word *Missing* written across it (an occasional Second Life bug). She slipped behind my couch to change outfits, into tight red boots, a red top, and a short black skirt. I invited her to take a seat wherever she felt comfortable. She perched on my desk, her virtual skirt hiked up, and I could see she had no underwear. I wondered what my real-world neighbors would think. I closed my curtains.

Aurora no longer worked as an escort, she told me, but she was willing to talk about her time as a virtual sex worker in Second Life. In real life, she had been born with a hole in her heart. "I also have leaky valves—like a car," she said, and laughed. As she bowed forward, her skirt hiked farther up her thighs. A year before she visited my office, when she was thirty years old, she was forced to convalesce for a long period after another heart operation, which was when she first logged on to Second Life. Within a month, she decided to become a madam.

She advertised in the Second Life classifieds for a few weeks, and built up a roster of eight employees. She schooled her "girls" in dirty talk, and gave them sexy "skins." And unlike many virtual escort agency owners, she let her workers keep the money they made. "I felt that if they were doing the work, they deserved the cash and the returning clients," she told me. I saw her rate card: "Exhibitionism," outdoor or in private, cost a thousand Linden Dollars (about three dollars) an hour; "couple-sharing," a foursome, cost four thousand Linden Dollars (about twelve dollars) for the same amount of time. There were some services she did not offer, including "Bestiality" ("Sorry, I love my 'bitches,'" her rate-card read, "but not in *that* way"). Payment was always up front. Working new johns alongside regulars, she earned the equivalent of ten dollars a day, although she put most of the money back into her club.

"Aurora" sounded like it could have been a Kiwi name, but, it turned out, she had never left the United States. She had stumbled on the Femme Fatale club's website and liked what she saw. "Although I have yet to even visit New Zealand, I found the club stunning," she said. "I also wanted a classy atmosphere for myself here."

In her real life, Aurora told me, she had had only one sexual partner. ("Many of my Second Life clients were shocked to learn of my inexperience," she told me. "I tend to have lived more erotically in Second Life.") She came from a strict Catholic background, and her virtual sex work had helped her come to terms with her own real-world lack of experience and confidence. Also, she felt it was safer than real-world experimentation. "This was a learning experience for me," she said. "I never willingly had anal sex. Now, I ask for it."

Aurora's real-world partner didn't know about her online escort work; he too lived a virtual life, but he preferred World of Warcraft. She was careful to keep her virtual life and real life separate—apart from one early slip. "I only allowed one person to see me on webcam," she said. "That became a nightmare. It was early in my online life, so to speak. We had even exchanged phone numbers. I haven't thought about this since it happened. He would call numerous times each day, for months."

Aurora ignored his calls. "Then I read he had committed suicide. He wrote me a letter the night before, asking why I wouldn't talk to him anymore." Still, there was, of course, no way to verify Aurora's tale.

According to her, the bad experience in the real world planted the seeds of doubt about her online profession. Also, she met another man, another Second Life resident; they had feelings for each other and considered meeting in real life. It was time to leave "the life" behind. Also, she had other plans. After six months Aurora gave up escort work (although her other girls kept working, so she left the classified ad in place) and she went into business. In her days as a madam, Aurora had offered virtual sex in the guise of a whole range of female stars. The girl might model for an hour, trying on different celebrity skins, until the client decided who he wanted. Of course, the celebrities have no idea this is going on and have no say in the matter. (I asked who was the most popular. "I'd say Pamela Anderson and Angelina Jolie are tied," she said. One client asked for "a transgender," and another asked for Jack Nicholson. She obliged both. Aurora found it remarkable—a sign of our times—when some clients wanted something other than a celebrity. "Interestingly enough, there were often clients who preferred the 'girl next door' look," she said.)

Now, along with one of her employees, she had left sex work behind, making a better virtual living selling these hand-sculpted celebrity selves to other residents. Business, she said, was booming. She showed me around her store, a three-level complex with a virtual porn theater and a picture of the porn star Jenna Jameson (with a caption, "Going Down?") in the elevator. On the walls were pictures of her celebrities (*Buffy* star Sarah Michelle Gellar, Janet Jackson, J.Lo) next to images of their real-world selves. Some looked more lifelike than others. (I couldn't resist; for 500 Linden Dollars—about $1.80—I picked up a copy of Drew Barrymore. Aurora, delighted at my custom, offered me a free Vin Diesel; I turned her down.) I asked what was included in the price; apparently, not everything. "Unfortunately, cocks are purchased separately," she said.

Like 'Alayne, Aurora told me her second life had improved her first one. "It's connected me with a new sense of myself," she said. "I've crossed paths I once was too fearful to cross even in my own imagination." I asked what kinds of paths. "Being sexually adventurous," she said. "Learning what pleases me. How to reciprocate."

Reciprocation was what Kyle Machulis, aka Second Life resident qDot Bunnyhug, had in mind when he built a vibrator that could be scripted to activate in time to Second Life virtual sex. In October 2006, Kyle, who a year and a half earlier had built a "homebrew" dildo attachment for Microsoft's Xbox console (the "SeXBox"), released his vibrator script to the Second Life public. (Kyle told me he had even made a sex toy controller for text worlds.) His field, he said, was "teledildonics": computer-controlled sex toys, linked together across the Internet. In a talk at Second Life Community Convention, a real-life gathering in San Francisco, Kyle told the crowd he saw no surprise in the surge of virtual fetishism. He mentioned "pony play," a sexual fetish where one or both partners halter up and act like a pony. In the real world, the harness and equipment would cost over five thousand dollars; in Second Life, it cost two dollars. In a presentation at the convention, Kyle demonstrated his vibrator. He pulled up an example avatar, a blue cube—"an ordinary cube. But if you *are* a cube, it's kind of hot," he said—and, in the real world, pulled out a "Rez Trance" vibrator, a customized add-on for an innocent PlayStation 2 game, Rez, which was originally intended to augment that game's synesthetic game play by vibrating in the player's pocket. In 2004, Jane Pinckard of the website Game Girl Advance wrote an article about having sex with one, and a thriving secondary market arose for the vibrators, which at the time fetched thirty dollars on eBay (although, after Kyle launched his Second Life plug-in, he joked, the eBay asking price doubled). At the conference, Kyle demonstrated his Second Life script; when the cube moved up, the vibrator moved up; when the cube moved down, the vibrator moved down.

"While this was mainly interesting to me from an engineering standpoint," Kyle told me, "I just happened to deal with sex toys—the actual need soon became much more apparent. There are quite a few people that use SL [Second Life] for sex. They might feel uncomfortable using a webcam or audio setup, or they might have certain needs that cannot be fulfilled through that medium."

Devices like Kyle's vibrator further blur the line between real and imaginary connection. Does virtual sex with someone who is not your real-world partner count as cheating? Talking dirty with a virtual self while having sex with a machine? I'm sure my girlfriend wouldn't be happy if she walked in on that. (Although I suspect no one would.)

Had my girlfriend been serious about her virtual two-timing worries, there were people who could help. Inside Second Life, for one hundred Linden Dollars an hour—plus virtual expenses—you could hire Marki Macdonald, a virtual private investigator, to set up a "honey-trap" and tempt your partner into virtual infidelity. Similar services were available in other virtual worlds, too. I found a listing on eBay: "Introducing: Sim Spies, at your service."

"Sure it seems innocent enough playing The Sims Online," the ad read, "but a person not necessarily looking for an affair can be drawn into the flirtatious world of chat and become a cheater. Beware! If your mate frequently stays up after you've gone to bed and they are doing more typing than clicking, it could be a warning sign.

"You do not need to spend another night lying awake in bed waiting for them to come to bed. You do not need to go weeks on end without making love or endure the gut-wrenching pain of longing for them to 'touch you like they used to.' If you're sick and tired of not being able to eat, not being able to sleep, and struggling every day with sadness and uncertainty . . . then we are here for you.

"This auction includes our team of Sim investigators going undercover to dig up all the dirt and expose those cheating Sims. We have a team of undercover Sim Divas that can try and initiate contact to see if they deny being in a relationship, or if they are looking for any fun on the side. You will receive screenshots of all chat and private messages and actions. You can finally have the proof you need to confront them and see the shock on their face when they know that they are busted and have been caught up in their web of lies."

In virtual worlds, players don't have to meet in motels to cheat; they can just close the door. People were attracted to sex virtual worlds because of the lack of real-world consequences, but instead they found new anxieties, fostered by marketers keen to make a profit. "Can you trust them?" the Sims Spies listing read. "Find The Truth Out Now!"

11

MY VIRTUAL SISTER

Beyond the nuclear family

In real life, sex builds families. In the virtual world, people are born whole. Second Life is over-eighteen only, and residents discovered to be underage are immediately banned. (In the early days of Second Life, some well-known virtual designers were ejected in this way.) There is another, separate Second Life, called the Teen Grid, open only to minors, but no connection is permitted between the worlds. When residents of the Teen Grid turn eighteen, Linden Lab transfers them to the main Second Life universe. They have to leave their younger friends behind, so Teen Grid residents have developed their own tradition: a "REZuation" party (based on the word *rez*, and coined to describe the process of making an object appear in Second Life), to say goodbye and commemorate their graduation from the smaller pond into the larger ocean of virtual adulthood.

In my strolls around virtual shopping malls, I had seen animated babies that cried and demanded attention. Residents who acquired these babies could even go through a simulated "birthing" process, with virtual doctors and midwives—and some women had claimed the process had helped them come to terms with miscarried or still-born children. Some residents, I knew, role-played as children for their virtual "adoptive" parents—but in any real sense, avatars couldn't have virtual offspring. In one survey, 80 percent of virtual world residents had no real-world children, though it could be that the demands of a second life preclude the spare time to devote to parenting. Still, virtual worlds, with their ability to conquer distance, were increasingly bridging familial gaps.

I had hopes that my own virtual life would make it a little easier to connect with my real family. My father, with whom I had connected through early computer games, still lived in another country, and we still connected occasionally through the Internet. For example, after I moved into my new apartment, we played a game of Risk online, and once I had set up my virtual office I invited him to come for a visit.

After my father had logged on to Second Life—he chose one of the default body shapes, a kind of futuristic cyber-Goth that looked a bit like an evil clown—I showed him around. (He hadn't finished the process of customizing his character into his own unique virtual self, and the bug that had made Aurora Walcott's dress disappear had infected his eyes; when I looked closely at his new face, each eye had "missing" written across the iris.) We sat down for a minute and watched a short film. Wanting to show him around, I took him to the spaceport, which modeled the history of space travel; my Goth-father and I swooped between scale models of Russian Vostok and American Apollo orbital launch rockets.

I wondered aloud what else he might want to see. "It's all right," he said. "I think I've seen enough." I felt sad. I had visited him in person two months before, but this was the first time we'd spoken since then. The "missing" tag across his eyes seemed ironic; since I was two, we had lived apart and I often missed his presence in my life. We had always had difficulty reaching each other, and even here, in Second Life, it wasn't easy to connect.

The oddness of my father's virtual appearance—especially the spiky leather wristbands—reminded me of the few times he and I had met in another virtual world. Months before he visited my Second Life office, I had visited him in his virtual world of choice: World of Warcraft. Some virtual worlds, like Second Life, offer you the chance to change almost every aspect of your virtual self. In others, like the phenomenally successful World of Warcraft (with some 8.5 million residents), there is less room to choose. You can elect to belong to one of six races (including elves, dwarves, and humans), and you can alter a few other small details, such as eye or hair color. Later, as you progress, you acquire new clothes and armor that help you on your way, but the overall effect is a world of near-identical residents, like a residential theme park where all the employees and visitors wear the same costumes. In World of Warcraft, tasks (hunt goblins, deliver this letter to the king) are set for your character right from your birth, so the world is full of people running back and forth on the same quests. My father had played World of Warcraft for over a year, and his character was far more powerful than mine; when I logged on to visit him, he agreed to meet me back near the beginner's town to take a look around.

My father lives in Germany, and for fun I gave my new virtual self a German-sounding name, Günter the Hunter. When I arrived— I flew down to land on the back of a griffin—he was waiting on the dock for me. "Hi," I said.

"Sorry, I can't talk," he said. "I'm waiting to meet my son."

After I persuaded him it really was me, we hung out in World of Warcraft for an hour or so. There was little to do apart from complete quests, so we ran around killing ghosts to collect gold. After a while, the tasks were so similar that all sense of our identities seemed to disappear. My virtual father could have been anyone.

Now that video games are not just for kids—half of U.S. households own a dedicated games-playing machine, and, in those households, 20 percent of gamers are over fifty, and more of them are eighteen to forty-nine than are under eighteen—virtual worlds have also become a place where generations connect. Despite my mixed success with my father, I had better luck with other family members.

My half sister, in her early teens, also plays World of Warcraft. In May 2006, for her birthday I bought her some virtual gold. I logged on to IGE.com, selected the World of Warcraft European Server, Onyxia, paid $36.90 from my credit card, and the next day—her birthday—she received five hundred gold pieces. With the character our father had helped her create, she went on a virtual shopping spree. A few days later I logged on again, and her character, an elf called Anela, invited me for a stroll through the deserts and jungles of Azeroth. My sister lived with my father in Germany; this was the first time we had hung out in six months.

She took me on a tour of her world, pausing considerately every few minutes to let me catch up as I walked the long distance from a graveyard after being eaten by a scarecrow or T. rex. (Her character was level 40; mine was level 1.) She showed me the new clothes she had bought with my virtual gift (her favorite was a new pointy hat), and her virtual horse, called Horse. She led me carefully through the rain forests of Stranglewood. The local fauna, scenting easy prey, pounced at every turn. A nearby "Murkgill Warrior," aiming for me, saw my sister and attempted to run away in fear; she killed him and stole his fish oil. She slayed and skinned a passing wolf.

She showed me a village, populated by enemy players, where she liked to hide and jump out to attack. One enemy, a dwarf named Grimbat, did walk by, but my sister was in a generous mood; she waved, and the nervous passerby waved back. "I don't kill him," she said.

"Ah," I said. "Very nice of you."

Another three enemies passed, chased by a pack of dinosaurs. My sister stepped in to help; the others escaped but my sister was killed. As she trudged back from the graveyard, an enemy player came up and knifed me in the back, killing me instantly. My sister wanted revenge but I hadn't had time to get his name.

Our father's birthday present to her had been a new PC. Up until then she had had to borrow our dad's to play. Now she could play from her room, and the two of them could play online together.

I was born in the seventies, in the decade where people—and especially families—drifted apart. (The seventies are a decade in which Richard Dreyfuss's character Roy Neary, in *Close Encounters of the Third Kind,* could believably trade his family for the company of aliens.) Like many children of the decade, I too experienced separation. When I was four, my mother and I moved into a commune, away from my father and much of regular society. I filled the void with my imagination, and twenty-five years later, it seems families are doing a similar thing.

In a January 2006 survey, 30 percent of parents said they play games with their children, and two-thirds of those felt the games had brought them closer. Now even estranged families can use online worlds to stay close. One father, Clay Thompson, explained to *Computer Games* magazine that he had arranged for a specific clause in his divorce decree to allow for three hours of online contact per week. "My son loves it when I make him invulnerable and spawn dragon after dragon in Neverwinter Nights," he said. "My daughters and I hit the shopping block in ToonTown and then go back to her virtual home to try them on together. It was the most fun I've ever had online, just hearing them giggle." In World of Warcraft, Thompson found he enjoyed the role of a healer; casting spells to keep his children alive felt good.

(Of course, virtual worlds don't always bring families together. In April 2006, in Dunedin, Florida, Joseph Langenderfer burst into his son's room after an argument, waving a pistol. Joseph thought his son spent too much time playing online games instead of doing the laundry. His plan: shoot his son's computer. The bullet hit the wall instead, and Langenderfer was held for attempted murder.)

My father had worked with computers his whole career, so he was comfortable with his daughter playing World of Warcraft, although he did limit her time online. But virtual worlds, with their capacity to distract children from the real world, make some parents anxious. Links between computer games and violence among children have been argued for decades. In December 2006, the German minister of the interior backed a law that, if passed, would criminalize the development, publishing, and playing of violent games. Under that law, my own experience inside Counterstrike shooting virtual terrorists would have been punishable by jail time. The concerns are perhaps understandable, given that in Europe 60 percent of children play video games every day, but the facts don't seem to support a moral crusade. U.S. video game sales doubled between 1996 and 2004; in the same period, violent crime halved. Some studies have shown that children with computers at home perform slightly less well at school, and other studies have shown that constant use of e-mail can dull our thinking as much as smoking weed. But there's an argument, too, that video games make us healthier, less repressed, by giving us a risk-free outlet for basic violent impulses that society cannot condone. Video games are perhaps, as a games store I once saw advertised, "Beyond Therapy." In early 2006, police in Edinburgh, Scotland, began a program to combat antisocial behavior: They hosted weekly video game contests between troublemakers and police. (The police tended to win at the driving games; the kids tended to win at virtual soccer.) Since the program began, the number of youth-related crimes in the area has fallen by half.

Virtual worlds offer children other positive forms of escape, too. A Portuguese organization called the Associação Recreativa para a Computação e Informática uses Second Life as a virtual refuge for abused children in Portuguese safe houses. They invite children into the game, then help them with social and technical skills.

Video games may well reduce the time we spend in our bodies. After all, an American child is six times more likely to play a video game than ride a bike. But new, mechanized forms of imagination have long been seen as threats to our children. Public cinema began in 1894; by 1896, in the French short *Le Coucher de la Marie*, actress

Louise Willy was naked on film. Early cinema "coin-up parlors" were seen as a moral threat, and laws banning them were debated in the U.S. Senate. Even early novels were regarded by some as a threat to the young; they might distract devout children from religious texts. But in each case the younger generation had helped us bring the new medium into the culture. Through play, it seems, children teach us the new opportunities and limits.

In November 2006, Linden Lab announced plans to open up its server software and allow others to set up and manage their own virtual universe. But driven by the political pressure of inhabiting someone else's world—and by the real-world financial pressure of virtual world subscription fees—smaller, homebrew universes had already sprung up elsewhere.

Years ago I read the work of Henry Jenkins, director of the Comparative Media Studies program at MIT, who called computer games "virtual play spaces": areas where young adults, in an urbanized world with scarce empty land, can find complete freedom of movement to explore themselves outside society's moral gaze. I have never seen as literal an example, though, as seventeen-year-old Todd Robertson. He and his friends, landlocked in the urban sprawl of north London, didn't build a clubhouse, or colonize a corner of a favorite pub; they built their own virtual world.

In July 2004, an employee of game software company NCsoft leaked the official Lineage II server files—the data that enables them to run a world. Soon, enterprising players realized that, with some time and money, they could set up private versions of the game and run their own universes. Two years later, private virtual worlds were a booming business. (In China, where broadband prices are low but game subscriptions relatively high, one private server had fifty thousand residents. In 2006, Chinese publishing company Shanda sued Actoz, the developers of Shanda's virtual world Legend of Mir II, after the source files were leaked onto the Internet; fewer players would pay for the "authentic" virtual world, Shanda argued, when they could play in the same world for free elsewhere.)

The most successful private universe—L2extreme, a version of Lineage II with five different server worlds—has had tens of thousands of residents online at a time. Websites such as Gamers 200 listed the top two hundred Lineage II servers, each advertised with basic travel-brochure copy, designed to encourage you to visit their world: "Shops!"; "Sympathetic ambience!"; "Fishing!"

Todd and his partners initially played online war games, including Counterstrike, but soon discovered Lineage II. After only a few months they moved to private servers, because there they had more fun and could advance their virtual selves faster. They moved from server to server, conquering and growing bored with each in turn, all the while talking about how they could do it better themselves. For a long time it was just talk, until one evening another player—whom they had fought alongside in Lineage II but never met in real life—liked their ideas and offered to bankroll their own server. They made plans, and another Swedish friend offered a high-end PC as a test bed. With some basic knowledge of C++, a programming language, and a lot of time, they chose a section of the Lineage II universe and sculpted it to their desires.

Then their shadowy financier pulled out. Still, it seemed a shame to waste the work, so they raised the money themselves, rented a server box, and christened their new world L2Supremacy.

When I first met with Todd to discuss his private universe, he and his friends had had their own server up for a month; they already had a stable peak-time population of a hundred or so players. As the tasks of managing a universe grew, Todd became the event manager. In a custom area called "The Coliseum," he organized virtual tournaments where players competed for virtual prizes.

According to Henry Jenkins, the reason our new virtual wastelands arose was to escape the prying eyes and order of society. In homebrew virtual worlds such as Todd's, rule-breaking, or attempted rule-breaking, came with the territory. They even had rivals. A group of their online friends split to set up their own server, L2Frenzy. "The day after we announced ours," Todd told me, "they coincidentally announced they were doing it, too." The other group has attempted to sabotage L2Supremacy by overloading their website and hacking into their world with GM privileges and wreaking havoc, killing players and stealing items. Todd insisted they didn't retaliate. "We're doing better than them," he told me, referring to their higher rank in the Gamers 200. "As long as we're on top, I don't mind."

Todd's older sister told me she worried about the time he spent in virtual worlds, about the lack of real social interaction and the possibility that Todd would meet strange men on the Internet. I told her I wasn't worried. He was at the forefront of a new movement that seemed only set to continue. (In August 2006, the latest Lineage II update, Chronicle 5, was also leaked. The rumor that Todd heard was that an NCsoft insider received ten thousand dollars; the site that bought the files set up their own server, and then, to reclaim some of their initial investment, in turn sold it for five thousand dollars—and soon the files were everywhere online.) Todd and his friends were learning to manage their own finances, as well as the economy of their whole world. Server space and bandwidth cost money, so most private servers offered their players the chance to "donate." In practice, most donations were rewarded with gifts of powerful items. (The ratio of effort to reward was greatly improved. L2Extreme sold weapons for between $50 and $130, and a level 80 character, fully powered up, for $150. For comparison, at Team VIP, a third-party broker for virtual items, a level 63 character on a U.S. commercial Lineage II server would have cost you $408.) The donation process was very popular—and cheap compared to playing the retail game. Some servers made serious money. In one week, L2Extreme reportedly pulled in $24,000; they regularly closed their donation process, Todd told me, so they could catch up on delivering the freebie items.

One of Todd's motivations for setting up his own server was an egalitarian ideal. Much like in real-world politics, those running these private virtual worlds shone favor on their friends and those who donated money. "On those other servers, there's a lot of favoritism," Todd told me. "In L2Supremacy, we're very fair." If virtual worlds were the new Wild West, they wanted to depose the corrupt sheriff and put the people in charge.

Todd and his friends had worked hard to build their world, and now they could enjoy their godlike powers. They could create any-thing, be anything, kill anyone. "We can make ourselves invisible," he told me. "I can turn myself into a tree, and watch people wander by." But it wasn't all fun. Todd had built an entire world, and now he had to manage it. Because he hoped for as many residents as possible, he realized they needed to slow the supply of powerful items so new players didn't begin at a total disadvantage. To reduce demand, he raised their prices.

Todd was learning to manage people, too. His world was growing faster than he could cope; he was forced to take on staff, and it fell to him to interview prospective new gods. I asked what kinds of ques-tions you ask a potential employee, someone who might help you run a world. He thought for a moment. "One question I asked," he said, was, "If you told someone to stop doing something disruptive, and im-mediately, right in front of you, they did it again, what would you do?"

"Ban them?" I guessed.

Todd shook his head. "We want people to stay on our server." The correct answer, he said, was "Turn them to stone for two hours, to think about what they'd done."

12

CORPORATIONS

Branding virtual dreams

When I first met John Lester inside Second Life, he showed me Brigadoon, the island refuge he had built for BrainTalk's Asperger's sufferers.

We met on top of the island's single hill, in a structure he had placed there before any residents moved into Brigadoon: a Greek temple, modeled on a real-world Temple of Zeus, overlaid with photos of original mosaics. "I remember I was telling someone about this Greek temple I had made," he said. "And I said, 'Wait, here let me pull it out.' You can store anything in your inventory, and so I pulled this Greek temple basically out of my pocket. I said, 'Let's sit in the temple and talk.' " (Brigadoon wasn't all so serious; later John showed me the beach hot tub, meant to encourage a more relaxed kind of interaction.)

John Prototype's amphitheater seemed appropriate, a metaphor for what many people hoped virtual worlds would deliver: a new kind of public-spirited civic society, where residents could still have a direct effect on the shape and function of their world. There, high on the virtual mountain air, amid the inspirational scenery, we loftily discussed the importance of fantasy life to the proper evolution of young souls.

I mentioned a book I had read not long before, psychologist Bruno Bettelheim's *The Uses of Enchantment.* "He talks about the importance of fairy tales, culture's dream-life, in the proper development of moral and psychic strength in children," I said.

"I will have to check it out," John said.

"He talks about how fairy tales speak to children's unconscious, and give them clues to life's essential, difficult dilemmas, in a way that an adult could never simply explain," I said.

"We watch other people's dreams on TV, in movies, and even in video games now," John said. "Our culture isn't growing the way it used to, from the people up. Nobody shares or makes up stories much anymore. That's what television is for."

"Yes," I said. My virtual self nodded earnestly.

"But in virtual worlds—well, in Second Life—everything here is created by people. There's no Disney," John said.

That was true—but not for long.

When I missed my first appointment with Rivers Run Red, Second Life's leading British virtual branding agency, I expected a rain check to be straightforward. A few days later, I received a reply from a company BlackBerry. "Finally out of the woods—scratched to bits and beetles in my hair!" The company clearly wasn't an everyday branding agency.

In fact, when I finally met Justin Bovington, co-founder with his wife, Louise Jorden, of Rivers Run Red, at their east London offices—painted entirely white, like their Second Life island—I realized we had met before. When I arrived, the pair handed me their business cards: On the one side were their real-world details, and on the other, their full-color Second Life selves. Justin, in a blue-and-black-checked shirt, looked like a groovy dad; Louise's other self, Jordie, looked like a stripper. Although this was the first time we had sat side-by-side in real life, Justin's Second Life avatar, Fizik Baskerville, had met mine, Errol Mysterio, in early 2004, over a chat with Wagner James Au (at the time, I think, we were hovering over a Dr. Seuss–like wonderland complete with giant purple-spiral candy sticks).

For a long time, corporations were surprisingly uninventive about how to extend their brands into virtual worlds. In July 2006, an in-game advertising company, Massive Inc., launched a kind of virtual billboard they called, snappily, "interactive advertisement technology" (essentially a 3-D model of a Toyota Yaris). In September 2005, Wells Fargo had dipped its toe a little deeper into virtual worlds, with Second Life's Stagecoach Island: an invitation-only corner of the virtual world designed to teach financial literacy to young people (while also promoting Wells Fargo financial services). It would seem, though, that companies who want a successful presence in virtual worlds have to try harder. People are attracted to virtual worlds because they want to take part; ads that try to press a message don't seem likely to grab their attention. "You don't walk into someone's house and demand they look at something," Justin told me. "So we don't do that in Second Life. What we do is corral it. We can set up areas where people can come and take part, enjoy themselves; they can opt in, or opt out."

In the early days of virtual worlds, brands ran free. When I joined Second Life, you could buy a virtual Adidas T-shirt for a hundredth of the price of a real one, and none of the money went to Adidas. Any virtual world developer would, when informed of copyright violation, remove any trademarked material—but back then, no one seemed to notice. By the time I met with Rivers Run Red, that had begun to change. Over the summer of 2006, after a rush of publicity about virtual worlds, and Second Life in particular—the tipping point may have been the May 2006 appearance of Second Life on the cover of *BusinessWeek*—corporations had begun to pay attention. (In one meeting of a multinational entertainment company, Justin told me, someone from top management, discussing their billion-dollar budget, turned to his creative director and said: "What's our Second

Life strategy?" The creative director had no idea what he meant, but he found out fast.) When we met, Rivers Run Red's clients included BBC and Disney; they had created a virtual premiere of *X-Men 3* from within Second Life, with a live camera feed from the red carpet in Cannes. (After this event, so many virtual snapshots of the event were uploaded onto the picture-sharing website Flickr that the Flickr management decided to ban virtual images from the front page of their site.) To help promote the film *The Hitchhiker's Guide to the Galaxy*, they built a virtual Marvin the Paranoid Android. Since the *BusinessWeek* article, Justin said, "everything has changed. Last year, eighty percent of our business was real-world business. Now, eighty percent of our business is virtual world business."

"Advertisers love Second Life," Justin said. "Second Life is fluid and quick enough, you can measure the results immediately. You can create something that's immediately relevant for that moment."

Still, taking up any kind of place in a virtual world often means upsetting those who are already there. As Justin reminded me, Rivers Run Red had its own difficult virtual birth. In December 2003, they bought the first Second Life virtual island at auction, for $1,250 — many times what people expected it to cost. The residents, defensive at the best of times, were outraged, and even more so when they discovered Rivers Run Red was a corporate agency. There were protests: Second Life residents held banners with crossed out Disney and Gap logos, and some conducted mock terrorist attacks on their island, Avalon. Over time, though, the company's commitment to working with residents became clear. They employed a whole group of full-time, virtual employees, spread across the real world, to build their clients' buildings, objects, clothes, beer kegs, perfume bottles — whatever a particular project required. By the time of my visit, their concern to respect the existing Second Life culture had calmed their detractors. "We've turned down a lot of work that wasn't right for the community," Justin told me. "One of the largest PR projects that has happened in there, we felt, was counterproductive to the creative aspirations of the residents. You can't just dump stuff in here and expect people to take an interest."

Their growing influence in the Second Life community was mirrored in their geographic location: Avalon, their sixteen-acre island, was right in the center of the Second Life map. After they spoke at the 2006 Second Life Community Convention in New York, their importance to the community, and to Linden Lab, was set. (Justin confessed he had even been given a few Linden Lab Second Life logo pendants.) "We made a promise to the community," Justin said. "We would never ever do billboard advertising, nothing traditional. We would always develop our ideas with the community." They work hard, he explained, to create something that gives both ways, so they are "engaging consumers in a conversation by permission." Their ethos is to make sure that consumers want to interact with the brands, distinct from what Justin referred to as the "interruption culture" of the TV commercial. "People I talk to think young consumers are apathetic," Justin told me. "They're not apathetic. They're just very well defended against advertising. They're too busy living their own lives."

Once again, it seemed virtual worlds had the capacity to help reverse the order of things. In the real world, corporations used people; in virtual worlds, perhaps, people could begin to earn back some control. For instance, Rivers Run Red was commissioned by Reebok to help build its virtual brand; keen to add value over existing virtual sneakers, they designed a store in which residents could customize Reebok shoes to their own desires. In the first month, Justin told me, the store sold eighteen thousand pairs. Their ultimate aim was to take the most popular virtual design and market it in real life. In May 2006, Rivers Run Red organized a virtual festival, inside Second Life, to coincide with a real-world BBC Radio 1 music event at Camperdown, Scotland. Six thousand people attended the virtual event, which was also projected onto real-world screens. "We watched it happening," Justin told me. "Every hour, a new time zone came online. As the Americans went to bed, the Koreans were getting up. People were wandering around Second Life, telling other people to come and see." They had planned the Second Life festival to last four hours, but after two days, they needed some sleep and shut it down. The next afternoon, Justin logged back on; even without the music, the party was still going. "Some guy arrived with his helicopter and got out with his posse. There was a guy with a wheelchair who was dancing with someone else dressed as [British cartoon candy mascot] Bertie Bassett. Then there was a bee craze; someone came dressed as a bee, then everyone left to get bee costumes. We didn't have to do too much; the avatars themselves became the theater."

Rivers Run Red made a living in the corporate world, and something of that world's awkward language occasionally leaked into their conversation. At a conference I attended, Justin broke humankind into marketing categories: passive recipients, active interpreters, engaged participants, and soon, apparently, we would all be "monetizing." Rivers Run Red was doing some monetizing of its own; *BusinessWeek* reported the company charged between $5,000 and $1 million per campaign (although Justin insisted most of the accounts were in the lower end of the range).

Justin told me he saw Second Life as broadband's "killer app." ("Shopping on the Internet turned out to be just catalogs online," he told me. "Second Life has the capacity to be so much more.") To Justin, virtual worlds are a place in which all our previously distinct modes of art and expression have come together. This is true for companies—"We are a games company, a film production company and a design company, all at the same time"—as well as for people, including himself. "Second Life has enabled me be the painter I've always wanted to be," he told me. "I can be a painter, a filmmaker, a writer, and a designer all in one place. I love it."

When I spoke with Bill Trost, lead designer of EverQuest, in 2002, he told me he thought virtual worlds could become the dominant mass media. "The more people play these types of games, the more variety we will see in the types of experiences they offer," he said. "I really believe that the variety and quality of content offered in

MMORPGs will soon rival that currently being offered on cable TV. I think Sony Online Entertainment is in a good position to become the HBO of the Internet."

When I visited the Rivers Run Red offices, the company was planning to explore these possibilities in depth. With Rob Marchant, a young TV director, they were setting up a virtual TV studio to film avatars in the same way as in a real studio. They planned to launch the first fully virtual TV channel, VirtualLife.TV, and make Second Life avatars TV stars within the world. They were in discussion with major TV networks, and planned to launch a twenty-four-hour service, with a thousand hours of original programming, including many films made inside Second Life.

Talking about their upcoming projects, Justin's face lit up. His fascination with virtual worlds was clear. "I never leave the island," he said.

No wonder his employees needed some time in the woods. They had been there, it turned out, for a survival course with the British television naturalist Ray Mears. It seemed like the perfect antidote to a virtual life, but even in their time off they found they had Second Life on the brain. Justin told me how he held up a stick, twisted per Ray Mears's instructions for making kindling, and had joked that it looked like virtual hair. "It reminded me of Second Life," he told me. "What people remember about Second Life, the most memorable thing they do at first, is to grab a texture, and bring something from the real world—a photo of themselves, their partner, or their cat—into the virtual world. They've projected a level of personality into their virtual surroundings. People automatically get it. It's like making things, even at the most basic level, out of twigs. Out in the woods, we were playing with fire, and we felt like we were reliving a key moment in human evolution."

I asked if he saw the emergence of Second Life as a parallel moment in evolution. "Absolutely," Justin said.

As virtual worlds like Second Life began to make headlines in corporate publications, big business began to take note. A week after I visited Rivers Run Red, I received an e-mail from Rory Caren, a media relations manager at IBM UK. IBM's global vice president of technology, Irving Wladawsky-Berger, was visiting England on a whistle-stop tour to promote the possibilities of virtual worlds.

In 1985, IBM was the largest computer company in the world. But within a decade, its losses were so high — $8 billion in 1993 alone — that the board considered breaking up the company. The world had shifted from centrally purchased, integrated solutions, to bit-by-bit solutions that focused on individual productivity. IBM was nearly left behind.

Wladawsky-Berger, born in Cuba, joined IBM in 1970. By the mid-nineties, he had become crucial to the company's survival, and led IBM's efforts to move into supercomputing, and to help clients achieve the business benefits of the Internet. IBM's "e-business on demand" efforts, which he headed, were central in dragging the company back from the edge of bankruptcy. Now, Wladawsky-Berger had decided that virtual worlds would form the next level of the Internet, and — perhaps driven by a determination never to go back to the difficult times — he wanted his company to be there: to ride the next wave of what he called "the leap from e-business to v-business."

The e-mail invitation I received to meet Wladawsky-Berger stressed how serious IBM was about virtual worlds. "IBM's chief technology strategist, Irving Wladawsky-Berger, is going virtual," the e-mail read. Irving saw virtual worlds as "signaling the next profound shift in how people use technology." Virtual worlds were "the next frontier." If that hadn't made things clear, the number of people in attendance did. When I arrived at the conference room, at an IBM building on London's South Bank, I was told it was "a global meeting." There were five others in the room itself, and listening in on a conference call were ten more. Even more were there, it turned out, although it took me a moment to notice: projected on the wall was IBM's virtual island inside Second Life, with at least fifteen avatars in virtual attendance, from real-world locations as far away as India and Australia. (One resident had silver skin, and a wide pair of fairy wings. "I see you've gone native," I said. She laughed. "Yep.")

Irving Wladawsky-Berger looked friendlier than I had pictured him: tidy gray hair and a round, cheery face. I asked why IBM was so interested in virtual worlds. In his marked Cuban accent, Irving told me he was the chairman of the board of governors of the IBM Academy, "a group of the top technical people around the world." A colleague, Chris Sharp, had approached Wladawsky-Berger to talk about virtual worlds. "At the time that took me a little by surprise," he said. "But I'd been around smart people enough that when you get advice like that, you listen very, very carefully." The academy study led to a more operational study by IBM's technology team, which led to a strong recommendation: Virtual worlds were something to which IBM needed to pay close attention.

Irving said he thought the crucial point of virtual worlds was that they shifted the role of the user from being controlled by the interface to being in charge. He thought of virtual worlds as the "immersive Web," with the potential for change "bigger than any before." Virtual worlds now reminded him of the Internet in 1994, he told me, "because around that time, the number of people using the then-fledgling World Wide Web was growing very rapidly, but business had not yet discovered it. And it seems like right now we are at the point of a massive initiative." Irving was convinced that along with the benefits of ubiquitous computing, there was a new kind of danger. How do we organize computing when computing is everywhere? "If you look at what's going on in IT, I don't need to tell you performance is going up in leaps and bounds, prices are dropping like crazy. IT is becoming embedded in everything, from medical technology, to cars, to RFID tags in consumer goods. This stuff is exploding.

"But I believe that the Achilles heel of this wonderful world is the complexity," Wladawsky-Berger said. "If you make what's going on complex enough, people won't be able to figure out how to use it. One of our biggest challenges is to make IT systems and applications far, far more usable to human beings. IT systems in business, government, health care, education, everything." Virtual worlds, he thought, were a way to integrate in this new era of distributed computing; a new metaphor, to unify networks just as the desktop metaphor—the one we use on our PCs every day—unified the file system. "I think that a lot of the complexity in IT is because systems and applications have really grown from the machine up," he said. "We do our machines, we do middleware, we do applications, then we put in a thin layer of human interface. We need to turn around our metaphor for design. The metaphor now has to be, for example, a hospital management system. How do human beings think about hospitals? What is a hospital? There are very few human beings in a hospital that worry about XML, and stuff like that. There are patients, and doctors."

I asked what specifically they were hoping to achieve inside virtual worlds. Wladawsky-Berger's early thoughts were that certain key areas would benefit immediately: customer service, telemedicine, prototyping, and education. (In India, where IBM is hiring thousands of new employees, the training procedure for recruits will include time spent in virtual worlds.) They hoped to "salami-slice" the marketplace, another IBM employee, Ian Hughes, told me: charge money for providing business services, such as interactive bookselling, that would apply to any virtual world. But the overall impression I had was of excitement that had yet to clarify into a concrete goal. A seismic shift was taking place, they felt, and IBM was determined not to be left behind this time.

IBM is a large organization, and like all large organizations it has learned to talk while saying nothing. "This next generation web will be a global consortium which means partnering within this grand experiment of technology is fundamental to the success of the 'immersive Web' and future business," my invitation read, which is another way of saying how nice it is to work with other people. At one point Irving used an acronym, "ERP applications," that I didn't understand. I asked him to explain, and he faltered. "ERP applications," he said. "Enterprise Resource . . . Enterprise Resource . . . What's ERP?" ("Enterprise Resource Planning," a disembodied woman's voice chipped in drily from the telephone.) Irving had never actually spent time inside a virtual world, but it didn't seem to matter. He was a visionary, not in the trenches. His presence and enthusiasm had driven IBM's efforts to "dip their toe in virtual waters," as he described it. When we talked on a more general level, his ability to grasp the overarching implications was clear. "People understand virtual stores much more clearly than, say, a catalog, which is how most e-business websites operate," he told me. In the same way, he said, "virtual worlds feel real. The virtual forces you to humanize."

I asked Irving about the geographic limitations of virtual worlds. Websites are, in one direction, perfectly scalable: one person or a million people can see the same page. Virtual worlds, on the other hand, can only pack as many people in a certain area as will fit. Wladawsky-Berger's perspective was that this would force corporations back into a focus on people. Virtual worlds are inherently democratic. One reason is that, relative to the real world, everything is so easily accomplished and so the competitive advantage of corporations is reduced. In other words, virtual worlds are a more level playing field. The second reason, though—and it was something I hadn't seen before Irving pointed it out—is that you can only make use of the vastly expanded mode of communication when others are nearby. "You're forced to think on a more personal level," he told me, and in a world straining to keep our corporations on a leash, this can only be a good thing.

"This is going to have a huge impact in business and in society," Berger told me, "in ways we do not yet understand at all."

Among the people in real and virtual attendance were members of IBM's Eightbar group—scientists, consultants, and executives who

held meetings and conducted experiments in Second Life. After we
met in the real world, I met with Ian Hughes, an IBM IT specialist for
sixteen years, member of Eightbar, and official full-time "Metaverse
Evangelist" at the IBM Second Life island Hursley. Ian's Second
Life self, ePredator Potato, looked like a predator—a human-hunting
alien copied from the film *Predator*—although his fearsome aspect
was undermined by what appeared to be a pair of fishnet tights. Hursley was like an IT department from the future. Ian showed me experiments with links to websites outside Second Life. A man stood in a
field and, via a link to Amazon.com, called up his search results in
the air in front of him; he could move them, like Tom Cruise's character in the futuristic thriller *Minority Report*, to find the book he was
looking for. I followed ePredator to a virtual tennis court. IBM managed the Wimbledon website, he told me. They transferred live ball
location data, recorded on custom keyboards by professional players,
and this virtual court replicated each shot. Virtual spectators could
watch the match accurately modeled inside Second Life with only a
slight delay. (To accompany the virtual Wimbledon, Ian had built a
copy of the bestselling real-world Wimbledon merchandise: a Wimbledon towel. It was a "virtual banner ad," Ian said, a kind of "avatar-
based marketing." People advertised Wimbledon, and paid for the
pleasure. In Second Life, though, the Wimbledon towel had an un-
advertised feature: You could throw it in the air and ride it as a flying
carpet.)

Hughes explained the day-to-day work of a Metaverse Evangelist.
He mostly met other IBM employees to explain virtual worlds such as
Second Life (apparently over two hundred "IBMers" were Second
Life residents), and there were also some meetings with IBM cus-
tomers to understand how they could use it, too. "So it's a lot of time
showing and explaining to people to help them 'get it.' "

The Eightbar group formed in February 2006 with two members;
when Ian and I met, in August 2006, there were over one hundred.
"Everyone wants to sit down in a virtual world, for some reason. It's
natural," ePredator/Ian told me. He pulled out something called a

"multi-gadget," made by another Second Life resident, Timeless Prototype. "This gadget creates chairs as you need them," he said. "The more people who sit down, the more chairs appear. It's a very useful tool to indicate to other people around that you're having a meeting. But it's not private; you haven't put walls and a roof around it. We can gather together and discuss things, and other people can join if they want to."

Meetings inside Second Life were more playful. In the real world, he said, after meetings were over, everyone left; after Second Life meetings, people milled around to experiment. "That's when much of the creative stuff happens," he said. (Earlier, Irving Wladawsky-Berger had explained why these kinds of virtual tools were so important. "In IBM, we have meetings around the world on every imaginable subject all the time," he said. "Today the bulk of the meetings are just conference calls. All of a sudden, we have a much richer environment, that can make our meetings far more productive." Also, he explained, they had to keep up with the competition.

"We're not playing, we're doing research," Irving had told me, but they were playing, too. I'd seen pictures of Eightbar members who had lined up a row of the recently launched Second Life Toyota Scions, placed a ramp on either end, then jumped the cars riding virtual motorcycles. The next time ePredator and I met, inside Second Life a week or so later, and with no senior IBM staff around, he materialized a larger-than-life version of the classic video game Space Invaders. The army of invading aliens, rendered in 3-D, began to wage war on a nearby Wimbledon billboard.

Later, at a real-world conference focusing on Second Life, I met another IBM Metaverse Evangelist: Roo Reynolds, young, clean-shaven, wearing a suit similar to the one his avatar wears. Despite his occasional adoption of large corporations' sexless jargon (in IBM, a "global innovation 3-D jam" was their idea of a party), Roo's enthusiasm for virtual worlds was clear. "In Second Life," Roo said, "designing and creating something becomes the same thing."

IBM has held meetings inside virtual worlds with more than

twenty major clients, including a telecommunication company, an aerospace firm, a petroleum giant, and "a major U.K. grocer" that, according to one Reuters report, "wants to build a virtual storefront that will allow consumers to buy real-world groceries online."

Both Ian and Roo told me that IBM had some concerns about the company's entry into Second Life. Inside Second Life, sensitive IBM topics such as patents, for which secrecy is paramount, are forbidden. Conscious that the world runs on Linden Lab's servers, they are wary of discussing anything that would harm IBM if leaked; they hope eventually to have an internal virtual world, maintained on servers they control, and accessible inside the company, for such secret work.

Robert Gehorsam, president of the virtual world developer Forterra, told me he had been approached by corporations who weren't comfortable operating inside Second Life because of that world's shaky response to its sudden growth. Robert was generous about Second Life's versatility, but had doubts about how robust that world was. "Ultimately, Second Life is a great consumer application," he said. "But it's not oriented to supporting what an organization needs. Security, reliability, highly defined applications, things like that."

Gehorsam had spoken with IBM, who showed Forterra what they were doing in Second Life. "I don't think they understand the difference between Second Life and an industrial-strength system," Gehorsam said. "How many times a week does Second Life go down? These are built-in problems. I will say that people are coming to us with prototypes they'd built in Second Life, and saying, 'We can't deploy with this.'"

Ian Hughes had told me the same thing. "That's something we're having to explore, access control in this environment," he said. "All companies who move in will have to think, what happens if somebody sits on top of your logo, strips, and takes a picture of themselves? On normal Web pages, that doesn't happen. You don't get someone wandering around your space, causing problems." Second Life resident Biscuit Carrol, who ran a start-up business giving Second Life tours and holding virtual conferences, also told me that for his corporate customers, security was paramount. "For example," he said, "people can fly around the windows and eavesdrop." His solution to that problem was to build his Second Life conference rooms so high that no one could reach them; you had to be invited to teleport in. "Even so," he told me, "someone could just strap on a jetpack."

Other businesses are also moving into virtual worlds. In June 2006, American Apparel set up shop in Second Life. The virtual outlet was designed to look just like a real-world venue, but on beachfront, the glass-faced store surrounded by casual, ethnic-looking benches made out of wooden logs. Inside, cheesy pop blared in an empty store. Wood veneer flooring was overlaid with rainbow racks of trademark colored T-shirts. The brand's outré sexuality had bled into the virtual world, too: On the upper-floor wall I saw stills from the website Beautiful Agony, a series of videos of real people's faces as they reached orgasm. For the first time, though, the corporate presence in virtual worlds led to real-world consequences; virtual T-shirts cost just one dollar, but—for a limited time only—each virtual purchase came with a fifteen-dollar voucher to spend in a real American Apparel store.

However, the launch of American Apparel inside Second Life was widely seen as a failure, or rather, just a PR success aimed not at the virtual community but at the front page. There were no storekeepers, and in the first ten days they sold a reported two thousand virtual items, which earned them $2,000, less than a day's sales in a single store. (Prices for virtual construction vary, but according to *The Wall Street Journal*, building a corporate Second Life presence costs around $20,000.) One resident, Dave Lime, part of a group called the "Second Life Liberation Army," stood around the store entrance and repeatedly pushed people out the door in protest at the commercialization of Second Life and the possible future erosion of residents' rights. It seemed an overreaction. A month later the store was deserted. For two days I lounged around the virtual sales floor, waiting to speak with a customer. Not a single soul walked in.

Around the same time, other multinationals began to latch on to the potential of virtual worlds. By October 2006, MTV, Coca-Cola, Sun Microsystems, Intel, and Warner Bros. all had a Second Life presence. In some ways, these businesses were following the money: In the United States in 2006, online ads made up about 6 percent of total ad spending, a little under the budget for radio ads but growing faster than any other advertising medium. A whole range of virtual businesses had sprung up to service the new corporate presence; one tour guide charged ten Australian dollars an hour.

Once again there was a rush to occupy the new territory, but rules of engagement had not been established. Residents worried, as I did, that corporations might take control of the virtual landscape in the same way they had taken control over the real one. The early signs, though, seemed to indicate that inside virtual worlds, the balance between corporations and consumers would be a little more even. Inside virtual worlds, at least at first, brands seemed less equipped to convince us they were the gatekeepers of the media that connected us. As Irving Wladawsky-Berger told me, the corporations that succeed will be those that focused on people—which could only be a good thing.

At that time, almost all the real-world reporting that came back into mainstream media was about the money: the scale of the economies, the virtual, "nonexistent" objects that could be bought and sold for real cash. This reporting simplified the revelatory capacity of virtual worlds, but there was a reason for this, too. It's not just that capitalism bribes every innovation to its own purpose, like an oil baron buying up politicians. It's that the figures themselves were startling. In 2005, residents of Second Life traded $1.47 million worth of virtual property in May alone. In 2006, the yearly market across all virtual worlds was estimated at $1 billion. These are huge numbers. To put them into perspective, *Titanic*, the biggest-budget film of all time, earned total domestic gross of $402.6 million. World of Warcraft made Blizzard Entertainment $300 million in 2005 alone.

It was no surprise, then, to discover that other big entertainment companies had joined in the exodus. For the "reality" show *Laguna Beach*, MTV had commissioned a modified version of the virtual world There—the same world Forterra had modified for the U.S. military. Billed with the tag line "Live It," that world was a chance for viewers to move into an Internet space modeled on the show, "alongside friends and fans," based on the show's real-world locations: "the whole Laguna experience in a parallel online universe." MTV even premiered the television show inside Virtual Laguna Beach before it aired on live TV.

In June 2005, *Titanic* director James Cameron announced his new film, *Project 880*, a "completely crazy, balls-out sci-fi flick." The film, later renamed *Avatar*, would be accompanied by a virtual world to be launched months beforehand to allow people to inhabit the story's universe before the film ever reached cinemas. Films, dreams, worlds: Cameron clearly believed, as I did, that the three constructs were related. "I create worlds, too, though mine are narrative-oriented," he said.

In an interview with *BusinessWeek Online*, Cameron expounded on his desire to see players create their own worlds. "I want to see developers create games in which players can add to the worlds as they go along, so you can see what hundreds of thousands of people in this game environment can create. It's like each is being handed a tool set. . . . Instead of creating a $50 million game, you're creating $2 million games and letting them grow themselves."

Cameron saw parallels between our new virtual universes and literature, specifically science fiction. "So much of literary sci-fi is about creating worlds that are rich and detailed and make sense at a social level," he says. "They force people to be more imaginative."

After businesses jumped on the bandwagon, more media followed. BBC reporter Paul Mason persuaded his company's flagship current affairs show *Newsnight* to shoot a segment inside Second Life, broadcast on January 5, 2006, with presenters' voices dubbed over the animations. In October 2006, Reuters announced a full-time Second Life reporter whose sole mission is to bring virtual news to the attention of the wider world. I met with Adam Reuters (in the real world, thirty-year-old Adam Pasick, of London), to talk about his virtual beat. "I cover Second Life exclusively," he told me, "with a focus on business and economy stories."

Then a group of odd-looking passersby—including a snappily dressed man with puppet hands, and a Grim Reaper—landed. In another leveling act, this time between the press and the people, they encircled Adam Reuters and began to taunt him.

13

VIRTUAL ART

Creating ourselves anew

Philip Rosedale sees virtual worlds as a remedy for the "Faustian bargain" of noninteractive media, such as television. "We all got TV, and it enabled us to see and learn many things, but unfortunately those things had to be centrally authored, without our participation, by a very small number of people," he told me.

Philip sees Second Life, built and managed by the residents, as a natural correction to our early, disempowering media—a better place, owned by us all. Perhaps that is why the Second Life community seems to thrive on drama: Virtual worlds help us reclaim control, from soap operas, cinema, and newspapers.

Virtual worlds could be a place where we remember ourselves, too. Wagner James Au reported on one Second Life resident, Duuya Herbst, who was among the last fifteen surviving members of the Deeni people, a small tribe living in Oregon. In a war with gold miners and the U.S. government in the late 1800s, the Deeni were almost wiped out. So, Duuya built a virtual replica of the dance hall that was host to his tribe's "Nadosh" feather dance, a solstice celebration of renewal. With just a handful of surviving pure-blood tribe members, he was trying to salvage the spirit of his ancestors and save their language, online.

There is a long tradition of writers and artists working with virtual spaces. In 1981, Robert Pinsky, later U.S. poet laureate, wrote about the close parallels—rhythm, meter, intensity of meaning—between poetry and computer code. His novel *Mindwheel*, in a text-only genre of collaborative prose-writing games now known as "interactive fiction," was an attempt to introduce surrealism to games. The late Douglas Adams, in partnership with Infocom developer Steve Meretzky, wrote some work exclusively as interactive fiction.

But virtual worlds cannot really be measured directly against other kinds of art. The open-ended journey that characterizes virtual worlds might make for terrible, say, theater. (As games theorist Espen Aarseth has pointed out, no one wants to play *Hamlet: The Game*, and "Fail—time and time again:—to avenge your father's death!"). Virtual worlds are not just interactive cinema, they are something new. David Mamet wrote, of the beauty of movies, "they are actual records of the light which shone on us." If so, then virtual worlds are actual records of the light we wish would shine.

Actors already earn a living from video game voiceovers, to the extent that, in May 2005, two Hollywood unions threatened a strike over actors' shares in game royalties. (Of the top ten games sold in 2004, nine were made with members of the actors' unions, including James Caan and Samuel L. Jackson.) But now virtual selves are so readily available, many are making films entirely in the virtual world.

Machinima, or machine-made cinema, is a genre that includes the virtually generated films I watched on my Second Life television. Machinima films are made by players acting out scenes in virtual worlds, with other players acting the parts of other characters, and one or more of the players recording the output of the screen to a video file. The video can be edited together, with sound dubbed over if necessary, to make a short film. In the early days of machinima, special software was required, but later, world makers like Linden Lab began to include special features to help residents record their antics for later editing. *The StrangerHood*, the show I first watched on my own virtual TV, had actually been commissioned by Electronic Arts as a promotional tool. Elsewhere, there have been machinima about love affairs inside World of Warcraft, and characters from the futuristic war game Halo musing existentially—and ironically—on the plight of being trapped in a life of eternal war. There are even live versions of machinima, more akin to theater than cinema. In August 2006, the American marketing company Millions of Us—"Virtual Worlds. Real Brands."—organized Second Life's first theater production: Virtual actors performed *From the Shadows*, by Enjah Mysterio (no relation to me), in a virtual version of a modernized Globe theater, as reimagined by the architect Norman Foster. (I had thoughts myself about staging *The Tempest*. At the end, for Prospero's farewell, the scenery, the Globe—even the surroundings, the earth, and the sky—would fade to nothing. "Our revels are now ended," our virtual players would say, as everything around them slowly disappeared. "These our actors / As I foretold you, were all spirits, and / Are melted into air, into thin air / And like the baseless fabric of this vision . . . ")

Publishing has entered virtual worlds as well. When I visited Rivers Run Red, they mentioned that they were working with Penguin Books inside Second Life. I asked for introduction, and within a few days I had invited Jeremy Ettinghausen, a digital publisher at Penguin, and also known as Second Life's Jeremy Neumann, to meet me in my virtual office. There Jeremy told me how he planned to bring the first cyberpunk novels—works of art that first envisioned shared virtual spaces—into the very worlds they had predicted. They began with Neal Stephenson, whose *Snow Crash*—a book that Philip Rosedale had used as a recruiting tool—was now a virtual book available inside Second Life. Or, at least part of it was: the first chapter, with an audio link, and another link to buy the virtual edition at a discount from Penguin online. Scheduled for a virtual appearance sometime in the future was William Gibson, the science fiction author who coined the word *cyberspace* after watching kids gaze, as I had done, into the blinking screen of a early coin-op arcade game. Plans were being made to re-create Blue Ant, the advertising agency from his bestselling novel *Pattern Recognition*. When Jeremy and I met, months before Gibson's scheduled appearance, Gibson and his agent were e-mailing Jeremy about Second Life daily.

"Because we publish *Snow Crash*, it seemed a really easy entry point to do something with that book," said Ettinghausen. "Though if I worked for a romance publisher, I'd definitely be setting up a 'romance novel' simulation in Second Life." Jeremy had been inside Second Life from March, and, he told me, he had never been gripped by anything so strongly. He had rented a small spot of virtual land inside an area of Second Life called The Future, "just so I can invite people to 'join me in the future!' " In April 2006, Jeremy began promoting Second Life inside Penguin, betting that his enthusiasm would spread; by the time we met, in October, his bet had paid off. "Over the last three or four months the U.K. press has gone mad for Second Life, making me look prescient," he told me.

I asked Jeremy if Second Life was a place where thought was less important than action. "I don't think it is less thoughtful—I go to quite a few discussions in SL and hear a high caliber of thought. But I think 'reading' is under threat generally as people increasingly go online for entertainment. Now that you can watch TV on your mobile phone while downloading music and firing off e-mails, reading old-fashioned linear text is a tough sell. And this is also why it is important that we establish a presence in here."

Jeremy took me to his land. The Future, it turned out, was high above the clouds, so to help get around, Jeremy gave me a jetpack. He showed me a crooked house, where floors twisted to become ceilings. Then he had to leave.

I strolled around Second Life, looking for other examples of in-world publishing. In one corner of the mainland, I came across a store called Pamela's Books, where Second Life self-publishers put up their books for sale. Browsing the store was a little different from a stroll around Borders: as I clicked on each book—a science fiction horror called *Dobbit Do*, a "*Dallas*-type tale" called *Cigar Box*—a larger version of the book, taller than the virtual me, appeared against the far wall. Elsewhere, I strolled into a meticulous copy of Paris's famous Shakespeare & Company bookshop, complete with worn sofas, and the shop's motto—"Be not inhospitable to strangers / lest they be angels in disguise"—written over an inside archway. Every wall was stacked high with virtual reading material. The store was more theater than commercial venture. It had been built by a woman from Pennsylvania, Sharon Ritter, who had never visited the real place. The books weren't readable, but it wouldn't be long, I thought, before our virtual selves would be able to stroll through an Amazon store itself. (Amazon's founder, Jeff Bezos, was an early Linden Lab investor.)

Other authors have appeared inside Second Life to promote and discuss their real-world books. Richard Bartle, the inventor of MUD, and Stanford law professor Lawrence Lessig sat on a virtual podium and inhabited avatars crafted to resemble their real-world selves to give virtual book readings and answer questions. The editor of the futurist magazine *Wired*, Chris Anderson, appeared as his virtual self to read from his bestselling book *The Long Tail*. Science fiction writer and technology activist Cory Doctorow made the entire text of his book *Someone Comes to Town, Someone Leaves Town* available as a free Second Life edition. Elsewhere, visual art, too, was being virtually explored. A few real-world galleries had built virtual Second Life equivalents, and in February 2006, Linden Lab offered a four-thousand-dollar scholarship to an art student willing to spend a term exploring art in Second Life.

In the meantime, the Rivers Run Red film festival had moved closer to a reality; they built a giant, floating blimp for the festival, which they planned to hold in conjunction with the charity Cancer Research. A celebrity patron, rumored to be the actor Ray Winstone, would appear in virtual form. I flew up to take a look at the blimp, which floated hundreds of feet above their island. On the blimp's upper story was a dance floor where, on squares of flashing lights, a group of people swayed in sync. I asked if they were waiting for the film festival. "No," one said. "We're waiting for Duran Duran."

In early 2006, Peter Wells-Thorpe, who worked with Duran Duran to develop their online and technology strategy, approached Linden Lab about creating a Duran Duran presence inside Second Life. Linden Lab referred the band to Rivers Run Red, who began talks about creating a whole new Second Life section for the band. In the meantime, word had leaked; groups of these fans, "Duranies" (a total of up to five thousand, Justin told me), had heard the band was coming; they logged in, and they waited. One "Duranie," JoJa Dhara from Holland, told me she had been a fan "from teenage to housewifeyears." They had heard about it after the band's co-founder and keyboardist, Nick Rhodes, did some interviews, she explained, and news of their virtual plans spread across the Internet. Now JoJa and her friends logged in every day to lounge around Avalon and wait for Duran Duran, staying awake sometimes until 5 A.M. When I visited, the fans had accumulated furniture: a candle, three deck chairs, a fishbowl, and a fax machine. The fish was a gift from Justin Bovington to keep them entertained; they named the fish Nick, after Rhodes. "Nick is a holy fish to us," JoJa Dhara told me. "NickFish is ours."

The band wouldn't be the first internationally renowned musicians to appear in Second Life—Suzanne Vega had already performed a virtual concert—but they would be the first band to embrace wholeheartedly the possibilities of the place. They planned to build a huge destination, Duran Duran's new virtual home, which would spread across four whole islands. In November 2006, over lunch at an Italian restaurant near his West London home, Nick Rhodes told me about the band's vision.

Nick had first stepped into Second Life six months before. Peter Wells-Thorpe gave him a tour, starting at Rivers Run Red's white-themed futuristic island. "The first thing that struck me was how fabulous it looked," Nick said. "I'd seen The Sims before, but this was a new level. Things had moved on.

"Then I saw a person take off and just start flying around. Then, I learned about teleporting. *Then,* I saw there was a search engine, where you could just type in whatever you like." Nick typed "Goth" and teleported to a Goth club. "There were great-looking Goth chicks." Nick clicked on a dance ball. "I never dance. But I found myself dancing around. I have to say it was a pleasurable experience—knowing that I'd managed to do it with a mouse."

Nick left the club, and flew over a field. "Then we went into a flower. And that sold me on the entire experience." Nick loved the intricacy he discovered inside Second Life. "I am an absolute obsessive about detail, to a painful degree. That's what keeps me awake at night." He had seen the flower from far away, and flew toward it, and when he finally arrived he saw that not only was the flower meticulously created, but also that someone had gone to the trouble of building a tiny bee to sit in the flower. "That was when I knew the place was for me. First, we thought, let's build a stadium. But after finding that level of attention to detail, we thought: Why not build a world?"

Nick and the rest of the band quickly decided they wanted to build virtual versions of their real selves, to inhabit the new world. The avatars would have the same names as the band. Nick—in the real world dapper, smart, with dyed blond hair—watched Rivers Run Red create the virtual version of himself. He delighted at their attention to detail: "They photographed our eyes, to get them right."

To Duran Duran, style was very important; they have worked with Vivienne Westwood and more recently with Giorgio Armani. "When we set out for this project, one of the questions we raised was, what are we going to be wearing?" Nick said. He spoke with a friend, the designer Antony Price. "Antony is an amazing British designer," Nick told me. "He designed a lot of the clothes for the artists we liked in the seventies, for Roxy Music and David Bowie. He did all of the outfits for our 'Rio' video. He's incredibly clever, technically. He's one of the few designers I have met who can draw something, and go and cut the pattern himself, and he can go and make it, and it will look exactly the same as the drawing. Very few people, even some of the major designers, have that skill on their own. Knowing how technical he is, I knew he would like this concept. In fact, we've asked him if he will open a boutique on our island."

Nick didn't like his Second Life version's round shoulders; he wanted a square cut. "Of course, that's not the way things normally work. Your clothes stick to your body. We found ways around that, by using building blocks to create straight lines." (Rivers Run Red added blocks of virtual wood to each shoulder and sprayed them to match the suit.)

Duran Duran planned to launch their Second Life presence with virtual gigs by their virtual avatars, which they would include in their real-world tour listings. They would prepare some elements of the show beforehand and play some elements live. "We will be able to improvise, and interact with the audience," Nick said. They were working with the American film company Giant Studios to use their motion camera equipment, also used in *King Kong* and the *Lord of the Rings* films, so Simon Le Bon, Nick, and the band would have access to their familiar dance moves.

Although the band's virtual selves would use their real names, they would, Nick said, be different people. "The avatars are going to stay in their personality from day one," Nick told me. "They won't be able to answer questions about 'Girls on Film' [one of the band's major hits], because they don't know about it. Of course, once we play the song live in-world, they can then answer a question about playing it in-world.

"I rather like the idea if you're going into this bizarre fantasy, that you keep it bizarre," Nick said. "I'd rather be talking about a twenty-foot eggshell that's just cracked open, than talking about something I did twenty years ago. Much more interesting to me at this time in my life."

The band had even written a song, produced by Timbaland and provisionally titled "Zooming In," from their avatars' perspective. "We thought OK, what's it like to be living in-world? What's the weather like? What do they feel like every day? Who do they fancy? What is their world about? I'd like to play it live in there. We could say, 'This one's for you!'"

In the meantime, the band was inhabiting Second Life anonymously. Andy Taylor, the drummer, became a virtual woman. "I think he's been rather enjoying it actually," Nick told me. "Especially when he says 'No' to guys. There's something going on there. I haven't asked yet. I know one of the other guys went in as a really short, big guy, and nobody would talk to him. Eventually somebody walked past, a big, tall skinny guy, who said, 'Hey there, little dude. How is it down there?' I quite like going in as an outcast. I think that'll be my next project."

Named after an evil doctor (Dr. Durand-Durand) in Roger Vadim's cult film *Barbarella*, Duran Duran have played with identity throughout their career. Nick traced the band's willingness to adopt new personae from the time they were just forming. "We grew up in the seventies. And for music alone, the seventies were about as inspiring as you can possibly get."

Nick cited other genres as further inspiration. "At various times throughout the decade, disco music, punk rock, heavy rock, pomp rock. We decided that we could be a rock band, but we could also be an electronic band. We could also play punky if we wanted to. We could play disco grooves and funk, and we could make really beautiful ballads, or we could make fast, raunchy rock tracks. And we could also do incredibly esoteric ambient things. I think a lot of bands find a sound and stick with it. We were fortunate enough in that Simon has a very distinctive voice, so as long as we stick that on top of whatever we're doing, we can go where we like."

Formed by Nick Rhodes and John Taylor in Birmingham, England, in 1978, Duran Duran has sold over seventy million records; they've had eighteen singles in the Billboard Hot 100 and thirty in the U.K. Top 40. Since their first album, *Duran Duran*, in 1981, the band has accumulated followers worldwide. When I met Nick, their fan club had over 150,000 dedicated members. Throughout their career, they have ridden the early waves of new technology. In the eighties they were among the earliest bands to issue extended remixes, "night versions" for club play. In 1984 they were the first act to build video screens into their tour shows. They were also among the first bands to embrace the Internet. "The first Duran Duran site was up in '96 or '97," Nick told me. The technology had yet to catch up with his vision. "The ideas I had, we did a lot of them, but nobody could operate them. We were doing these things in Flash, and creating these animations, but everyone was on dial-up. Nobody had a computer. And so it was an absolute catastrophe. But I liked it! Because I could play with the demos."

Duran Duran were also the first band to offer paid music downloads. Through the online service Liquid Audio, they sold their 1997 single "Electric Barbarella" for ninety-nine cents. "When people were cursing Napster for ruining the music industry, I have to say, I thought completely the opposite," Nick explained. "I didn't like our songs being taken free. I still don't particularly, I'd rather people paid for them. But I saw what would happen. It was like the Wild West at the time, and inevitably police come along, and sheriffs, and they sort the thing out. But the labels didn't see that. It took them a long, long time to catch up. I'm glad we did it, even though it sold so few copies."

Their next album, *Medazzaland,* was hit by pressure from stores, who were threatened by the new distribution, in the same way Wal-Mart recently declared they might stock fewer DVD copies of movies offered for download on Apple's iTunes Store. "If that record ever had a chance to be a hit," Nick said, "it was completely destroyed by the fact that some of the main chain stores in America refused to stock our record, because we were selling direct. And they were afraid they were being cut out."

In more recent years, the band has overlaid animation on live footage of concert crowds; the audience reaches up to touch the non-existent figure they can see walking across their heads.

Duran Duran's Second Life selves were an extension of this digital curiosity. They were already working on the technology to have their avatars projected on the back walls of real-world gigs, a technology tested in October 2006, at the British Academy Video Games Awards. Projected on the back wall, in a clear, soft-edged white room, Nick's avatar opened a virtual envelope and read out the nominations. "What a great pleasure it is to be here this evening, in your world," Nick's avatar said, his voice modulated as if to come from some other, digital place. As the virtual Nick was about to announce the winner, Nick's real self walked on the stage. Waving a remote control, he pressed a button to freeze his virtual self. "I'm sorry," the real Nick said, pointing to the screen. "But he's not to be trusted. The winner is . . ."

All virtual lives, I had discovered, were in a way a kind of theater. Jeremy Chase had played the mafia role with an almost camp commitment; Aurora Walcott's story could have been real, or it could have been imagined, but the tale interested me either way. People were inventing themselves; at times they seemed to take that reinvention too seriously. It was a relief to talk with Nick, who approached virtual worlds from a much more playful angle.

"The one thing that I guard rigorously is naïveté," he told me. "I think if you lose that as an artist entirely, you're sunk. And so every time I see something new, I feel almost like a child with a new toy. I feel as though there's some beautiful thing to explore there."

The Duran Duran area of Second Life consists of four islands, themed so visitors could start in a city, then stroll from the urban to the rural to the pastoral—somewhere between a surreal theme park and an interactive Duran Duran version of *Yellow Submarine*. One area, Sanhedralite, was named after an early Duran B side. ("Simon invented the word," Nick told me, "and because we were inventing a world, I thought it would be quite poetic to use that.") Azizi, the main city, was Duran Duran's vision of "our sort of downtown New York, with our lofts and our tall buildings. That's where it all happens." Another area, Tlön, was named after the world from Jorge Luis Borges's story "Tlön, Uqbar, Orbis Tertius," about a fictitious country that comes to life through the single copy of its made-up encyclopedia. "In deference to him, somebody else who had created a world, I thought it would be nice to have that name, too," Nick said.

Justin at Rivers Run Red gave me access to the Duran Duran island, a work in progress, and I took a brief flight around their vision. I flew into a towering lipstick skyscraper, to visit the still eerily empty Japanese restaurant at the top. Around me ran conveyor belts of virtual sushi. Through the windows I could see the clouds drift over the rest of the Duran Duran world. On the floor below, in a ghostly bridal suite, a wraith leaped at me from a mirror, and, when I lay on a virtual bed, I rose flailing into the air as if possessed. Lower still was the "Barbarella Apartment," a pink and purple hotel room with pop art above the bed. In the more remote, wilder areas of the Duran Duran world, a cherry-red ray gun spouted water into a pool, where oil paints leaked from flattened tubes into the sea. Above the pool, a 3-D Dalí painting wriggled disconcertingly, as if distorted by the heat. Towering above the world was a Mount Rushmore–style monument to the band, the face of each member carved in a virtual stone. Around the cliff flew Nick Rhodes's origami birds.

To honor their influences, the band planned to include a walk of fame, with people—Jean Cocteau, Liberace, Orson Welles, William Blake—important to them. Elsewhere there were mirrors that reflected unusual things out of the corner of your eye, black swans and panthers, and a haunted house. There was an underwater nightclub.

("Of course!" Nick said.) There were flowers that, when picked, had a psychedelic effect on your virtual self's view, and a tent for a fortune-teller to act as a guide for new visitors.

Nick was paying close attention to everything in the island, from the tiny to the huge. "I'm ready to build the virtual bees," Nick said. "I'm ready to build the virtual subway line." Both Nick and Justin Bovington had planned the island to a meticulous level. ("I thought I was obsessive," Nick said. "I've met my match in him.")

"I've spent days making noises in the studio, for what the jellyfish will sound like as you swim past them," Nick told me. "And the noises the cable cars will make as they go through the mountains, and when they stop." In the end, for the cable car, Nick ran a coin slowly down the length of a guitar string.

In general, Nick tried to create sounds rather than record them. For the island's virtual cars, he had tried at first to sample a real car but eventually decided the artificially generated sounds worked better: virtual sounds for a virtual world. There were things he just couldn't record. "What should a cold winter sound like?" Nick said. "I've been trying to work it out."

For fun, Nick had also recorded himself, modulated into his avatar's voice, reading a series of oddly phrased voice messages, made for the Duran area of Avalon, to enliven the virtual fax machine. "Hello: Where am I?" the voice asks when you press the "messages" button. "Who are you? Why are you talking to me? What am I doing here? I need to know the answers." "I have no idea where I am. If I did, then I would tell you." "I think I'm almost ready. I'll be there, with you, soon." "All the dreams I have ever had have all come true — here, with you, in this place."

"In a way, it's like playing God," he said. "You are creating your own world, and you can make what you like in that world."

But if virtual worlds are medicine for a broken world, sometimes people have taken too much. In the summer of 2005, in his favorite all-night games café in Kangju, near Seoul, twenty-four-year-old Kim Kyung-Jae decided to play his virtual character for as long as he could. He told his mother he was going camping with his friends, and settled in at a café. He ate noodles from a vending machine, drank complimentary cups of instant coffee, and played games. Eighty-six hours later, still inhabiting his virtual self, deep-vein thrombosis set in. A blood clot formed and moved to his heart, and Kyung-Jae died in his chair.

Was the medicine worse than the disease? Were these new virtual émigrés holding themselves back from the suffering of the world, too? Or were they plunging into a new mode of being, one that would deliver a new perspective on our plight? I decided to travel to Korea, where the mania for virtual worlds, and their capacity to generate both pleasure and pain, had reached its peak. In 2005, more people visited Korean-made virtual worlds than visited Korea. I would do both.

14

KOREA

King of the world

Until I met the king of the world, I had become convinced the trip had been a waste of time.

Our flight from London to Seoul was long. My girlfriend popped a Valium; I didn't. She slept; I didn't. On the plane, I read my guidebook. South Korea is a place of contradictions, it informed me. Koreans are proud of their country, but readily adopt other cultures (50 percent of South Koreans declare they are Christian). South Korea is a successful, affluent nation—the fourth-largest lending nation in the world—but under constant threat. I mentioned to the young Korean in the next seat that I was from London. South Korea is about the same size and population as the United Kingdom, he told me, but Seoul has the second-largest metropolitan population in the world. He took my map of Seoul and carefully described each region: the business center, City Hall, the student areas near the national universities, the rowdier area near the U.S. Army base. He smiled at me. "Seoul is a very friendly place," he said. "Also, very near North Korea. One nuclear weapon . . . Boom!" He grinned and swept his hands across the map.

At Incheon International Airport, after eighteen hours of traveling, my girlfriend and I argued. For half an hour we dragged our bags through the ranks of expensive black "luxury" cabs, shouting the whole time, to find a stand with normal-priced taxis. From the window, we watched as we crossed the reclaimed land around Incheon airport and Seoul drifted into view.

I had been expecting the bright LED towers of Tokyo or Hong Kong; Seoul looked more like Birmingham, England. There were no steel high-rises, no hectic snake-vending street markets. Thanks to the government's vision of Seoul as a "hub of Asia," even the road signs were in English as well as Korean. There were apartment buildings, rickety houses, and cars. Then more cars. Then we were stuck in traffic. The cabdriver pointed out the window and spoke in heavily accented English. In our delirium, we thought he was agreeing with us. "Shitty Hole!" he said. Our despair took on an edge of hysteria. (He meant, we later realized, City Hall.) My girlfriend had wanted to go to Hong Kong, but at the last minute I persuaded her to come to Seoul "for the experience." In the cab she gave me a look that told me I was going to have trouble keeping her happy for the whole week. Or even for the first day. I slumped lower in my seat.

On the subway we read the English-language *Seoul Times*. The South Korean government had recently decided to move the capital from Seoul to the area of Yeongi-Kongju. The new capital, scheduled to begin construction in 2007, was controversial (and in fact, after legal challenges, has yet to begin). On the subway were government-sponsored ads supporting the move, highlighting all the problems with life in Seoul. My girlfriend pointed one out, above her head. "Look," she said. "Just as we arrive, everyone else wants to leave." Seoul, it seemed, was a place where people found disappointment.

In our hotel room—which consisted of a bed—the Internet wasn't working. The room's only distinctive feature, mounted in the center of the far wall, was a short orange cord wrapped in bright emergency-red plastic and labeled "Escape Rope." We were on the seventeenth floor.

We had a remote control that worked the television but also, according to no apparent logic, the lights and other room features; one button turned off the ceiling lamp, but turned on the TV and the bathroom fan. Another turned off the fan but switched on the bedside light. In Korea, as more than one helpful vendor informed me, they didn't sell English power adapters; to get one, apparently, you had to pop over to Hong Kong. I finally lied through my teeth to get hold of just one from the Westin Chosun Seoul hotel. So each night, as if the jet lag and light show weren't enough, I had to set my alarm to wake me every two hours to charge my laptop, minidisc recorder, camera, and phone in shifts.

Halfway through my stay, the day before I visited NCsoft, and over a sorrowful, solitary "surf-'n'-turf" salad plate at an empty Sizzler—the nearest open restaurant—I chastised myself for coming at all. I should have just written about the games themselves. Or gotten another job entirely. Builder. Taxi driver. Elsewhere, at exactly the same time, my girlfriend was by the hotel pool with two English teachers from New Zealand. When she said she was in Seoul for a holiday, they choked on their drinks and told her to get out while she still could.

As my journey went on, and I made my appointments to see games professionals, it became clear that the BBC had arrived in Seoul weeks earlier, and had spoken with some of the same people. Were they scooping me? Did they ask better questions? As the days went by, it grew worse. I bought an expensive digital camera, but forgot to take photos. I forgot to call that guy back. I'm a bad person. I should have been a musician. I'm lazy compared to these lean-looking Koreans. I have no stamina. In the hotel mirror, I stared at my slack physique. I seemed to be in even worse shape here than I was back in London.

That night, back at the hotel, I flipped between channels dedicated to mysterious cartoons, shopping, and computer game tournaments. There, indecipherable armies of space tanks attacked one another and insectoid shapes scuttled and scuffled over an alien landscape; the players were surrounded by dry ice. Sports-style commentators sat behind a desk, apparently discussing timing, reactions, and tactics. At the end of each match, it seemed, the loser was nearly crying; although the winner too seemed close to tears, and it was hard to tell whether their eyes were red from emotion, or from years of staring at a video screen. Then there was the porn: channels and channels of Koreans fucking like crazy. Of course, my girlfriend and I were getting none. I was taking pills for exhaustion, given to me by a Chinese doctor in England: small balls apparently made of iron, which bruised my throat as they went down. Not long before, there had been SARS outbreaks across Asia. Was it me, or had a lot of people back at the airport been *sneezing?*

In Seoul, the line between dream and disappointment seemed paper-thin. I arranged to spend some time with a team of professional gamers, who turned out to be a group of Canadian kids sharing a cramped apartment. They played StarCraft, Korea's most popular spectator game: a futuristic military strategy contest in which two players control opposing armies of space tanks with frenetic mouse clicks and flicks of the wrist. The Canadian gamers showed me replays of famous matches, mistakes made under pressure, tactics never seen before. "More people in Korea know the rules of StarCraft than know the rules of chess," one told me, although I had no way to check.

These people lived off savings, shared bunk beds, and argued over whether they could afford takeout pizza. In Korea, it seemed, the disappointment and the dream offered by virtual worlds balanced out almost precisely.

When I finally reached the headquarters of NCsoft (makers of Lineage II), I spent almost the whole day discussing the financial end of massive online worlds. I kept trying to steer the conversation to something salacious or even surprising, but they only wanted to talk business.

I had been told in advance that the NCsoft server room was the most secure nonmilitary installation in South Korea. Every teenage hacker in the nation dreamed of penetrating their vaults. It was, I had been told, protected by guards, steel doors, and fingerprint scanners, like the Bellagio vault in *Ocean's Eleven*. The reality, I discovered, was more like *Being John Malkovich*: a hidden elevator button, an unlabeled second floor. We pulled on antistatic slippers and strolled around the server room: racks of silver boxes lit by halogen lamps and cooled by a frigid breeze. It could have been the heart of the data management strategy of any multinational business. Back in the meeting room, under the watchful eye of NCsoft's head of international public relations, one of their games masters read a prepared statement welcoming me to "the exciting world of Lineage II." We toured the call center, which looked just like a call center. I had hoped to overhear inane queries like "I've teleported myself into a tree, how do I get out?" or "This elf is stalking me . . . " but I heard just standard business issues: bounced payments, missing passwords. Everything was business-focused. I knew the stories, but the reality seemed more prosaic. I began to think that this was a dead end, a business that suckered millions into paying regular fees . . . not a shared dreamworld but a racket, a knowing illusion peddled on children by businessmen. I was still not convinced there was a story.

Then, in came Kyu Nam Choi. He plugged in his laptop and logged in, and the transformation happened in front of my eyes: The owner of a struggling hamburger restaurant became the king of the world.

When I met the king of the world, he ran a restaurant in northern Seoul. He woke up around 9 A.M., showered, pulled on sweatpants, sandals, and a T-shirt, and walked to his restaurant to open up. If you saw him on the street—a stocky, black-haired, thirty-two-year-old South Korean with a weary face, which he hid behind a wide, black fringe—you might have thought he was down on his luck. His shoulders were slumped. He looked tired. Sometimes he couldn't help but look over his shoulder. There is always someone who wants to kill a king.

No wonder he looked tired. Like any world leader, he found it hard to get enough sleep. Most days, along with his brother, he ruled his kingdom for twenty hours out of twenty-four; that was not including the time it takes to run his other business. Since he had been crowned, the restaurant had suffered. He found it hard to keep up with the paperwork. On top of running a restaurant—and ruling the world—he made ends meet with an additional range of odd jobs. He had no wife to make additional demands on his time, but even so, there were never enough hours in the day. He barely had time to manage his staff, and lately there had been fewer customers to even serve. By about ten-thirty, the restaurant was usually still empty. He walked upstairs to his office, sat down on his padded swivel chair, and became king.

There were other kings in the world of Lineage II, but he was the king of kings, and so perhaps the loneliest. The world he ruled over was home to almost three million people; still, at ten-thirty most mornings, his castle was empty. Each morning, the king usually strolled down to the gate, along the stone corridors, down the carpeted stairs of the castle's great hall, and out into the huge sloped floral courtyard. He walked down below the colossal battlements, among the royal flower gardens, and commanded the guards to open the gates, which only his royal court were allowed to enter. Flanked by guards, he stood outside the gates and gazed out over the hills. The members of his court were out there somewhere, on a hunt—for sport, for furs, for honor—or in battle with the king's enemies.

Later, he would join them. For now, though, he had to go downstairs, fire up the oven, light the grill, and serve breakfast.

His subjects knew Kyu Nam Choi as Archirus. His kingdom, Lineage II, was thousands of square miles of mountains, desert, forest, and sea. To walk across the virtual subcontinent would take days. When I met him, Archirus's kingdom, with its three million inhabitants, was the most popular virtual world on the planet, more densely populated than Brazil. All of the residents, like Kyu, led other lives: They were bankers, students, cabdrivers, housekeepers, hairdressers, and businessmen. All of them paid around fifteen dollars per month to enter a fantasy-themed virtual world where hunting parties gathered to stalk monsters (from lowly wolves to near-invincible dragons). The more monsters they killed, the more powerful they became. And, as the most powerful inhabitant of this realm—the king of kings—Kyu ruled over them all. He had the power to change laws, to raise taxes, to end their lives. When he walked by, they cheered. When he taxed them, they suffered. When he died—in the virtual world, not the real—they mourned.

South Korea is the country where mania for virtual worlds is at its most extreme. In part because of a mid-1990s government drive, South Korea is per capita the most Internet-connected nation on earth. (When I visited, in late 2004, 60 percent of households had broadband, compared with just 33 percent in the United States.)

In Korea, professional gamers can earn the equivalent of six-figure salaries, have three TV channels dedicated to them, and be recognized by screaming fans on the street. Pop songs are written about on-line games. Almost all of Kyu's three million subjects are Korean and, of the 25–30 million people worldwide who then played these games, a third were Korean and nearly half—around 12 million—played Korean-made games. Each year, more than twice as many people around the world visit Korean-made virtual worlds as visit Korea. A week before my visit, the Chinese government—which had recently banned foreign animation from prime-time TV—announced that Chinese companies should develop similar games, since too many Chinese people were spending their time in Korean-made virtual worlds, and too much virtual world profit ($117.4 million in 2005) was leaking from China to Korea. To correct the balance, the Chinese government pledged $1.8 billion over the next five years to develop one hundred "domestically devout" virtual worlds, such as the forthcoming "Chinese Heroes," based on a Mao Zedong–era model soldier. According to the South Korean Culture Ministry's Game Development Institute, online games revenue in Korea was worth $1.5 billion in 2005.

Before my trip, I had read up on the craze. Apparently, gaming café owners had been convicted for putting amphetamines in the watercoolers to keep kids playing their games. Runaways had reportedly supported themselves entirely through in-game fraud. In Asia, the scale of the phenomenon meant the retreat from life and body had reached its peak—to the point where some end up leaving their body entirely. (The same month Kim Kyung-Jae died in his game café chair, twenty-eight-year-old boiler repairman Lee Seung Seop also died, from cardiac arrest, after fifty hours inside World of Warcraft. During 2005, in total, ten South Koreans died in similar ways.)

Although Kyu was a player, not an employee of NCsoft, South Korea's most successful game developer (corporate motto: "Create the Next Culture. Build the Next Game. Imagine the Next Life."), the king and I met on the eighth floor of their Seoul office building. In a meeting room, Kyu—particularly weary from a long battle to recapture his castle the night before—brushed his fringe from his eyes, leaned back, sipped plum juice, and explained the double bind of his double life.

In the real world, on a good week, Kyu's restaurant served two hundred customers; online, he was the ruler of three million subjects. In the real world, he had trouble paying his bills; online, he could raise taxes. Still, this was not always a trouble-free source of funds. When taxes rose too high, his people revolted. Each Monday morning, on the eighth floor of NCsoft's real-world offices, the Lineage II team met to monitor inflation rates. If Kyu was a king, these people were gods, even if they often felt more like tax inspectors. To keep the economy in balance and stop in-game fraud, they audited the books of anyone who had acquired a suspiciously large amount of money or property.

Kyu sighed. Last night, he told me—with something of the calm self-deprecation of a movie star—had been the climactic battle of four months of struggle against a coup attempt. His most loyal subjects were a core of around a thousand people who effectively made up his government. They formed a chain of command, filtering the problems of his subjects up through the ranks. His court, his most loyal subjects, doubled as his defense force in case anyone tried to take the throne. They were so strong, he said, that no other group in the game had the power to conquer them in battle. They began to take for granted that the Castle of the Kings would remain theirs. Then, two weeks ago, his enemies had banded together to form a great temporary alliance, an axis of virtual evil. In a colossal battle, his cohorts were beaten—thousands were killed—and his enemies captured the throne. Many of his court took the defeat personally. Hundreds left his service. He went from an entourage of a thousand to fewer than four hundred dedicated followers. Then, last night, he said, he and his subjects returned to lay siege to the castle. They conjured two huge stone golems to break down the doors, and fought their way up the sloped garden, under a hail of arrows from archers lined along the battlements. They fought up the stone staircase of the main hall, along the corridors, into the throne room, where they reclaimed the seal of the king.

I asked him why his subjects had been so disappointed to be beaten. He explained it was because many of them died. Although in all virtual worlds, including Lineage II, if your character dies you are simply reborn, with all the same powers, in a safe place, many of Kyu's subjects took virtual death personally. "Many gamers think the character is another me. So in fact when my character dies, I feel so sad. If somebody kills me, I feel like revenging the killer. It happens a lot."

As the most powerful Lineage II character, Kyu was even at risk of real-world violence. Inside the virtual world, Kyu could defend himself. His fighting skills were appropriate for an all-powerful warrior king: Alone, using his bare hands, he could kill ten players at a time. In the real world, those ratios didn't apply. When I asked if I could visit his restaurant to take photos, Kyu smiled sadly and shook his head. "There are unpleasant people in the game," he said. "Like any king, I have supporters and opponents. I can't risk my face being disclosed in case someone from the game used the photos to find me in real life."

Instead, he logged on and showed me around his castle. On the screen, in a flash of blue light next to his throne, his character appeared: a silver hunter, with a curved sword, edged with jagged swirls, taller than him.

It was 9 A.M. and, at this early hour after such a huge battle, his subjects were likely still asleep. The throne room was empty, except for his trusted royal secretary, Logan, who, he explained, always attended him. Logan, a creature of habit, greeted him with "How are you, my highness? How may I help you?" Most mornings, the king explained, he handled his chores first. He asked Logan to check that the castle gate was secure, and that no one had made an assault on the walls overnight. He then asked after the castle safe-deposit box, the store of weapons, gold reserves, and general state of repair.

The upkeep of a castle was expensive. As king of kings, Archirus's assets—and bills—extended right across the world. Some mornings, when the defenses were depleted or the coffers low, he asked Logan to increase taxation rates. Logan put the word out, and across the whole kingdom, the tens or hundreds of thousands who bought or sold anything at all that day would pay a little extra into the pockets of the king.

Sometimes, when taxes approached 15 percent, Kyu explained, citizens marched on the castle to protest outside the gates. But the king always made a point of going out on the battlements to explain the pressures he was under. They never understood. Only the king knows the true responsibility of being a king.

I asked Kyu whether he was tempted to cash in on his success. No one has ever sold a character as powerful as his. With the deed to his castle, with the account of the highest player in the game, with all his royal cash reserves, there would be millions of potential bidders. He could earn tens of thousands of dollars. When I asked him if he had ever considered making real-world money from the game, though, he looked hurt. No, he said, he never considered it. It would be dishonorable. His supporters had helped him attain his money, items, and power. If he sold them, it would be a betrayal of their trust.

Kyu's virtual reign gave him real power: If he asked his followers to vote a certain way in real-world government elections, he said, they would. In fact, Kyu compared his network of thousands of supporters—his royal court—with a political party. Much of his time as king was spent preparing his castle against attack, solving problems, and mediating disputes between his subjects. Not just anyone could walk up to the king and petition for his help; the requests were passed up through his commanders. And enough problems filtered up to keep him more than busy. For example, on hearing that Kyu was visiting NCsoft that morning, one of his subjects, a level 75 player, asked Kyu to see if he could persuade NCsoft to give him a virtual gift for his upcoming virtual wedding.

Kyu admitted the pressure was becoming too much. The more time he spent as king, the more his restaurant suffered; the more his restaurant suffered, the more he wanted to spend time as king. Until he discovered Lineage II, his whole life had been the single-minded pursuit of success. He worked in restaurants, then managed them, then ran whole chains. His life, he told me, was nothing but work. He was successful, he made money, but he trusted no one. The people he met at work were usually looking to use him in some way. He had never had a close friend.

Then one afternoon, with two hours to kill after a canceled appointment, he wandered into a branch of PC Bang, a twenty-four-hour Internet café dedicated to online gaming, and saw rows of people playing Lineage. He played it, and liked it. That night he bought his own copy of the game and installed it on his office PC. He was one of the earliest players, and he played for the most time, with enough skill, to become the first to make it as the king of kings. As his online life developed, he began to find the friendship he had missed all his life. Now he was making up for lost time. Kyu told me he had never had a girlfriend, but he hoped one day to meet someone online, get married, and settle down. Until then, despite his struggling business, he wouldn't give up Lineage II for the world. He had tried every other pastime he could think of, but nothing helped him forget about his problems—the restaurant, being alone—as much as playing the game. Nothing else, Kyu said, gave him the same feeling of belonging.

Now, though, because of his second life, his first one was suffering. If it weren't for his subjects, he said, he would have to quit. But he felt he couldn't; they depended on him.

He depended on them, too. "People feel happiness and satisfaction through online communication, especially those who feel loneliness in real life," Kyu told me. In the games, he said, people talked to him. In the streets of Seoul, nobody even said hello. It was funny, though, he said, of meeting his online friends in the real world. Sometimes the most talkative characters turned out to be the most reticent. "Some gamers are really shy in real life," he explained. Even so, Kyu trusted the people he met through Lineage more than those he met through work. The people he met through the game were interested in him as a person. "We meet," he said, "with no conspiracy."

This virtual community is real enough—and it has been known to save lives. In 2004, not long before my visit, the friend of one Lineage II player began to hemorrhage while giving birth. Her blood type, O negative, was shared by only one in two hundred Koreans. The player logged on and advertised his friend's plight and, within the hour, an O negative Lineage player showed up at the hospital. Mother and baby survived.

The sense of community provided by virtual worlds seems to resonate with a particularly Korean need to keep in touch. When I visited, communications technology was everywhere. On underground trains, people chatted on cellphones, and at Korean convenience stores—LG25 and LINKO ("A place for buying fun")—you could drop off your phone battery and pick it up forty minutes later, fully charged. As my translator explained, many Koreans thought "cyber-electioneering"—website chat room, text message, and e-mail campaigning—had swung the 2002 election in favor of the now-ruling liberal party. "In war, families were separated," my translator told me. "Now Koreans like to be in contact."

But the sense of community in virtual worlds had a downside, too. Gamers came to rely on the game to provide companionship, and the Korean government had begun to recognize the addictive effect of this powerful pull on Korean youth. In 2004, a law was passed limiting online gaming to those over eighteen, and the game companies now (reluctantly) enforce the law by linking online accounts to government ID numbers. Still, the kids find ways around the ban.

In 2002, the South Korean government established the Internet Addiction Counseling Center, whose staff visit schools to measure Internet addiction and offer advice and education for those who feel they are indeed addicts. I decided to visit. Outside, as I left the taxi, the driver asked me for the center's telephone number, and asked which floor the addiction center was on. He told me about his son, a high school student who never left his room. He used the Internet every day, from 10 A.M. to midnight, the driver said, mostly in chat rooms and inside Lineage II. His son wasn't alone. According to Lee Sujin, a clinical psychologist who greeted me at the addiction center, more than two-thirds of South Korean teenagers play online games. Over a quarter think of themselves as Internet-addicted.

Lee Sujin told me about a recent visit to a psychological conference on the subject, where her international colleagues viewed the Internet addiction problem in terms of chat rooms or online gambling (in the United States, the Center for Online Addiction, founded in 1995, lists chat room and cyber-sex compulsion as the top addictions). In South Korea, Lee said, the main problem is online gaming. I suggested that, besides distracting kids from the world, these games also provide a sense of community they lack in the real world. She agreed but pointed out that at the addiction center they see only the ill effects: depression, nervousness, absence from schools, and cyber-crime — the theft of game accounts, for example. In South Korea in 2004, there were approximately 64,000 cyber-crimes, about half related to online gaming. There were nearly 10,000 arrests, resulting in some 5,000 convictions. (For comparison, the number of equivalent arrests in the United States in the same year was precisely none.) Most young Koreans who commit cyber-crimes are sent to the Internet Addiction Counseling Center rather than to prison. The center puts offenders through a reeducation program, then gives them community work, for example, renovating old computers for charity. They try to instill self-respect in the children, Lee Sujin told me, and to help them develop self-confidence in the real world. "It's not easy," she said. "It's so much easier to achieve things in the game. When these kids face problems in the real world, they give up."

I asked Kyu Nam Choi what kept him playing, even as his business slid toward bankruptcy. Was he addicted? He shook his head. It was the endless possibilities that most attracted him to live in a virtual world. "It's not addiction. It's a way to live a different life," he said. "Real life doesn't often live up to our expectations, but in the game, anything can happen. I have killed, I have been killed, I have been reborn. In real life, I don't own a car, but in the game, I can fly."

Kyu turned to the laptop. Fingers rattled over the keyboard. On the screen, in his castle, his character began to yelp in strange magical tongues. Green and blue flames rose up to fill the throne room as the king of the world levitated into the air. NCsoft's head of international public relation gasped in what sounded like genuine admiration. "Fabulous. I can't do that with my character," she said.

Kyu logged off. As he unplugged his laptop and prepared to return to his hamburger restaurant, I asked him one last question. In order to play the game, you have to live in the real world. But what if that weren't the case? If he could liberate himself from all the computer hardware, and become just one person, Kyu or Archirus, the real or the virtual, which life would he choose?

He leaned back, folded his hands behind his head, and closed his eyes. "In real life, even though I own my business, I am just an ordinary person. In the game life, I rule the world. Which would you choose?"

After Kyu Nam Choi and his NCsoft escort left the room, I asked my translator what she thought of him. Her eyes were bright. "He's amazing," she said, almost breathless. "He had the feeling of a real master. Didn't you see his hands? They were artist's hands."

Although Kyu has never had a girlfriend, it's not necessarily for the same reasons that a thirty-two-year-old computer-obsessive from the United States might be single. Rather than being dismissed as nerds, in South Korea successful players become stars. In his book, *Game: The Revolutionary Power to Change the World*, the Korean critic Park Sang Woo argued that the difference between Korean and Western residents of virtual worlds is that Koreans identify much more with their virtual selves.

In a Starbucks in the huge underground warren of COEX Mall, Asia's largest shopping mall, I met Park Sang Woo to talk about Lineage II. Park turned out to be a young man with a meticulous beard and an intense stare. When I arrived, his nose was deep in a Japanese book on postmodernism. In online worlds such as Lineage, players can kill one another. "In the West, death means nothing; you are instantly reborn," Park told me. "In Korea, players feel the death of their online player keenly. There is honor and reputation at stake.

"In other countries, alter egos are necessary for online games. The focus is on building 'another me,' which is different to the 'me' in real life. But in Korea, the real life and the game life are very much connected. The higher level our characters are, and the more splendid items we can get, the more praise we receive. In Korean society, people like to be noticed."

I kept hearing this phrase: Koreans like to be noticed. In a country where the family name comes before the given one, and the middle floors of apartment buildings are the most desirable—because you are surrounded by the most people—every young person seems to want to stand out from the crowd, despite the strong traditional Confucian pressures to conform that make it very difficult to leave the pack. Online gaming has become a way for young South Koreans to remain conservative in their lives, but also stand out among their peers. (Megapass, South Korea's ultrabroadband Internet service, advertises with the English slogan "I'm the champion, 100 percent different.") One of the games masters of Lineage II told me she started playing the game because in the street, she wasn't supposed to laugh. In the game, she could laugh wherever she liked.

Because virtual worlds have penetrated Southeast Asian culture so thoroughly, the attendant crime has also reached a peak there. Two days after I arrived in Seoul, I read a newspaper report about two policemen who attempted to arrest a suspected rapist, Hyuong Kim, and were stabbed to death, allegedly by Kim. Kim became Seoul's public enemy number one. Police distributed a thousand leaflets with his name, photo, and citizen ID. Two days later they received a tip. Kim was accessing an online game from the Samsung apartment block in northern Seoul. Police barricaded the building and searched every apartment, scouring even the insides of washing machines. They found nothing—even though their computers showed Kim as still logged on. The next day, police discovered the culprit: a fourteen-year-old boy had seen Kim's ID number on the wanted posters, and used it to access an over-eighteen gaming site. Word spread. Soon, Hyuong Kim was logging on to play Lineage II from all over the city.

In South Korea, this kind of identity theft is widespread. An estimated 30 percent of South Korea's ID cards are fraudulent; in June 2006, the ID numbers of President Roh Moo Hyun and Prime Minister Han Myeong Sook appeared on the Internet. The IDs were used to gain access to online games and hundreds of pornographic websites. In another case, in July 2006, South Korea's National Police Agency began investigating ten people, including a garage mechanic and an employee at a credit report company, both of whom had access to databases of private information, for their role in the sale of private ID numbers. The owners of seven gaming cafés allegedly bought the information and set up 280,000 virtual world accounts. They hired part-time gamers to work inside worlds such as Lineage II to earn virtual currency, which they sold for real money on Korean websites such as itemBay for an estimated 14.2 billion won ($15 million). The Cyber Crimes Police also investigated a senior NCsoft executive who allegedly knew about the false IDs, but—worried his company's revenues would go down (each of those 280,000 accounts paid a subscription fee)—kept quiet.

NCsoft, however, is on the lookout for such crime. They have 150 employees monitoring for "bots"—automated characters designed to make virtual money without anyone having to sit at the actual keyboard. But the odds are not in their favor. When I visited, NCsoft spent $10 million a year on cyber-security, less than the $15 million made by one virtual crime ring alone. South Korean police said they were investigating an additional 900,000 fraudulent accounts, which they believed were linked to operations in China making similar profits. (Of these accounts, 120,000 were later closed.) In 2004, NCsoft accidentally leaked the account details of over 8,500 Lineage II customers (the company failed to encrypt a single log file that contained the customers' IDs and passwords). NCsoft was ordered to pay each affected customer half a million won (about five hundred dollars) in compensation.

I met Inspector Kim Gi Bum, of the Cyber-Terror Unit, in his Seoul headquarters. Kim, his ranks pinned on a black ribbon to his shirt pocket, led me to his desk. With a serious, bespectacled frown, he explained how his department had been established to handle criminal hacking attempts, in many cases North Korean attempts to disrupt South Korean business and government. Not long after, a Seoul politician had decided the unit's responsibilities should include virtual crimes. Now over half their workload was related to on-line games.

When I visited, Korean law did not yet recognize virtual items as assets with legal value. (Nor does it still, although a number of attempts have been made to pass laws that would change this fact.) So, if you sold someone a virtual item but you didn't get paid, no crime would have been committed. You could bring a civil suit, but the game company would probably close your account before restitution could be made. If the tables were turned—if you paid someone and they didn't cough up the item—a crime would have occurred, and the seller who didn't deliver would be convicted of fraud. Another common crime, the inspector explained, was hacking, where one user obtained access to another user's account and cleaned out his or her items. These cases were covered by existing Korean laws against identity theft; the crime was punishable by up to three years in prison, but it still took a civil suit to get back your virtual sword. As Kim and I spoke, the matter of whether virtual items should have legal value was being debated by the South Korean parliament. The inspector told me that he and his colleagues hoped value wouldn't be determined by law. In one stroke, their games-related workload would double. Also, such a ruling would criminalize all Korean online gambling sites, which were currently only valid for cyber-cash—gambling for real money was illegal. Every one of the millions of virtual gamblers would become outlaws.

Inspector Bum confirmed the rumors I had heard that Seoul cyber-café owners had been convicted of spiking watercoolers with amphetamines to give their customers more energy to inhabit their virtual selves. He talked me through some other recent cyber-police cases. In one, a fourteen-year-old runaway they recently arrested had slept in a gaming café for an entire year. During that time he had made 128 fraudulent deals, where he promised items in return for money, but never delivered—for a profit of over $10,000. In another case, a girl met in the flesh a friend she had made through Lineage II; she felt she knew him but, when they met, he raped her and forced her into prostitution. Inspector Kim told me that other common cyber-crimes included violence against the families of games players, and hacking attempts to steal passwords and items—as well as many of the offline attacks Kyu feared.

After meeting with Park Sang Woo, my translator led me through the depths of the twenty-four-hour COEX Mall. South Korea has rebounded from the financial hardships of the mid-1990s to become a creditor nation. Around us, the coffee-and-sugar-fueled, Gap-clothed business of modern capitalism seemed to be churning healthily on. Having shed their military dictatorship less than two decades before, squeezed between the two often hostile nations of North Korea and Japan ("As a peninsula, we feel like an island," my translator told me), Korea came to modernization late, and in a hurry. The Korean people seemed aimed like a rocket for the dream of capitalism: the primacy of the self. My translator wore Chanel shades, and her self-confessed role model was Audrey Hepburn. Nicolas Cage was marrying a Korean woman he met while she was working as a waitress, my translator told me. "See? It could happen to me."

She led me near the center of COEX to the largest games and Internet café (known in Korea as a "PC Bang") that she knew. The proprietor gave us each a card, good for an hour's play, and we typed our numbers into two adjacent PCs. Around us in rows sat hundreds of young men, their bright eyes gazing through computer screens into their virtual worlds. In that moment, fazed as I was by jet lag, caffeine, and crowds, they seemed not addicted but calm, a cool eye at the center of COEX Mall's hurricane of consumer abandon. I watched their fingers skitter across keyboards. I admired their skill. I wondered whether they were perhaps not escapees but misunderstood pioneers, determined to communicate with like-minded but distant souls, to share their visions of another kind of place.

Carl Jung called alcoholism a low-level search for God. Virtual worlds, even for those addicted to them, seemed like a low-level search for one another.

With my translator's help, I decided to log on and try Lineage II. I did my best to make my character, a wizard, look like me, but ended up with a pointy-eared, silver-skinned elf. It would do. Like everyone else, I was born fully clothed, in a windy castle with a stone-clad inner sanctum, where four wizards taught me how to move around and cast spells. Soon, bored of wizard school, I wandered out of the castle and down to the local village, to take my place among thirty-odd players seated in loose groups around the village well. With my translator's help, I struck up a conversation with another wizard who, he explained, had recently proposed inside Lineage II to his real-world girlfriend.

After half an hour watching me watch the players watch their PC screens, my translator made her polite goodbyes. With nowhere else to go, I stayed. The conversation inside Lineage II was in Korean — still, I waved, and they waved back. I wandered outside the village, cast a few spells, killed some wolves, delivered some letters for other players. For a while I sat by the edge of the sea, under a waterfall. When I looked up from my screen, four hours had passed. It was 2 A.M. I blinked. Around me, lit by the glow from the monitor screens, were all the same faces. Now, at this early hour, their virtual adventures took on a darker edge. The landscape seemed to be a territory of nostalgia, not optimism. Like fantasy fiction, the game seemed to declare a longing to regress. Still, I could feel the appeal of the delusion. The point of life is rarely certain; in the game, your goals are always clear. In life, we risk everything; in the games, we risk nothing at all.

I thought about what Kyu Nam Choi had said: Real life doesn't often live up to our expectations, but in the game, anything can happen.

The power of this alchemical transformation, of awkward life transmuting into a coherent and plausible dream, has brought virtual worlds into the heart of modern Korean culture. In 2002, a Seoul primary school burned down with the children inside. In response, a charity was formed. It commissioned a virtual world as a memorial. Grieving parents could wander in a small, peaceful city in memory of their kids. It was a tiny and particular heaven, devoid of crowds, traffic, and loss.

The mania for virtual worlds began in South Korea, but soon spread across Southeast Asia. In Thailand in 2004, a surge in subscriptions to another fantasy world, Ragnarok Online—then that country's second largest virtual universe, with well over 2 million subscribers—led the Thai government to implement a temporary Internet café curfew. The same virtual world boasts some 1.5 million residents in the Philippines alone. In June 2005, World of Warcraft opened in China. Timed with the launch, the game was featured in a TV commercial for Coca-Cola. Within a month, that virtual world had 1.5 million Chinese residents—then almost half of the total World of Warcraft population. That month, the first Chinese Internet addiction clinic opened, and a month later the Chinese government introduced an "anti–online game addiction system" to protect virtual residents against mental and physical harm. Every local Internet company now has to agree to limit their customers' time inside virtual worlds: After three hours of consecutive play, a resident begins to lose virtual experience; if they play for five hours straight, their virtual self is reset. They would have to wait five hours before they could continue. (A year later, one in seven Chinese gamers admitted to opening extra accounts to get around the limits.) Even with the limitations, the Chinese government estimates that 24 million Chinese people log on to virtual worlds—as many as the rest of the world combined. If you include more basic, Web-based online worlds, these numbers expand hugely. One such world, Westward Journey Online II, based on a famous Chinese novel, claims 83 million registered residents.

The inevitable crime had also begun to spread across Asia. In September 2005, a Chinese exchange student living in Kagawa prefecture, southern Japan, designed and programmed an automated virtual character, a criminal virtual robot, that logged on to Lineage II and played for him. His robot self automatically attacked and robbed passersby for the priciest of their virtual possessions—rare items such as the Earring of Wisdom or the Shield of Nightmare, which conferred special virtual abilities on their owners. The student then sold them on a Japanese auction site for real yen. He was arrested by the Japanese police, though no virtual charges were brought against the virtual robot.

In November 2006, a twenty-three-year-old Chinese student was arrested in Japan for selling virtual weapons and currency online, earning real-world income in contravention of his student visa. (Police estimated his earnings at 150 million yen—about $1.3 million.)

In China, one player in the virtual world Dahua Xiyou II (inspired by a traditional fairy tale) managed to obtain a temporary job at the game's developer, NetEase. By faxing forged ID cards and resetting passwords, he obtained control of over thirty accounts, which he plundered for items and gold in exchange for real money—a total of around 4,000 yuan ($510). Yan Yifan, of Guangdong in southern China, was caught and convicted. He appealed by arguing the items weren't real and therefore weren't covered by law. In March 2006, the court found that the players from whom he stole virtual items had invested time, energy, and money to gain them, and that Yan Yifan had profited in real terms, and therefore the virtual items did deserve legal protection. They upheld his fine of 5,000 yuan (about $640). In another case, two ex-employees of Shanda, the company that developed Legend of Mir II, were tried for copying and selling virtual items for a profit of 2 million yuan ($250,000).

In Asia, as I had discovered, the consequences of virtual crime weren't always financial. In February 2005, Qiu Chengwei, a forty-one-year-old man from Shanghai, lent his twenty-six-year-old friend Zhu Caoyuan a hard-won virtual sword, a dragon saber from the online fantasy game Legend of Mir III, in which hundreds of thousands of Chinese players gather to fight monsters and earn virtual booty. Instead of returning the sword, Zhu sold it on to another player for

7,200 yuan—about $900. Qiu Chengwei approached the police, but because the sword existed only inside the game, no law had been broken. So one morning a month later, in the real world, Qiu broke into Zhu's house. Zhu barely had time to put on his underwear before Qiu stabbed him to death.

When questioned by police, Qiu Chengwei confessed, and in June 2005 he was sentenced to death. The sentence was suspended, and Qiu will now spend at least fifteen years behind bars.

But the tales of virtual mania tempting Southeast Asians into crime are only part of the story. In other ways, the facility of virtual worlds to connect us has also started to take root. I read reports of Chinese dissidents who had begun to congregate in far-flung corners of the Chinese World of Warcraft. There, among the more remote digital hills, where their conversations would be difficult for their government to monitor, gnomes, dwarves, and elves had begun to gather to discuss democracy. It took the Chinese government two years to catch on, but in December 2006 it announced it would be monitoring virtual worlds more closely, after it discovered some worlds were carrying "antigovernment messages."

On our last night in Seoul, to make up for the disappointment of the trip, I decided my girlfriend needed a treat. My translator told me that Seoul's five-star Park Hyatt hotel was running a half-price deal for local residents; to make sure we got the discount, she called to make the booking for me.

In the lobby, a grand cube of gold and indigo, a jazz singer sang "Let's Stay Alive," "Brighter Days," and "Breaking Up Is Hard to Do." At the check-in desk, though, they weren't happy with our reservation. They didn't believe we lived in Seoul, and it took half an hour to persuade them to give us the half-price rate. From then on, I was convinced, they tried their best to hustle back the difference. The staff served us snootily. The music was too loud. A small bottle of Perrier cost eight dollars. On the next table, a spoiled British family nagged at one other incessantly. The place felt tacky, hassly, and over-rich. I thought about logging on to play Lineage II, but Internet access—free in every other hotel—cost a dollar per minute.

In life, Chinese sage Chuang Tzu wrote, we each have our hearts broken seven times. The Talmud said it differently: "God is not nice. God is no uncle. He is an earthquake." Virtual worlds, because they are a part of the real, must teach us that, too. I found it out again, in a city thousands of miles from home.

Life was hard, even at the Hyatt.

15

CONCLUSION

Back to life

When I began my journey, the media were largely ignoring virtual worlds. But as Second Life, World of Warcraft, and all the others took up more of the global conversation, the media started to pay attention. In October 2002, when I first set foot in EverQuest, the virtual world was featured on *Icons*, a gaming show on the cable channel G4—reported to be the least viewed cable channel in America. By October 2006, another virtual world, World of Warcraft, was the theme of an entire episode of a more popular TV show: the cartoon comedy *South Park*. The episode, called "Make Love Not Warcraft," was watched by 3.5 million viewers. Inspired by cartoonist Trey Parker's observation that half his staff were World of Warcraft addicts, it featured the series' cartoon cast becoming addicted to—and conquering—that virtual world. The *South Park* trio of Stan, Kyle, and Cartman wandered among the world's huge population, which by that month had reached seven million: twice their own viewership. ("I bet half these people are Korean," Cartman says.) The addiction spread throughout the fictional town. Even Kyle's normally strait-laced dad succumbed.

Throughout 2006, a wave of press rose about virtual worlds, particularly Second Life. *BusinessWeek* reported on Anshe Chung; *The Wall Street Journal* reported on the Tringo game's move to mobile phones. Driven partly by this wave of press, which focused on the money to be made inside virtual worlds (consumption, after all, was a metaphor our society could easily grasp), interested parties of all kinds—journalists, venture capitalists, documentary makers, and multinational entertainment corporations—rushed to dip their toes into the new virtual waters. The charities Fight Hunger and Comic Relief both planned to hold events in Second Life to raise funds and awareness of their causes. Another charity, the World Development Movement, had built a house-sized billboard counting preventable child deaths since Second Life had opened, under the slogan, "Don't forget the real world." Harvard, the University of Texas, and the University of California at Berkeley had constructed virtual lecture halls. In World of Warcraft, academics had begun to attend symposia: Whole gangs of trolls and night elves gathered in virtual wooden shacks to split hairs. In October 2006, Endemol, the production company behind the reality TV show *Big Brother*, announced they planned to film a version of *Big Brother* inside Second Life. In the virtual version, as with the real show, residents would be forced to remain inside the confines of the *Big Brother* house and face a weekly popular vote for eviction.

Across the board, the stakes were rising. As of October 2006, at IGE.com you could still buy desirable accounts on EverQuest for over $2,000. (That much would buy you a level 75 Necromancer, "from the original owner!") Economists revised their revenue projections: In 2006, virtual worlds were set to earn their creators over $5.2 billion. When I visited Linden Lab in March 2005, around 20 people made over $20,000 a year from their virtual lives; by September 2006 there were around 500. But those making money were in the minority. That same month, just 10,267 Second Life residents made a virtual profit at all, and the majority of those earned less than $10 a month. Still, the promise of a virtual fortune—what looked to be easy money—continued to captivate new residents. The Second Life annual GDP was now $64 million, and everybody wanted a piece.

In August 2003, to protest in-world taxation, a group of Second Life residents had marched in-world, built replica tea crates, and set themselves on fire. Next time, they might have to march on the real Capitol Hill: In October 2006, a congressional committee began to investigate how virtual assets should be taxed. This was perhaps the first step to removing one of the main reasons to emigrate from the real into the virtual in the first place.

Former Virginia governor Mark Warner, once rumored to be considering a run for the Democratic nomination for president in 2008, appeared for a talk inside Second Life. (He later announced he wouldn't run.) As big business saw it, technology, communication, and profit were already merging into one. The newspaper finance pages were full of digital distractions: Sony's new PlayStation 3, Nintendo Wii, Microsoft's iPod-competing Zune music player. For years advertisers had taught us to seek comfort in machines, and now entertainment machines, designed to replace the real world with something more comforting, had become corporate battlegrounds on which money and power competed both for our cash and for our desires. I heard rumors that IBM was considering buying Linden Lab. British newspapers like the *Guardian* published Second Life stories at the rate of sometimes two a day, and a *Guardian* technology editor, Vic Keegan (he had edited some of my own early journalism) published his new poetry collection, *Big Bang*, exclusively inside Second Life.

As I drew to the end of my journey into virtual worlds, the worlds themselves were picking up the pace. When I visited Linden Lab in March 2005, Second Life had 700 servers and 25,000 residents; in January 2006, it welcomed its 100,000th resident. When I first met Philip Rosedale, he had told me, "I don't know why we don't have a million residents in Second Life." Then, on October 18, 2006, at 8:05:45 A.M.—around the same time the population of the United

States reached 300 million—the millionth resident entered Second Life. That was a tenfold increase since January—and the same day another 30,000 signed up. In a celebratory e-mail, Linden Lab apologized for how crowded their Orientation Island had become. Within a week, another 100,000 had joined, and two weeks later, there were 1.2 million Second Life residents, twice the population of Boston. Along with the huge numbers, there was renewed discussion of what those numbers meant. Less than half of all residents had logged in to Second Life in the last two months, and Rosedale admitted to me that as few as 10 percent of first-time Second Life residents stayed to build a virtual life. There weren't a million real-world people playing Second Life regularly, but the world was unarguably growing. There were now 2,006 privately owned islands, and 52,463 acres of rented virtual land; in total, the Second Life soil was now three times the size of Manhattan. In late November, Anshe Chung Studios issued a press release: Anshe's Second Life property and virtual cash holdings, not including her company's real-world assets—which she had parlayed from a $10 Second Life account—now had a total worth in excess of $1 million. Anshe was the first virtual millionaire.

Anshe called a virtual press conference. The venue had been built by the Anshe Chung Studios team in Wuhan, in the style of a traditional Chinese palace: silk partition screens, bamboo-print silk lampshades, a faded pink-and-yellow-flowered rug, and virtual white china cups placed hospitably by every chair. At a long desk on the stage, complete with theatrical microphones, sat Anshe and her husband, Guni, a pointy-eared elfin man with flowing brown hair.

Before Anshe spoke, I turned my head to look at the crowd. There were many faces I recognized: the Second Life Herald owner Urizenus Sklar—who in real life, I knew, was Peter Ludlow, professor of philosophy and linguistics at the University of Michigan, the man who had first exposed underage escort Evangeline's exploits in The

Sims Online. Also there, in a smart brown suit, was Adam Reuters, who mimed scribbling in a virtual notebook throughout. There were a handful of residents wearing identical default clothes and faces: reporters who had joined Second Life that day, simply to attend the conference. Catherine Smith was there, too, as her virtual self, Catherine Linden, with a bright red bob and tortoiseshell glasses. Also in attendance, it seemed, was Wonder Woman, and for a while a humanized fox danced in the aisle.

Not long before, Anshe told us, she had plowed back a large portion of her virtual profits to extend her empire. "Before November 15th I used profits from this business and made one big investment of $250,000 U.S. to expand Dreamland, our largest residential project. I think this might have been the largest investment in virtual real estate," Anshe said. The million figure, she told us, "is the net value of me, Anshe Chung, as a resident of one virtual world. It is all assets that are inside Second Life. It is not money that my creator, Ailin, has put on her bank account." (Throughout the conference, Anshe referred to Ailin as "my creator," and in fact she requested those present focus their reporting on Anshe, the virtual self, rather than Ailin Graef, the real person.) Anshe thought she had probably made more than a million dollars worth of virtual assets much earlier in the year, but she announced it now as her virtual land assets alone, which, at that day's market prices, were worth over $1 million. "I predict that in 12 months there will be at least 10, probably more, real-life millionaires in Second Life," she said.

In a previous interview, Anshe had said her move to China had been a relief; she could work with a government that better understood the virtual economy. I asked her to elaborate. "The situation is simple: In China there is a *huge* industry of companies that work in virtual worlds," she said, "usually game worlds. This of course makes the administration take this much more seriously and have developed special laws and procedures. In Germany the administration is not used to this. They just treat you as whatever they classify you as. Basically, not being alone when it come to virtual profits helps." Anshe paid real-world taxes on any virtual earnings she took out of Second Life, and she wasn't averse to in-world taxation, either.

But Anshe's rise hadn't been entirely smooth. "The hardest part was that when I started to become successful, I met an established elite of business people who were here longer," she said. "This created some friction."

Despite the in-rush of corporate power into Second Life, Anshe believed there was room for new virtual entrepreneurs. "There is still much opportunity for people who are innovative and creative," she said. "The nature of virtual economy is that it is hard to maintain margin when you do something that everybody does. You compete on the global level. But when you are innovative you have even more opportunity than in the real world."

Like Linden Lab, Anshe hoped self-governance would emerge in virtual words. She even believed those governments could act as examples for real-world countries. "Ideologies could be tested in virtual worlds," she said. "Some might fail, some might work. I think it depends on the people who participate."

As the conference went on, people left their PCs, either out of boredom or from the more mundane demands of the physical world. To indicate this, various avatars slumped forward as if asleep. It reminded me of my own posture at the occasional real press conference.

Prompted by this reminder of the real world, I asked Anshe if she thought the exodus into virtual ones reflected some rising difficulty — loneliness, dissatisfaction with the body, financial struggle. "Errol, imperfection in the real world always has existed," she said. "This is why people kept working hard to change the real world or to create things like literature or movies. I see virtual reality as one very powerful tool to enable people [to] do things that they could never do in real life."

Anshe thought the exodus into virtual worlds might eventually attain legal status. People could be citizens of one virtual reality country and only tourists or visitors in RL (real-life) places.

"I am still amazed that all this could happen," Anshe said. "I think Philip and the whole Linden team are big visionaries."

Even Linden Lab, seemingly last in line for the virtual gold rush, was making money. After an investment of nearly $20 million, Philip Rosedale told me, they were heading for a profit. Second Life had been criticized for being opaque to virtual debutants. (One "update message," shown to all residents when the Second Life software changed, included the unfathomable sentence "* Added PARCEL_FLAG_RESTRICT_PUSHOBJECT to llGetParcelFlags, and REGION_FLAG_RESTRICT_PUSHOBJECT to llGetRegionFlags()." Another time I logged in and, because of a database error, my virtual self—along with thousands of others—had become a woman. Some days, it was difficult to log into the world at all. Nonetheless, our need for a new place was strong enough to overcome these obstacles.

Still, the drama continues. In November 2006, a British man was jailed for a real-world assault after an online argument—on a Web page, but it didn't seem like it would be long before the United Kingdom saw its first real assault linked to virtual worlds. Linden Lab has recently tightened its disciplinary procedure (they now hold any accounts reported for abuse until they can verify that resident's real-world identity), but for a while the global attacks continued, including one with a series of self-copying gold rings that crashed the grid in early 2007. As of November 2006, the latest hot topic was an object called a "CopyBot," effectively a copy gun that could duplicate any Second Life object. People armed with a CopyBot strolled into virtual shops and made copies of all the available merchandise for free. Nimrod Yaffle, the resident who had previously been banished to the cornfield, was spotted wandering the Sandbox building area copying everything in sight. In an odd synchronicity, at the same time in the real world, Bath University's Adrian Bower announced a real-world CopyBot: a refrigerator-sized "self-replicating rapid prototyper" that forged objects from downloadable designs. The machine had already made a belt buckle, an architectural model, and one of its own parts. Michael Hart, founder of the free online library Project Gutenberg, predicted a future where the virtual and the real drew closer together; when consumers would download objects—a pizza, a Ferrari—just as they downloaded books from his website.

In the virtual world, the CopyBot could even copy avatars. Both Philip Linden (who told me he'd seen it coming) and Adam Reuters were hit, and found themselves face-to-face with their virtual doppelgängers. Across Second Life shop owners faced with the threat of an end to virtual income waged war. They built objects to block off CopyBot vending machines, and in some cases, they surrounded those still using the device with placards that read "Shame!" Many shops closed down to weather the storm, until Linden Lab could figure out how to handle the problem. (Interestingly, its first recommendation was a reminder that residents could cite the Digital Millennium Copyright Act—a real-world U.S. copyright law—to force other residents to stop using their intellectual property without permission.) Once again Second Life residents—each one armed with an opinion—hit the bulletin boards.

I began my journey with a visit to the real-world Boston, to meet Wilde Cunningham, a group for whom the enchantment of virtual worlds was unequivocally a good thing, and their example had inspired many others to follow behind. There was now a handful of similar support groups. For instance, John Palmer, a practicing Buddhist from Dorset, England, built Support for Healing, a virtual island, a haven of Zen gardens and waterfalls where those suffering from depression could visit and share their burdens. Simon Stevens, a real-life consultant and activist for the disabled, who has cerebral palsy himself, set up a nightclub called Wheelies, which, he said, "aims to make guests feel comfortable about disability as well as dancing and just plain having a good time." When, on Simon's invitation, I visited his checkered-floor dance club for Turbo Tuesday, his virtual self,

Simon Walsh, had huge red dragon wings and waved blue and red rave-style light sticks. His avatar wore a virtual version of his real-world head padding, and there was a wheelchair still attached to his behind, although he was dancing on his feet. Above his head, his title read "Proud Spaz." He had applied for the virtual *Big Brother*, he told me, although he had yet to hear if he would appear in the house.

When I first met Wilde online, they had wondered what might happen if the technology existed to connect them more directly to virtual worlds, without the awkward obstacle of the keyboard. Real-world technology was fast catching up with their hopes. Back in 2004, at the University of Pittsburgh, scientists had demonstrated a robotic arm controlled by the brain signals of a monkey, monitored via electrodes. In March 2006, at the Centrum der Büro- und Informationstechnik (Center for Office and Information Technology) exposition in Hanover, Germany, researchers from the Fraunhofer Institute in Berlin and the medical school of Berlin's Humboldt University unveiled a more specific version. The "Berlin Brain-Computer Interface" was an electrode-dotted shower cap that enabled humans to type with their minds. Then, in July 2006, researchers at University College, London, successfully tested a helmet that measured brain activity and could control a virtual self. After a swimming accident in Greece, Tom Schweiger, a thirty-one-year-old Austrian man, was made paraplegic. Using University College's helmet, he explored a simple virtual world (a simulated "cave" room, with sound and projected images) through goggles, by imagining moving his arms and legs. An electrode cap measured the EEG readings from the motor areas of his brain associated with arm and leg movement. "At first it all felt strange, having the cap on and being asked to think about moving my feet," he told the *Observer* newspaper, "but gradually I felt as if I was in that world. At one point I completely forgot it was a virtual world and that I was part of this experiment." Robert Leeb, a researcher at Graz University of Technology in Austria, planned to develop this technology to allow disabled people to control their wheelchairs through thought.

And this kind of technology was popping up everywhere. In November 2006, Australian engineers at the Commonwealth Scientific and Industrial Research Organisation built a T-shirt that turned air guitar into real sound by sensing hand movements and feeding them to a synthesizer. In the arms race between the three main game console manufacturers, Nintendo was gambling that it could beat Microsoft and Sony with its new console feature: a controller with movement sensors, in a small white stick that could stand in as a sword, a golf club, or anything the games' designers could imagine. A Korean company had developed a wearable "personal digital assistant," which, through what it called the Body Area Network, let users touch computing devices to interact with them; you could touch a printer to make a document, or touch another person to transfer a file. Even the dead could now remain connected. One Second Life resident offered, for a fee, to continue your virtual self's life after your real death; and, in the real world, cemetery stones had been designed that, through a satellite connection, linked the resting place with memorials in virtual worlds (a website, an online photo book, a place inside Second Life). Our first forays into a virtual world seemed to involve abandoning the body, but now, the body—alive or dead—was making a comeback.

Once, at a party, a man told me he was insane. Not long before I left, he leaned close and said: "I'm psychotic, you know. Yeah. I'm schizophrenic. I'm on drugs. I'm basically OK, except—I believe the universe is man-made."

My eyes had widened, and I had moved away. After a year inhabiting virtual worlds, though, I found myself relaxing into a similar feeling. Sometimes, as I walked through a shopping mall or cycled down the road, I felt a strange, sideways motion, a fault slide in my vision. I could almost see the constructed, perfect, other world—the smooth solids and cluttered polygonal curves—emerge here and there behind the real. The schizophrenic I met had spoken truth in his delusion. In our urban environments, almost everything—the roads, the buildings, the concrete slabs under our feet—is already man-made, a constructed buffer against the wild earth. Virtual worlds only extend the real world's already psychedelic quality—literally, from *psyche* and *delos*: the capacity to make ourselves visible.

On the boards around a building site in Hackney, England, near my real-world home for most of my virtual journey, graffiti read: "Write your MySpace name here." Over some months, I watched the list of names stretch from two to over thirty. At first, to me and to others to whom I pointed the graffiti out, this seemed nothing special, but that lack of surprise only shows how we have already begun to take our virtual spaces, and how they interact with the real, for granted. MySpace names become a way to connect in the real world. We can start up Google Earth, gaze through our monitors—or even into the screens of our mobile phones—and look down onto our selves, or even our pasts. Google has released its latest Google Earth software, with historical maps of places, including my hometown, London. We can zoom down in a satellite view and look onto the topography of our past.

Virtual worlds are not other universes; they are new continents, extensions—like the past and the present—of now. And like Roger Rabbit escaping from his cartoon, virtual worlds have begun to crop up in our real spaces, too.

In August 2005, I attended an event that was an augury of the ways our virtual and real lives might begin to interconnect. As part of the Game Developers Conference in San Francisco, Linden Lab threw a party at the downtown Varnish Art Gallery. At the same time, they built a Virtual Varnish, a re-creation of the real-world gallery; people celebrated simultaneously in the real and virtual worlds. Then—the first time this had ever happened—the two worlds joined. On the wall of the virtual club was a video feed from the real-world celebration; on the wall of the real-world club, a projector showed the virtual party.

Philip Rosedale was inside the virtual version, as Philip Linden.

"Coming to you live!" he announced, then sat down on a virtual couch and said very little—perhaps busy enjoying the real party instead. Philip had told me about his plans for the event. "It will have this whole Alice in Wonderland quality. You're in the virtual and you're looking through the window to the real, and you're in the real and you're looking through a window to the virtual." The idea had been a wonder; the reality was a confusion. The dialogue around me was a mess of crossed wires: "Hi Philip!" "Maxx is dandruffing!" "Stand up Marcos!" "Yay!" For some, the video played off-center; others saw only half the picture, or the whole image reversed—and yet it was a thrill. There we were, in a virtual world, watching the real, and the real was watching us back. I waved, in a jerky motion that was reduced to a crawl by the overloaded servers. I was sure someone in San Francisco—the real San Francisco, which we could see on our screens—waved back.

It seems that soon all lines may become blurred. We already have "alternate reality" games, such as Perplex City: a subscription service that immerses subscribers in a story, through e-mails, websites, text messages, and real-world events, to bring them a near-virtual experience. Theme park environments like MagiQuest in Myrtle Beach, South Carolina, use a blend of low-frequency radio and infrared to create a real environment that works like a game: Point your wand at real things and they spring to life.

Our journey into virtual worlds so far has been about conquering geography, replacing it with something that more closely fits our desires. The whole initial purpose of virtual worlds was to ensure that where you were in the real world didn't matter. The next phase in the early growth of virtual worlds will reintegrate the real, to bring the two more closely into line.

In 1991, John Ellenby and his son Thomas were sailing off the coast of Mexico. It was night, and they were lost, and John Ellenby had a terrible sense of direction. They decided that what they needed was a compass, a GPS device, and a pair of binoculars, all tied together; then they could point it at any landmark and it would tell them what they could see. Fifteen years later, their company, Geo-Vector, in partnership with three Japanese cellphone firms, launched a version of their dream. So today in Tokyo you can point a GPS cellphone at a building and your phone will tell you what that building is. Ask your phone for a nearby hotel and it will lead you there. It can't be long before the range of information linked to a particular real-world place expands; we'll have access not only to what the hotel wants us to know, but also to what previous residents have said—not just at a website, but right there in front of the building.

When we can define our identities online, it seems, we start to be able to redefine ourselves offline, too. Philip Linden had told me about one virtual resident who used the virtual versatility of his second self to reshape his real-world body. Over the course of a year—spending seventy-five hours a week inside Second Life—he customized his virtual self piece-by-piece (refining his face, buying a virtual earring or tattoo), until he realized he could do the same with his actual body. He spent the next year remodeling his real self the same way—losing weight a pound at a time, remaking his style garment by garment—until he was as happy with his real body as he was with his avatar.

My own experience was the reverse. My virtual life felt liberating, but my real one suffered as a consequence. I was already inclined to neglect my body, but as I spent more and more time online, my gym membership lapsed. (The gym, another monetized corner of the world, cost $160 a month—ten times as much as my virtual office.) For me, virtual activity meant real-world inertia, but perhaps that wouldn't remain true for long.

Kyle Machulis, the man who invented teledildonics for Second Life sex, planned to modify an exercise bike so that by pedaling in the real world he could move forward in the virtual one (he couldn't find a stationary exercise bike). Another World of Warcraft fanatic set up a treadmill by his PC and ran while he played. (In case you wanted to go the other way, too, you could use your virtual character in EverQuest II to order a real-world pizza without leaving your chair.) In 2004, twenty-five years after Pac-Man first appeared in arcades and barrooms, researchers at the University of Singapore constructed a version of the game that takes place on a university campus. Wearable wireless-networked backpacks and virtual reality goggles put real people in place of Pac-Man and the ghosts, and university pathways in place of the haunted hallways. The players saw both the real and the unreal worlds; instead of collecting virtual yellow dots, they collected real sugar jars. These are the very early signs of a collision between our world and the virtual, and very soon they might leave us unsure about which is more important. Soon, as the technology improves, we may be able to choose whether to see people as they want to be seen, or as we want to see them. (That might not be a bad thing, given how many pizzas EverQuest players might end up eating.)

Virtual worlds also have the capacity to change our urban landscape. Our communication technologies already mean more people can work away from their colleagues than ever before. Virtual worlds may well extend that trend: As we are transported by these software engines into another place, distance will continue to decrease. Just as warehouses for physical distribution in urban centers have become increasingly obsolete, offices—places where we travel simply to come together—may become useless, too. We may perhaps shift into a two-tone life, with a local, physical existence and a global, virtual one.

In November 2006, I called Philip Rosedale to see how he was coping with his runaway success. He told me he shared this vision of a real world shaped by our virtual lives. "It's already happening," he said. "What's interesting will be how many people choose to live in New York or London when they no longer have to."

In fact, Philip believed our exodus into virtual connection would go further: The real world, he told me, would fade into the background. "All of our creative energy will be directed there. The futurist in me says that the real world will become like a museum very soon. So it'll be fantastically cool to go to New York, but in the same way that it's cool to go see the Mayan ruins. Because the big buildings will still be there, but they'll be covered in dust. Because no one will bother too much with them anymore."

Paradoxically, although virtual worlds seem to promise physical isolation, this capacity to conquer distance without travel may help save us.

In most European languages, the words for time, work, and distance share common roots. In virtual worlds, the software engine—so named because it does the work of calculating and displaying the 3-D world—also transports us. (Young men still tinker with engines, but of a different kind: The car in the driveway has been replaced by the PC in the bedroom.) It is no surprise, then, that virtual worlds have the capacity to transform our ideas about travel. One of the first things people do when they enter Second Life is buy a new vehicle: an airplane, a parachute, a spaceship, a jetpack, a UFO. But then they leave the vehicles behind and grow wings. In Second Life, I owned a Ferrari, but I kept it in my pocket. If I wanted to travel, flying was faster—and if I needed a mechanical boost, I would put on a jetpack. In most virtual worlds I visited, you could simply teleport yourself; traditional modes of transport were redundant. That didn't stop our real-world car manufacturers from trying to persuade us otherwise. Toyota was the first to make a real-world model, their people carrier Scion B, inside Second Life. They originally planned to give the car away, but, afraid of alienating existing virtual car dealerships, they charged the equivalent of two dollars per Scion. In September, Audi premiered a new TV spot inside Second Life, and in October 2006, General Motors, who eighty years earlier had bought up streetcar lines, bought sixteen Second Life islands—256 acres—to help extend their brands into cyberspace. A month later, Nissan built a four-car-high virtual store, modeled on a soft-drink vending machine. Despite their efforts, and those of other car manufacturers, I saw no one drive the virtual cars. In fact, as my life in virtual worlds developed, even my own real car began to seem outdated. As I made my way around the city, I carried along with me, in the shape of my car, a ton of glass and metal. It seemed a waste.

James Lovelock, the environmental biologist who coined the term *Gaia* for the earth's living ecosphere, has suggested that virtual worlds might be part of the solution to global climate change. In his book *The Revenge of Gaia,* Lovelock suggests that virtual worlds may become an integral part of a more sustainable future, and an unconscious migration to low-energy activities. The figures are indisputable. A thousand-square-foot retail outlet in the real world uses around 280 kilowatt hours of electricity each week; the server technology behind an island-sized virtual outlet—set over 412 acres—uses the same amount of energy in a year. When I traveled to Boston to visit Wilde, my air flight produced about two tons of carbon pollution for my seat alone, equivalent to running a car for two and a half years. When I traveled to meet Wilde in Second Life, I produced almost no carbon pollution; it was equivalent to leaving my refrigerator door open for five minutes. If, as it seems, we face a new global challenge, the worldwide analogue to the challenge of managing our own unhappiness—the management of the health of the earth—then perhaps virtual worlds can help. Besides the possibility of continued neglect of the real, they also contain the hope that we can save ourselves. If we do end up in a future where oil is scarce we may have already discovered a different, more efficient means to conquer distance: to project our selves but leave our bodies behind.

Connections made in virtual worlds without any physical contact can certainly feel real, as they at least did for me. Although Marsellus Wallace had never followed through on the job he had given me, I liked him and I wanted to play along. I had e-mailed Tommy Fitzsimmons, the target of my "hit," to come clean to him about the job and to see if we could in turn arrange a setup for Marsellus—who, it now seemed, had taken my money and run. I'd found out more about Fatallty, the player whom Jeremy Chase claimed to be as famous as:

He was the world's most successful Quake player, Jonathan Wendel, who made his name in international video game tournaments. Wendel had earned over a million dollars in cash and prizes, as well as sponsorship money, and had his own line of PC equipment. Well . . . Chase had at least earned a hundred bucks off me. I e-mailed Marsellus a few times to set up the double-cross. Each time I was convinced he knew about the setup. I e-mailed Tommy Fitzsimmons, who now believed I was working with him. I considered a double-cross, or a triple-cross, or something. Either way, they would both have to trust me. I had continued my mafia homework; now I felt like Donnie Brasco, undercover, infiltrating the family. Any badly told lie could break the whole story. In fact, Marsellus only half took the bait. After congratulating me for taking the initiative, his e-mails tailed off again. The meeting never took place. Still, Tommy didn't think I had given anything away; I forwarded the e-mails I had sent Marsellus, and Tommy paid me the ultimate mafia accolade: I could have been a made man. "You'd make it pretty good doing this type of stuff," he told me.

Although Marsellus was evasive, I did finally catch up with Raymond Polonsky, Chase's more legitimate virtual self. He was branching out into designer jewelry, he told me. He had kicked out almost every member of his virtual crime family. And, he said, Linden Lab had started clamping down on his virtual mafia. "I got suspended for the first time ever," Polonsky told me. "No appeal. They wouldn't even return my e-mails asking for specifics." Even some of Polonsky's friends turned their backs. "I started getting the cold shoulder from regular associates of mine that are Linden Lab employees."

Chase was still contorting to keep his legitimate characters separate from his mafia selves. I was asked to help set up a short interview about Second Life for NBC's *Today* show, and the presenter wanted to be a pirate. I scoured the virtual world, but couldn't find a parrot for his shoulder. I mentioned my dilemma to Polonsky, who sent me a parrot immediately. "Handy knowing a mafia don," I wrote back. "What? Who do you mean?" Polonsky replied.

Noah Burn, the EverQuest forger, was also getting out of the life.

At one point he had come up with another virtual business also on the edge of the law. An EverQuest II resident who had heard about his previous forgery exploits had approached him with a new business idea. The resident had found a small spot on a cliffside in EverQuest II where they could attack monsters but the monsters couldn't reach to fight back. They could stand there all day, and earn "experience"—points they can use to develop the characters' powers—at a far higher rate than normal. They began to charge other residents for earning experience for them; those residents would lend their account passwords to Noah and his business partners—like handing over their car keys for their virtual selves. Noah and his partners would stand on the ledge and fight all day, earning in three days the experience points most people would manage in a year. By working with three borrowed characters at a time, they earned about a thousand dollars a day, split between three of them. It worked, until one of Noah's partners—whom he had met only inside the virtual world of EverQuest II—gave in to temptation and looted all the items from one of their borrowed virtual selves. "There's no loyalty in virtual scams," Noah told me. Sony customer service got involved, the thief spilled the beans, and the plan came to an end. Now, Noah said, he spent hardly any time in virtual worlds. "The joy of killing a monster that takes twenty minutes to beat for the off-chance that you may get a few gold pieces has really lost its luster once you've been on the other side," he told me. He now ran a vinyl business, making car signs and stickers with a friend, and hoped to return to school for a creative writing degree.

Each individual I met had found something new in virtual worlds, something they lacked in real life. Still, Second Life remained awkward and obtuse. "What's so great about Second Life, is that with all this attention, it still doesn't really work all that well yet," Philip Rosedale told me. "And as we improve the technology, things like search, frame rates, crash rates, and all that stuff—as we improve that, good grief. You think it's growing now!" As the visual realism improves, as physical interfaces allow us to bring our bodies, as well as our minds, into virtual worlds, how will things develop? What will happen when the technology catches up with our eyes and sense of motion? What will happen when virtual worlds are hard to distinguish from the real? How will we find our way home? Will we be in danger of forgetting our bodies completely?

For some, this abandonment was a hope, not a fear. "Without reality, you die," Anshe had said, but Philip Rosedale didn't quite agree. When we spoke in November 2006, after he talked excitedly of the next big Second Life audio innovation—residents would be able to talk to one another with their real voices, and the volume would rise and fall as you passed by—the conversation turned philosophical. Philip shared some of his science-fiction-inspired dreams. "I think— and science backs this up—that Second Life has as much computational power as a human brain," he said. He told me he envisioned a future, perhaps not too far away, in which people could upload their entire minds into a global, networked machine.

Rosedale wasn't the only one to feel this way: that the mind can, in some circuitous way, conquer itself. For some people, the temptations of an entirely virtual life remain seductive. Toward the end of his life, LSD guru Timothy Leary began to dream about a new kind of digital immortality: He would upload his mind onto the Internet and conquer death through electronic storage. This movement, known as "transhumanism," which has taken root through the work of California critics like Ray Kurzweil, seems a particularly American dream. After all, the right to the pursuit of happiness is enshrined in the Constitution. And if you can't find happiness in this world, why not send yourself entirely into the next?

Philip shared his belief that we might eventually leave our bodies behind. "There's a reasonable argument that we'll be able to," he said. "As you could probably imagine, we think a lot about the nature of the brain, and whether computational substrates can be dense enough to enable thinking within them. I can tell you that I'm quite sure the answer to that is yes. We're not there yet, obviously. The computational density of Second Life is not enough to support thinking.

Although I should note as a side point that the combined computational capacity of the aggregate Second Life grid, running twenty-four hours a day as it does now, is in excess, by almost any measure, of at least one human brain at this point. Second Life is dreaming. It could be looked at as one collective dream. In an almost neurological sense."

To Philip, even the most powerful emotion, love, is a product of the mind. "I mean, people kill themselves over love, all the time. And that is purely an artifact of the interaction between two minds."

I put it to Philip that life and feeling have their roots, not in the mind, but in the body. He slipped the question with science talk. "As many modern thinkers would assert, and I would assert it at a neurological level, we are not localizable," he said. "Your body is a part of your memories as well. It is mutable, like a synapse; it's actually changeable. If, out of pleasure, I decide to work out, my body is changed—so your body is an extended aspect of your mind."

I didn't agree. No one confuses the photograph with the camera, but some people confuse the mind with the self. Wilde's wisdom had come not from their minds, but from the struggles of their bodies, and the dream of a digital mind seemed a particularly California kind of hubris. In Silicon Valley, which Philip Rosedale called home, a whole generation had grown to associate technology with money and power. To them there was nothing technology could not conquer. Just as the Western world, brought to its success by the powers of the mind, has raised the mind above the body, so these technologically inspired Californians are susceptible to raising the machine over the self. The appeal was clear: a new kind of heaven, the promised perfection of virtual worlds taken to its logical extreme. Without a body at all, our minds would have nothing to hold them down. Then, everything would be easy, and there would be *no more death*. However, if we did somehow make it, so would the W-Hats, and Marsellus Wallace. Trouble will follow us there, too. We'd have to build a fourth life, to escape our third one. In either case, you can leave me out.

On my visit to Linden Lab, I had given Philip a copy of my previous book, and when we spoke again in November 2006, I remarked on the similarities between the disciples of my mother's guru and his employees—two groups of people out to make a better world; the new names, the logo pendants. (Except in Linden Lab's case, the seventies mantra "Be here now" had been replaced with a new kind of remote presence: "Be there now.") To my surprise, Philip laughed. Before they settled on Second Life, he told me, Linden Lab had considered giving their new world a Hindu name. Inside Second Life, near their first Linden headquarters, there was even a shrine to their ideals: a temple, with an inner sanctum of a slowly turning logo. In 2003, Rosedale first met James Currier, a dot-com entrepreneur who later became a Linden Lab investor. "When he met me—this was in 2003, when we had five hundred people inside Second Life—he said, 'You know what? You know what you have to decide?' I said, 'What's that, James?' and he said, 'What color are the robes going to be?' "

"That was always his thing. That was what he said when he first saw it. He said, 'This is a religion.' "

I liked Philip. He had forged a world I had dwelled within. His world had given me a new name, and his dream was a good one. Still, like all messiahs, he couldn't see the dark side of his dream. "We always joke that it's like the *good* cult," he told me.

"Take it from me—that's what they all think," I said.

When I began my journey into virtual worlds, the people addicted to them were stereotyped as loners. But the loneliest world, I discovered, is the real one. In June 2006, a study at the University of Arizona linked use of the Internet to a decline in close friendships. Between 1984 and 2004, the number of people who said they had no one to talk to about personal matters had doubled, and the average number of close friends had fallen from three to two. "I think behavior online is more supportive than in real life," Philip Rosedale has said, and in other ways, the figures back him up. A 2002 study showed that using the Internet has positive effects on communication, social involvement, and well-being.

Still, for now, I decided to leave virtual worlds, or at least spend less time in them, use them as a place to meet, not as a place to live. Perhaps I would take a keepsake back with me: For $75, plus $8 shipping, a Second Life resident called Hal9k Andalso would craft a five-inch-high real statuette of my virtual self. On the website, I noticed, John Lester had ordered one.

Virtual worlds seem to be simply an extension of the human gift and curse. We can imagine the world to be different, which is our strength—we can begin to journey from the imperfect present to a more perfect future—but also our weakness. The world we live in never measures up to our idea of heaven, which instills in us an insoluble yearning, what Tennessee Williams called "that long-delayed but always expected something that we live for." Virtual worlds are a new picture of an old affliction, the basic human wound, whatever it was that drove humanity away from the real world and into our imagination.

Dreams give us hope, to inform our real life, but we have to be awake to make use of them. Like our dreams—like all our stories—our new virtual worlds have something to teach us. And again as with our dreams, we can only begin to put those lessons to use when we wake up and leave our sleep behind. The people I had met in my journeys had found a new way to dream, and some had tried to lose themselves in fantasy worlds completely. But, as in all fairy tales, only the disenchanted are free.

Walking is controlled falling. Without the pull of the earth, and without the resistance of the ground, we would remain still. That's why, in our dreams, we can fly, and that's why, in our dreams, we find it hard to run. We need gravity and friction to move forward.

When I was nine years old, eager to leave the confines and struggles of the communal world I found myself in, my favorite thing to do—when I wasn't at the arcades with my father—was to read Nicholas Fisk's *On the Flip Side*. The book's basic premise was that one day, out of the blue, people started to disappear. They packed their bags, closed their affairs, and then disappeared out of existence. Animals, too, started to vanish. Pet tortoises, squirrels, lions at the zoo; they all left, and made a discreet "pop" in doing so. As it became clear what was happening, people started to discuss their departure plans: "Are you ready to go?" "I'm thinking of leaving myself." It was something like the Christian Rapture, except the decision to leave was entirely each person's own. And no one knew what lay on the other side. The idea gripped me. I too wanted to leave behind the heartache of this world, to abandon my troubles and vanish into some other, easier place. I willed it to happen to me. I blinked my eyes, frowned, and concentrated furiously, but I couldn't seem to find the right thought or secret word that would send me through to the other side. I recently reread Fisk's book and found the story just as powerful. The book seemed to me to tap into a basic human longing for some other, better place, where what we lack is suddenly plentiful.

In one way or another we all have this hope, the yearning to transcend, to reach up, to let go of our skins and find a new place without sorrow and loss. Virtual worlds have the capacity to promise that redemption, to entrance us, to make us forget ourselves until it's too late. They can encourage us to neglect the real, in favor of the virtual, until our lives—like Kyu Nam Choi's restaurant—slide into ruin. On the other hand, virtual worlds can provide something that is missing, a balm for our wound: a place to take our sad hearts other than the supermarket.

ABOUT THE AUTHOR

TIM GUEST is a journalist and the bestselling author of *My Life in Orange: Growing Up with the Guru*, about his childhood on communes around the world. Guest's articles have appeared in *The New York Times, The Guardian, The Telegraph, New Scientist,* and *Vogue.* He lives in London.

ABOUT THE TYPE

This book was set in Electra, a typeface designed for Linotype by W. A. Dwiggins, the renowned type designer (1880–1956). Electra is a fluid typeface, avoiding the contrasts of thick and thin strokes that are prevalent in most modern typefaces.